Jim Tucker's
Bilderberg
Diary

One Reporter's 25-Year Battle
to Shine the Light on the
World Shadow Government

American Free Press
2009

Jim Tucker's
Bilderberg Diary

First Printing: July 2005
Second Printing: April 2008
Third Printing: May 2009

Published by: American Free Press
645 Pennsylvania Avenue SE
Suite 100
Washington, D.C. 20003
1-888-699-6397
www.americanfreepress.net

ISBN Number: 978-0-9818086-8-0

To contact the author:

James P. Tucker Jr.
c/o American Free Press
645 Pennsylvania Avenue SE
Suite 100
Washington, D.C. 20003
Tel: (202) 544-5977

Table of Contents

Powerbrokers Meet ...

2000—Brussels, Belgium: Christopher Bollyn photographed slash-and-burn speculator George Soros talking with Carl Bildt, the former prime minister of Sweden and the UN special envoy to the Balkans. Following the U.S. bombing of the former Yugoslavia in 1999, Soros was looking to invest heavily in the Balkans in 2000. Most likely Soros and Bildt were not discussing the latest baseball scores.

FOREWORD 2005

Life in the Shadows
With a Bilderberg Hound

hen I began working with the populist news-paper, called *The Spotlight*, in June 2000, my very first assignment was to accompany Jim Tucker, the paper's senior reporter, to the annual meeting of the secretive group known as Bilderberg, which was taking place in a five-star resort near Brussels, Belgium. Although I had heard about Bilderberg, I knew very little about this secret gathering. I had read Jim's earlier reports, but I wondered how such high-profile figures could meet with no mention in the mainstream press.

And that's how I found myself, for the next four years, attending the annual gathering of Bilderberg, photographing those elite politicians, power brokers and bankers, who gathered every year to talk candidly about the most important issues—matters that affect all of our lives—behind locked and heavily guarded doors.

Upon arriving in Switzerland on May 31, 2000, I took Jim's advice and followed his usual routine. The day before the group was scheduled to arrive, I traveled to Genval, near Brussels, Belgium, and checked into the site of that year's meeting at the Chateau du Lac. However, I was told I could only stay for one night as this multi-million-dollar resort had been completely booked for the weekend by a group of important people.

I poked around the grounds and hallways to see if there was anything that might confirm Tucker's information that this was actually the place that Bilderberg would convene. Though hotel staff claimed not to know anything about the group, which would be taking over the hotel for the next four days, I could see that conference rooms were busily being prepared and I sensed that the employees had been lectured to keep their mouths shut about the caliber of individuals who would be attending that coming weekend.

As I've learned, this is always the case.

It was not until early the next morning, however, that I began to notice the extent to which this enigmatic group goes to lock down the site.

I looked out the window and saw a team of special security agents walking around the front of the hotel. It certainly looked like something very important was about to take place.

After breakfast, I checked out of the hotel. Taking my camera bag, I went for a stroll along the lake. There was a road that passed directly in front of the hotel and beyond the road was a small park and lake. There were several benches conveniently located in front of the hotel. In the beginning I was by myself, but as the morning progressed more and more people began to stroll past the hotel. It was Thursday, June 1, 2000, and because it was a bank holiday in Belgium many local people had the day off. As I was perched with my cameras in front of the hotel, passers by would ask me if I knew what was going on. A Belgian journalist thought that a famous football team was staying at the hotel. I had some copies of *Spotlight* material about the Bilderberg group with me and explained that it was a very different kind of team that was expected at the hotel. I told him that this team included people like Queen Beatrix of Holland, Henry Kissinger, David Rockefeller, and perhaps even President Bill Clinton. He came back later and actually wrote a story about Bilderberg. The local people became quite interested in the possibility of seeing celebrities and would

2004—Stresa, Italy: Henry Kissinger, a perennial Bilderberger, walks along Lake Maggiore, the scenic venue for the 2004 meeting. That year, Kissinger joined Bill Gates and other luminaries in this northern Italian town.

return to ask who had arrived. Some American women who had memberships at the hotel's fitness club looked at the Bilderberg material and recognized Vernon E. Jordan Jr., the famous lawyer, political advisor and confidant to Clinton. They had seen Jordan in the spa talking on a phone wearing only a towel and had noticed the scars he bears from having been shot outside a Fort Wayne, Ind., motel in 1980.

When word spread among the locals that the high and mighty of the world were really coming to the Chateau du Lac, a crowd began to form along the road in front of the hotel. Whenever a car would drive up, I would try to position myself for a photo with my telephoto lens. People would come to me and ask, "Who was that?" Often, they would tell me who they thought they had seen.

While the local people enjoyed the party atmosphere, I could see that Bilderberg security was becoming very uneasy with the scene in front of the hotel. The unexpected crowd had completely ruined their plans for the Bilderberg guests to slip into the hotel unnoticed. With dozens of people crowded around the front of the hotel there was very little Bilderberg security could do without drawing even more attention to the secretive group. A few Bilderberg hounds, like Tony Gosling from England, were on hand and a young boy with a camera was even waiting by the front door trying to take photos of the rich and famous guests.

The next day, things were different. I arrived at the hotel early to find that two tents had been set up by the front door of the hotel. When a car arrived it would drive into one tent so that the passengers could pass into the hotel without being seen. With President Clinton scheduled to receive the Charlemagne Prize in Aachen, on the Belgian-German border, there was anticipation he would suddenly show up to meet with the Bilderberg group.

At midday, the Bilderberg attendees began to come out for a break in the fresh air. John M. Deutch, the Belgian-born former Director of the Central Intelligence Agency, came out with two Americans and walked right into range of my camera. I was busy running around trying to get photos of the individuals and groups as they walked near the lake. As long as I didn't get in anybody's way, there was very little Bilderberg security could do; the roadway was public property. Then two individuals came out from the tented doorway. There were security men all around these two. They walked quickly toward the side of the hotel. I immediately recognized these two Bilderberg men: the infamous currency speculator George Soros and Carl Bildt, the former prime minister of Sweden and the UN Special Envoy to the Balkans. I spoke politely to Bildt as the two made their way to the side yard of the hotel. Not wanting to offend, I didn't ask Bildt the question that I should have:

"Mr. Bildt, what do you know about the smuggling of Soviet weapons on the Estonia ferry?"

That question would have certainly shocked Bildt, who was Sweden's prime minister when the ferry sank with the loss of 852 lives on Sept. 28, 1994.

Soros was visibly uneasy about being photographed with Bildt, who was serving as special envoy for the UN secretary general in the former Yugoslavia. Bildt was serving UN Secretary General Kofi Annan, who is married to Nane, a Wallenberg and niece of the disappeared Raoul Wallenberg.

The photographs I took of Bildt and Soros are my favorite photos from four years of covering Bilderberg conferences. They were also the last photos I was able to take that year. The conference had just begun, but Bilderberg security decided that I had to go.

In front of the hotel—on public property—the security chief came up to me and stood directly in front of me with two of his thugs on each side of me. "If you don't stop running behind people and taking pictures," he said, "I'm going to jump all over you."

I took my camera bag and went to the nearby restaurant, which I knew was not owned by the man who owned the hotel. I called Jim from the restaurant and told him what had happened and he advised me to leave. On the street, two Belgian security thugs were watching me. I called a taxi and waited for what seemed like ages.

Finally the taxi arrived and took me to the Brussels train station. I remember having to run across the tracks in front of the locomotive and jumping on a train at the very last minute. The conductor quickly came to see if I was alright. I breathed a sigh of relief as the train pulled away from Brussels.

When the pictures were printed, Jim and I went through them to try to identify the people in the photos. Although I had only taken photos for a day and a half, I had gotten a lot of good shots of who was attending Bilderberg 2000. I also came away with a much better understanding of what Bilderberg is.

At the next year's meeting, in June 2001, we found ourselves on Sweden's west coast when Bilderberg gathered at a hotel near Stenungsund, near Gothenburg. Bilderberg had learned from the exposure at Brussels and probably chose the Quality Hotel Stenungsbaden because it had a perimeter fence.

On the first day, while I was taking pictures from private property adjacent to the hotel with the permission of the owner, Swedish police seized me and drove me six miles into the wilderness and left me on the side of the road amidst farmers' fields. I could see that with a large number of Swedish police helping Bilderberg, this was not going to be any easier than Belgium.

On the other hand, thanks to our efforts, in Sweden there was more media coverage of the secretive group's meeting than in any other country I have seen. We found articles about Bilderberg in the Swedish press unlike any we had seen before. When Jim and I arrived at our hotel in Gothenburg there was a welcoming committee from several independent magazines. At the hotel gate through which the Bilderberg cars had to pass there was a group of witnesses from a variety of organizations. Patriotic Swedes were aware that Bilderberg was meeting and were very interested to know who was attending and what was being discussed.

I spent the next three days high up in a tree or on a breezy bridge overlooking the hotel waiting for a Bilderberger to come into view. When the group went for an afternoon cruise I got some excellent photos of the assembled group of Bilderberg 2001. Having cultivated a connection with a hotel employee, I was able to provide Jim with the full list of participants on the last day of the conference. Once again, we were able to show exactly who had attended Bilderberg.

Compared to the event in Sweden, Bilderberg 2002, held at a Marriott hotel in Chantilly, Va., was a very lonely event. Just a few miles from Washington, there was not a soul to be seen. It was completely different than in Europe.

The Westfields Marriott is surrounded by trees, but Bilderberg 2002 didn't need much security because, apart from us, nobody seemed to care that the most powerful people in the western world were meeting in secret for three days at the hotel. We met only one young man who had taken a bus from Phoenix, Ariz., to witness the Bilderberg meeting in Chantilly. As a long-time reader of *American Free Press* and *Spotlight* he was very aware of the importance of what was happening in the Marriott hotel that weekend. As usual there was no coverage in the U.S. media except for Jim's stories which were published in *American Free Press*. But we know the U.S. press knew about the meetings. I personally photographed NBC News chief foreign affairs correspondent Andrea Mitchell dropping off her husband, Federal Reserve Chairman Alan Greenspan, at that year's meeting.

The last Bilderberg conference I covered with Jim was the 2003 event held at the Trianon Palace Hotel at Versailles, near Paris, France. While the French press was a no show, two Norwegian journalists from the business daily *Dagens Naeringsliv* covered the event.

On the edge of the grounds of the famous palace of Versailles, I was able to get photos of the assembled Bilderberg group when they went for an afternoon tour of the palace. I was waiting in the park with some French students when I saw Rockefeller come walking back to the hotel with his bodyguard. I introduced myself and he allowed me to take a few photos.

Over the course of those four years, I enjoyed being a part of the only American team of journalists that works to get inside Bilderberg and do what reporters are supposed to do: act as a watchdog for average Americans by disclosing truly important news. I have taken great pride in the work I did covering Bilderberg meetings with Jim; it has been a pleasure to be able to share with the world some truly revealing photographs of Bilderberg attendees.

The experience has left me with the feeling that Jim truly is a part of history, exposing year in and year out the machinations of this secretive cabal that works closely with the Establishment media to keep the world ignorant of its plans. I look forward to the publication of Jim's book on Bilderberg, and hope that this will once and for all blow the lid of this shadowy group. Cheers, Jim.

—CHRISTOPHER BOLLYN

DEDICATION

BY JAMES P. TUCKER

This book is dedicated to the many supporters and readers, first of *The Spotlight* and then *American Free Press,* who have been so helpful in locating and penetrating Bilderberg for so many years. Readers within reasonable proximity of Bilderberg meetings have alerted their local newspapers and broadcasters. In Europe, especially, this has resulted in heavy coverage by reporters who pool their information with me. Readers have met planes and driven me to Bilderberg sites. Thank you. You are all my co-authors.

Above, Jim Tucker outside the Dorint Seehotel Uberfahrt in Rottach-Egern, Germany, at the 2005 Bilderberg meeting.

The Walls Have Ears ...

1997—Lake Lanier, Georgia: This is the listening device a supporter, who wishes to remain anonymous, found in the room of my hotel, adjacent to the Bilderberg meeting site. Big Brother wanted to know how I was planning to get inside the meeting, closed to all but the wealthiest and most powerful. Below, Prince Bernhard of the Netherlands presides over the first Bilderberg meeting in Oosterbeek, Holland, in 1954.

PREFACE

What Is Bilderberg?

he Bilderberg group is an organization of political leaders and international financiers that meets secretly every spring to make global policy. There are about 110 regulars—Rockefellers, Rothschilds, bankers, heads of international corporations and high government officials from Europe and North America. Each year, a few new people are invited and, if found useful, they return to future meetings. If not, they are discarded. Decisions reached at these secret meetings affect every American and much of the world.

This book examines the history and actions of the secret group that calls itself Bilderberg and the efforts of one courageous reporter—James P. Tucker Jr., who has been trailing Bilderberg for nearly 40 years—to focus the spotlight on the actions of what many have called "the world's shadow government." This is his story.

Bilderberg:
Its Long & Secret History

The roots of Bilderberg go back centuries, when international moneychangers would secretly manipulate the economy to enrich themselves and enslave ordinary people.

The Rothschilds of Britain and Europe have met secretly with other financiers for centuries, as did the Rockefellers of America.

In the beginning, the Rothschilds were "Red Shields" because of the ornament on their door and the Rockefellers of Germany were "Rye Fields" because of their crops.

One of the most significant such meetings took place in the spring of 1908, led by Sen. Nelson Aldrich of Rhode Island, whose family married into the Rockefeller clan, accounting for the late Gov. Nelson Aldrich Rockefeller's given name. It was held on Jekyll Island off the Georgia coast.

The late B.C. Forbes, editor of *Forbes* magazine, reported what transpired at this meeting of the world's wealthy. With Aldrich were Henry Davidson, of J.P. Morgan and Co.; Frank Vanderlip, president of the National City Bank; Paul Warburg, of Kuhn Loeb and Co., and A. Piatt Andrew, assistant secretary of the treasury.

They emerged from this secret meeting with a plan for "a scientific currency system for the United States." They had the power to pressure Congress into establishing the Federal Reserve Board, a private group of bankers who meet to shape the money supply.

But in 1954, the international financiers decided that the world had become so small, and their interests intersected so often, that they must have regular, annual meetings. That year, they met at the Bilderberg Hotel in Holland, and took the name "Bilderberg" for themselves.

They have met behind sealed-off walls and armed guards at plush resorts ever since. Secrecy prevailed briefly, until the late journalist, Westbrook Pegler, exposed Bilderberg in 1957. However, Chatham House rules have remained in effect, whereby meetings are held privately and attendees are prohibited from talking on the record about what transpired.

Pegler devoted two of his nationally syndicated columns to Bilderberg in April 1957, although he did not know the group's name. *(See Appendix 2, page 231.)*

"Something very mysterious is going on when a strange assortment of 67 self-qualified, polyglot designers and arbiters of the economic and political fate of our western world go into a secret hud-

FROM WHENCE IT GOT ITS NAME: Above is a photo of the Hotel de Bilderberg, the hotel that hosted the first Bilderberg meeting all the way back in 1954. Bilderberg meetings have been held every year since then, with the venue sites getting more lavish every year. Bilderberg has at times taken to meeting on islands, ostensibly because it's easier to keep reporters and photographers away so no one can document those participants who attend.

dle on an island off Brunswick, Ga., and not a word gets into the popular press beyond a little, routine AP story," Pegler wrote.

Pegler reported that Ralph McGill, the late editor of *The Atlanta Constitution* and Arthur Hayes Sulzberger, publisher of *The New York Times*, had attended on their promise of secrecy. Since, the publisher and associate editor of *The Washington Post,* Donald Graham and Jimmy Lee Hoagland, respectively, have been regular participants. All network news channels have attended these meetings. All promise to abide by the rule of secrecy.

Bilderberg, which typically meets at a luxury resort near a small town, provides a short "press release" to the local paper—preferably a weekly. It is designed to reassure natives as armed guards arrive, motorcades roar by, yachts dock and helicopters land, delivering unidentified people behind closed-off walls.

The "press release" is the same each year; only the site and dates are updated. It says individuals will meet privately to do nothing for three days. Otherwise, they try to impose a complete blackout.

The blackout is virtually complete in the United States. When giant newspapers and broadcast outlets say they do not want the word "Bilderberg" to appear, the pressure on Associated Press is obvious; they are the biggest customers, paying far more than a small-circulation local paper.

Small-city papers depend on AP for all out-of-town news, even for their state legislative coverage. They run hard to stay ahead of the city council and high school football team. Unless informed directly, they have no knowledge that Bilderberg exists.

While Bilderberg denies its meetings are significant, the record proves otherwise. The now defunct *Spotlight* wrote advance stories on the end of the Cold War, the downfall of Margaret Thatcher as prime minister of Britain and of President George Bush the Elder's breaking of his pledge to not raise taxes based on what transpired among Bilderbergers.

More recently, while the mainstream media in 2002 was asserting that the invasion of Iraq would come by late summer or early fall, *American Free Press* reported that there would be no aggression until 2003. The war began in March 2003.

Learning what transpires at Bilderberg can provide a glimpse of what the future holds.

Bilderberg:
Conspiracy 'Theory' or Fact?

When international financiers, heads of state and high government officials are exposed conducting public business in secret, they whimper about "conspiracy theories." But I will soon provide you with names and telephone numbers you can check yourself. Challenge these Bilderberg conspirators to deny that:

• They meet at a secret location each spring, normally in late

May or early June. Their exclusive resort will be sealed off at high noon on the Wednesday before Bilderberg starts meeting on Thursday through Sunday. The resort will be emptied of all non-Bilderberg people. Armed guards will seal off the resort to prevent anyone from approaching.

• All Bilderberg participants and their staff people, as well as all of the resort personnel, are sworn to secrecy. They will report nothing. Collaborating newspapers, including *The Washington Post, The New York Times* and *Los Angeles Times,* will report nothing. They keep their vows of silence so fervently they allow their own newspapers to be factually wrong rather than risk exposing Bilderberg. Participants will deny that Bilderberg even exists. You will almost never read the word "Bilderberg" in these newspapers or hear it on national network news, which have all participated in vows of secrecy. (Because of extensive coverage in Europe in recent years, *The New York Times* published a "humor" commentary after the 2004 meeting in Stresa, Italy, denouncing "conspiracy" theories.)

Chasing Bilderberg for 28 years has been the most exciting assignment of my lifetime newspaper career, the first 20 years of which were in the mainstream press. I had held some high positions—night editor of the now defunct *Washington Daily News,* editor of the *Martinsville* (VA) *Bulletin,* copy editor at the Richmond (VA) *Times-Dispatch* and, finally, assistant news editor of the Akron (Ohio) *Beacon-Journal.*

So a moment that came in the spring of 1975 is forever photographed in my mind. I was being interviewed by Willis Carto for the job of starting a newspaper to be called *The Spotlight.* Carto was officially "treasurer" of Liberty Lobby but he was more than that. He *was* Liberty Lobby, having founded the populist institution in 1955.

He asked me what I thought of Bilderberg. I had never heard of Bilderberg. He gave me a brief oral summary and a lot of Liberty Lobby's research material to examine. The materials contained not only the institution's newsletters—*Liberty Letter* monthly and

Liberty Lowdown —but also copies of the columns of the late, great newspaperman, Westbrook Pegler, who had first observed these mysterious meetings from afar and written about them in the 1950s.

I was dumbfounded. How could I have spent my adult life with Associated Press, United Press International and other newswires ticking at my ear, and serve on newspapers with far-flung staffs across the globe and not know of these characters? The *Daily News* had been a Scripps-Howard newspaper; its headquarters on the same third floor as the *News's* staff. Scripps-Howard covered the world. I edited its copy for the *News* and had much communication with the Washington staff of Scripps-Howard.

And that was the year—1975—that started my career as the only reporter who, for three decades now, has worked earnestly to hound this secret meeting of the world's most powerful business-men, powerbrokers and politicians and expose it to the light of public scrutiny.

I soon learned that Bilderberg had recruited the media moguls into its secret conspiracy and dictated an absolute blackout in the United States. There was much *Spotlight*-generated and now *American Free Press*-generated Bilderberg publicity in Europe, but the near total blackout in the United States persists.

Bilderberg is a powerful assembly of the world's leading financiers, industrialists and political operatives.

It includes such internationalists as banker David Rockefeller, heads of state in Europe and high officials of the U.S. government—White House, Defense, State, Congress and others.

Past U.S. presidents—Bill Clinton and Gerald Ford—have attended Bilderberg. But a sitting president cannot because White House paperboys are given his complete schedule each day—the size of a paperback novel, accounting for every minute. Even his schedule on "working vacations"—the only kind a president takes—is provided. There is no way a president can disappear for three days without accounting for himself and if a sitting president attended Bilderberg, even the controlled media would be hard-pressed to explain away the president's absence from the limelight, hidden behind the locked gates of the Bilderberg meeting.

High officials of *The Washington Post, The New York Times,* and *Los Angeles Times* and of all three major networks have attended Bilderberg many times, on the promise of secrecy, to report nothing and to not use the word "Bilderberg." Except for some minor, inconsequential accidents in which the word "Bilderberg" has suddenly appeared in print—after all, you can't call a staff meeting and tell all 900 *New York Times* news staffers about the blackout—the promise has been kept.

The only time "Bilderberg" ever appeared in *The New York Times* came when one of the luminaries died at a meeting and the obituary writer, and his editors, innocently let the word slip through. And, as mentioned earlier, *The New York Times* responded to a blizzard of publicity and criticism in Europe with a "humor" story in 2004 reassuring the world there is no "conspiracy."

Four times the word slipped into *The Washington Post*—which has been represented by successive publishers since Bilderberg's first meeting under that name in 1954. One came in a worshipful profile of Bilderberg luminary Vernon Jordan.

In another instance, in a multi-part profile of then-Vice President Dan Quayle, the fact that Quayle had attended a Bilderberg meeting was mentioned in passing, buried deep in one of the articles in the series. (Not incidentally, the *Post* mentioned that David Rockefeller himself had been quite impressed with Quayle at that meeting.)

Another came in an inside-page story celebrating how Austria was being economically penalized for holding a fair election in which Joerg Haider's Nationalist Party enjoyed significant gains. In a laundry list of important meetings that had been scheduled for Austria, but changed, the *Post* mentioned Bilderberg—but said it had been moved to France when it actually would take place in Belgium, outside Brussels.

Then, in a Dec. 3, 2004, obituary for Prince Bernhard of the Netherlands, The *Post* said: "He is also credited with establishing the Bilderberg Group—a secretive annual discussion forum for prominent politicians, thinkers and businessmen, which he chaired from 1954 to 1976." The *Post* made no mention of its own long-standing involvement in the secretive international body.

And in 2005, Virginia Gov. Mark Warner's attendance at the Bilderberg meeting in Germany was written up in a series of reports across Virginia. Warner is a Democratic governor in a state that has gone Republican since 1952, with the exception of 1964 when Lyndon Johnson trounced Sen. Barry Goldwater (R-Ariz.). His presence signals that the global elite considers him to be a potential president.

Bilderberg and its brother group, the Trilateral Commission, are good at picking future presidents. Actually, they like to own both horses in a two-horse race. Here is the line-up: Jerry Ford, Bilderberg; Jimmy Carter, Trilateral; President Bush the Elder; Trilateral and Bill Clinton, Bilderberg.

Warner, respecting the rules of secrecy, kept the trip off his public calendar. When an Associated Press reporter heard an off-guard comment, Warner admitted attending but refused to divulge information. AP was given the *American Free Press* edition that carried Bilderberg details and the list of participants.

How can such a near-total blackout be imposed on what were, not so many years ago, 1,800 daily newspapers (now down to 1,200) in the United States, all of which thump their chests as protectors and practitioners of freedom of speech?

When the major newspapers are intimidated, it affects all papers and the wire services. Most of the nation's newspapers depend entirely on the wire services for news outside their own cities—state, national and world. If Bilderberg is not on the wires, the local editors are as ignorant as I was for 20 years. They work hard to stay ahead of the city council, high school football team and all local news. Similarly, small broadcast outlets depend on their wire services and network affiliates which, in turn, also depend largely on wire services.

Wire services operate like farmers' co-ops. Big-city newspapers pay many times as much for the services as small-town papers. When they tell the wire services to keep silent on Bilderberg, the pressure is obvious.

Newspaper participants go to any length to keep their vows of silence. It's a heady experience for these journalists to clink cocktail glasses with the rich and famous. They do so at the price of the credibility of their own newspapers.

A recent example came at the Bilderberg meeting in the spring of 2002 at Chantilly, Va. At that time, *The Washington Post* and the entire mainstream media were predicting that the U.S. invasion of Iraq would come "in the late summer or early fall." But, to appease Europeans who opposed the invasion, Secretary of Defense Donald Rumsfeld assured Bilderberg that the invasion would not come until the next year—2003.

Jimmy Lee Hoagland, associate editor and columnist at the *Post,* has escorted his publisher to Bilderberg for years. He had to hear Rumsfeld's assurances. But he let his own newspaper continue with the "late summer or early fall" prediction, knowing it was wrong. He would not even steer his paper straight on the pretense of getting the information elsewhere—too much risk.

But covering Bilderberg is more than a spring adventure—it is a year-round operation. Two of the most significant Bilderberg exposés occurred during the "off-season" and in unlikely ways.

In March 1985, *The Washington Post* carried a few lines of type in its society section, noting that David Rockefeller and Henry Kissinger had a meeting with Mikhail Gorbachev, head of the then-Soviet Union. The *Post* described the meeting as productive, and that was all. A check of the Soviet-controlled media revealed enormous details.

Rockefeller and Kissinger had told Gorbachev they were sympathetic with the economic stress suffered by the Soviet Union and could arrange for U.S. financial aid to its puppet state of Poland if Americans could observe a "free election." So it was arranged that Poland would have a "freely elected" national legislature with only one-third of the seats reserved for the entrenched Communist Party.

Could you imagine a U.S. election where one-third of Congress is reserved for only Democrats or Republicans?

Another one-third of the seats were reserved for the Peasant Party, a wing of the Communist Party that had voted in lockstep with the Kremlin's dictates for 40 years.

But when the "election" was over, young Turks in the Peasant Party seized the moment and voted with members who were truly freely elected to form the government, ousting the communist regime. The fires of freedom then swept Eastern Europe, bringing an end to the Cold War. Based on this information, the still-flourishing *Spotlight* did an advance story on the downfall of communism in Europe, long before the mainstream media had a hint.

Another significant event occurred when NATO celebrated its 50th anniversary in Washington in April 1999. Kenneth Clark, former chancellor of the exchequer in Britain and a longtime Bilderberg luminary, agreed to what he thought would be a "sweetheart session" with a small group of reporters at the National Press Club. I asked the first question, pointing out that he would be attending the Bilderberg meeting in Sintra, Portugal, and inquired about the agenda.

The question stunned him. He was too embarrassed to deny Bilderberg when he had been told the city, country, resort and precise dates. He was pounded by questions. Before the hour ended, he had openly acknowledged that Bilderberg intended for the Western Hemisphere to become an "American Union" similar to the European Union. The American Union's common currency would be the dollar.

Clark acknowledged Bilderberg's plan to develop an Asian-Pacific Union with a third common currency. The world, he confirmed, was to be divided into three great regions for the administrative convenience of the world government emerging under the United Nations. All of this, he said, would come "sooner, rather than later."

Every year, as *Spotlight* and now AFP have pursued Bilderberg, readers have learned what to expect in advance of the mainstream media because those who know are under a vow of silence and the others are ignorant.

It was *Spotlight* readers who turned the beam of publicity on Bilderberg in the European media. That year, 1994, we learned early that Bilderberg would be meeting near Helsinki, Finland. European readers inquired if they should alert the media and the answer was a quick "yes." The result was extensive press and broadcast coverage that stunned Bilderberg luminaries. Bilderberg has suffered extensive coverage in Europe since. However, media and security control is so tight in the United States that readers have had only limited success in exposing Bilderberg here.

Having built a track record of history confirming our reports, the Washington press corps has become intensely interested in what it cannot report. After each Bilderberg meeting, I carry a load of copies of *American Free Press* containing Bilderberg reportage with me to hand out to reporters who can't report. Many tell me directly that they consider the mainstream cover-up a scandal.

I normally dislike it when a question is answered with a question. But I have found it effective, over the years, to respond to reporters who say Bilderberg is just a golf outing with:

"If 120 film stars, or 120 professional football players, gathered secretly each year, in a sealed-off resort patrolled by armed guards, you would bust your [expletive deleted] to learn what transpired. Why, then, no curiosity when 120 of the world's most distinguished leaders in finance and politics gather in that way?'

That question has never been answered.

Not Buying it ...

2004—Stresa, Italy: That year a large contingency of Bilderberg security had been given photos of me and knew in advance I was not "Etienne Davignon" as I had wryly told them at the front gate of the meeting site. I promptly turned around and formulated another plan of attack, inevitably gathering vital information about the meeting from sources inside Bilderberg he has been courting over the years.

CHAPTER ONE

1975-1982

The Early Years

From 1975 to 1982, I supervised Bilderberg coverage by reporters in the field collecting reports on the world's shadow government. When Bilderberg met in Europe, a European correspondent would be assigned. Similarly when meeting in North America, a staff reporter or a local correspondent would be assigned. It was not until 1983 that I began personally covering Bilderberg and it has been a lot of fun ever since. Over the course of those seven years, I accumulated reams of information from multiple sources, of which I have compiled in this first chapter.

he Trilateral Commission was created in July 1973 at the suggestion of Rockefeller during "an earlier Bilderberg meeting," Forrest Murden, a spokesman for the organization, admitted in a telephone interview with me on Dec. 14. Murden, who headed a public relations firm Forrest Murden Co., said he handles "administrative duties" for the Bilderberg organization in the United States on an "at-cost" basis. Its offices occupied the fifth floor of a building at 39 East 51st Street in Manhattan, New York.

Jimmy Carter was recruited for the Trilateral Commission immediately in 1973 because the new organization viewed the obscure Georgia governor as a rising star, Murden said.

The Trilateral Commission is an Asian-oriented counterpart to the Bilderberg organization (which has been oriented toward the interests of the nations of the North Atlantic Treaty Organization) and there is a heavy cross-membership among those two groups and the Council on Foreign Relations (CFR). The CFR is broadly viewed as the U.S. auxiliary to the Bilderberg group. Murden mentioned the overlapping memberships in the three groups while agreeing that characterizing the Trilateral Commission as "an Asian Bilderberg group" was "analogous" because the Japanese are included.

Murden's link with Bilderberg was first uncovered by investigators from the now defunct *Spotlight* in New York. In two telephone interviews, Murden acknowledged his role, which included handling the arrangements when Bilderberg meets in this country, although the group meets annually in different countries.

Murden said, in both interviews, that "Jack Heinz," head of the Bilderberg Steering Committee, was present in his office. Murden was referring to the now-deceased Henry J. Heinz II, head of the Heinz pickle-and-ketchup fortune, who had attended Bilderberg meetings for 21 years. Murden first suggested that Heinz participate in the interview. In the second interview, Murden said Heinz was "in conference." Heinz's son Henry John Heinz III was elected to the U.S. Senate in 1976 after spending $2.9 million—a record—of his own money.

Sen. Heinz later died in a plane crash, and his widow, Theresa, married Heinz's Senate colleague who ultimately became the 2004 Democratic nominee for president, Sen. John Kerry of Massachusetts.

Murden said the next Bilderberg meeting was to be "next spring in England" but the exact site and date were not yet fixed.

Murden acknowledged that the Bilderbergers discuss policy matters affecting the entire world. Asked if Bilderberg discussions had led directly to upheavals in world policy, Murden expressed the opinion that they had. But Murden said he "can't document" the direct results because of the secrecy agreement under which the Bilderbergers meet.

Murden took the official line in his unusually candid interview when pressed on whether policy discussions, which included heads of state, such as U.S. Secretary of State Henry Kissinger and other high government officials, violated Logan Act prohibitions against private citizens trying to influence foreign policy. Murden insisted that such "discussions" are common and legal.

The most significant comments by Murden were his confirmation that Carter was sought out by the Trilateral Commission as a potential political star and that Rockefeller was the power behind the establishment of the Trilateral Commission.

Observers of the world intrigues have long speculated that the Bilderberg organization was the umbrella with the CFR and Trilateral Commission as ribs, citing the heavy cross-membership referred to by Murden.

Rockefeller was first named as a major force behind the Bilderberg organization by Liberty Lobby in its publication, *Liberty Lowdown,* in 1971 and again in 1975. He was publicly suspected of extending his world manipulations through the Trilateral Commission. Murden's comments are the first known public confirmation of this by the Bilderbergers.

When Carter first rose from obscurity, the preliminary observation by opposing Democrats in the early primaries was that he never ran low on funds. It soon became known that he was an early recruit of the Trilateral Commission.

There was no plausible explanation for the high-powered Trilateral Commission to recruit the unknown Georgia governor. In 1973, Carter was totally unknown outside Georgia, and the state was far more widely recognized as the home grounds of former Gov. Lester Maddox and the late Sen. Richard Russell.

Thus, Murden's confirmation has weight that Carter was recruited as a "rising political star" (these words were suggested by *The Spotlight* and accepted by Murden) and not because of some desire to expand the input of the commission. Murden's words amount to tacit admission that the Trilateral Commission was grooming Carter for big things—such as the White House. This would explain Carter's ever-flowing fountain of funds.

Murden himself suggested, during the second interview, that the Dec. 20 edition of *Time* magazine be examined for a "better understanding" of the Trilateral Commission.

Henry Grunwald, then *Time* managing editor, was a Bilderberger. He consistently collaborated with Bilderberg and never broke faith with the group's instructions to suppress information about its meetings. He refused an invitation from Liberty Lobby to be interviewed about his Bilderberg activities.

The *Time* story of Dec. 20 is a sympathetic account of Carter's drawing on both the Brookings Institution and the Trilateral Commission for talent in the new administration.

Time reported:

"Historian Arthur M. Schlesinger Jr. reported in *The Wall Street Journal* that only last month he tried to persuade a Paris audience composed of intellectuals and journalists that the [Trilateral] Commission was a respectable organization and not a 'horrible bankers' conspiracy" dreamed up by the Rockefellers."

Rockefeller Defends Secrecy

Vice President Nelson Rockefeller, running hard for president in 1976 by "not running" with great speed, was having a typical sweetheart session with the left-wing press until the Bilderberg question left him fumbling his way to an incoherent defense of secrecy. The perennial smile disappeared, and a grim expression dropped over his jolly face. His reply was lengthy, incoherent and no response at all. He was visibly shaken.

The knowledge of the Bilderberg history appeared to flash into Rockefeller's mind when the question was posed; his face was jovial until the word "Bilderberg" was uttered and then clouded instantly.

He quickly began replying:

"I went to one . . . an exchange of views among such groups is, uh, uh, essential. It is, uh, very useful if we have people . . . some public . . . some private."

Rockefeller paused, and looked grimly about after that incomplete sentence, then charged on:

"We had some opposition leaders from other countries who would hesitate to express opinions if the meetings were open. I can understand the desire of the press, uh, this is a matter of great concern to the Senate."

Another pause—this time, his eyes appeared to be searching for help: Rocky's long-time Bilderberg collaborator and policy advisor, Secretary of State Henry Kissinger, was not present.

"If a staff memo is subject to subpoena, how can, uh, it's a very serious problem. The 'sunshine laws' [a reference to laws requiring public business to be conducted publicly] have a great deal of appeal, but we must examine it in the light of these issues and, uh, find some balance in this field."

This reply was intended as a response to my question:

"Mr. vice president, you have testified to attending the Bilderberg meeting in 1974. Your brother David has attended many, and another is scheduled April 22-24 in Hot Springs, Va. Since high government officials discuss U.S. policy with leaders from other nations and have their expenses paid by federal funds, do you believe these sessions should be open to the press?"

Some observers viewed it as significant that Rockefeller's lengthy but unresponsive reply failed to take issue with my observation that "U.S. policy" is discussed. But they were unable to determine if that was intended by Rockefeller or merely overlooked in his confusion.

Rockefeller's tacit acceptance of the policy discussion point is considered significant because the Logan Act prohibits private citizens from negotiating U.S. policy.

'Media Cop' Involved in Bilderberg Cover-Up

The publicly acclaimed, self-anointed "media watchdog" that posed as policeman of the national media actually pursued only the jaywalker journalists while participating in covering up one of the major stories of the century: the secret Bilderberg meetings where international policies are developed.

Heading this so-called "Accuracy In Media" (AIM) organization was the late Reed Irvine, who, in 1975, was receiving an annual stipend of $37,000 from the privately owned manufacturer of U.S. money and international monetary policy, the Federal Reserve.

The "Fed," in turn, is allied with the Bilderberg group, which is composed of the world's biggest moneychangers—led by the Rockefellers and Rothschilds.

Liberty Lobby spent years gathering evidence by procuring documents and taking long-range photos of principals attending Bilderberg meetings at sealed-off, heavily guarded sites, which finally forced the internationalists to admit their existence and Associated Press and United Press International to offer bland, "sweetheart" stories.

Now the cover-up, which involved specifically *The New York Times, The Washington Post, Newsweek, National Review* (founded by self-styled "responsible conservative" William F. Buckley, Jr., an heir to a substantial international oil fortune who spent some years in the employ of the CIA) along with certain syndicated columnists, was aimed at portraying the secret Bilderberg meetings as harmless talk-sessions of no consequence.

But the same media moguls who showed such initiative and energy going after selected targets such as former Vice President Spiro Agnew and former President Richard Nixon now show no curiosity whatsoever about the fact that the world's top bankers and politicians would gather under extreme conditions of secrecy—armed guards, flushed-out hotels and other security measures that suggest a summit of heads-of-state—for harmless chatter.

Nor do they show interest in obvious correlation: the devaluation of the dollar and upheavals in foreign policy that have followed Bilderberg meetings over the years.

Irvine's position as head of AIM while on the Fed's payroll was analogous to a police chief taking Mafia bribes.

AIM's raging inertia is an understandable paradox. It would cost Irvine his $37,000 yearly salary from the Fed if he upset the Bilderberg cover-up, and to some extent, his working for the Fed made him part of it.

Leaders of the giant liberal press were part of the cover-up. Grunwald, managing editor of *Time* magazine; Buckley, syndicated columnist and editor of *National Review*; Osborn Elliott, *Newsweek*, Frederick S. Beebe, a *Washington Post* official; Gardner Cowles, Cowles Publications; syndicated columnist Joseph Kraft, *Look* and an armada from *The New York Times*, including the late Arthur Hays Sulzberger, C.L. Sulzberger, James Reston, Max Frankel and Thomas Wicker, were all invited guests at Bilderberg meetings, where they hobnobbed with the sacrosanct international moneychangers.

So close is the marriage between the Fed and AIM that Irvine sometimes corresponded on behalf of AIM using Fed stationery. But Irvine would follow orders: a plum of $37,000 annually was a tidy income for a part-time or no-time job in 1975, in addition to his AIM salary. Since he was working for basically the same outfit (the Fed-AIM) and drawing two checks, Irvine behaved.

Irvine performed his Bilderberg mission well, but not well enough. Each year, more and more was being written about the Bilderbergers by independent, enlightened newspapers and periodicals in the United States and Europe led by *The Spotlight* and now, following the demise of that newspaper in 2001, by *American Free Press*.

Bilderberg's Founder . . .

Prince Bernhard of the Netherlands: Above, in a rare photo of the prince, Joseph Desire Mobutu (left), then-president of Zaire, is seen wagging a finger at Bernhard after the prince presented him with a medal, in 1973. Following World War II, Bernhard founded the secret group known later as Bilderberg. When he died on Dec. 1, 2004, the Associated Press's obituary credited him with "establishing the Bilderberg Group—a secretive annual forum for prominent politicians, thinkers and businessmen—which he chaired from 1954 to 1976."

CHAPTER TWO

1983

Quebec, Montreal

In my first year covering Bilderberg from the site of its annual meeting, the world's shadow government was forced to admit its interlocking relationship with the Trilateral Commission while gathering near Montreal in 1983.

ilderbergers went to a great deal of trouble to assure a "sweetheart press" in 1983 that they're just a bunch of "good ole' boys" having a little private party—in which, matters troubling your heart and mine will undergo sympathetic, sensitive discussions. Translated, of course, it means that the houses of Rockefeller and Rothschild, and their colleagues, are plotting to rip off the American taxpayer.

Four Bilderberg luminaries sat at a table behind water pitchers to bestow condescending smiles and words on a room jammed with toadying "journalists" and broadcasters.

Even the location was tactical. The press conference, held May 12, one day before the three-day conference, had been scheduled for the swanky hotel at Mirabel Airport. That's the international airport 30 miles from the remote Montebello resort, the site of the gathering that year.

But the scene was shifted to the Chateau Champlain in the heart of downtown Montreal. That was more convenient to the sweetheart press and 30 miles farther from Montebello—a town the Bilderbergers insisted would be of no news value that week-end.

Theodore Eliot Jr., the honorary secretary-general for the U.S. Bilderberg subgroup and dean of the Fletcher School of Law and Diplomacy at Tufts University, Walter Scheel, former president of West Germany and current Bilderberg chairman, Victor Halberstadt, professor of public finance at Leyden University and honorary Bilderberg secretary-general for Europe and Canada and Willem F. Duisenberg, president of the Netherlands Bank and honorary Bilderberg treasurer, were the Bilderberg officials meeting their adoring press.

The practice of holding "press conferences" was introduced in April 1975 when the Bilderbergers met in Cesme, Turkey. It came only after relentless reporting by Liberty Lobby's *Liberty Letter* had prompted respectful stories by United Press International, Associated Press and the *Washington Post-L.A. Times* wires.

Although the establishment stories were, and have generally remained, in the nature of cheerleading and hardly of substance, considering the nature of the issues discussed behind closed doors by the global elite, the Bilderbergers felt compelled to drop the pretense that they did not exist.

They began holding press conferences in advance of the meetings, providing incomplete lists of participants, which they insisted were "complete," and saying that they would be doing nothing significant for three days. Later, they would hold a post-meeting press conference to announce that, indeed, they had done nothing.

Scheel opened the press conference by reading a prepared statement in French to the effect that there would be an innocent exchange of ideas that would never, never be translated into tangible results.

"Why meet at all?" he was asked.

There was some uncomfortable squirming before Eliot came to the rescue: "George Ball said that, by the time he became No. 2

2001—Gothenburg, Sweden: A member of the Swedish SWAT police force confronted me personally this year. The Swedes weren't taking chances with security and one of their concerns was keeping me away from the meeting site.

man in the State Department, thanks to the Bilderberg meetings, he had come to know the European leaders he worked with."

You could perceive the relief felt by the establishment press and the Bilderbergers.

Nor was the answer really as silly as it sounds. Ball was among a swarm of Bilderbergers placed at the top of the government by President John Kennedy in 1961. By the time of Carter's election in 1976, it was Rockefeller's other group, the Trilateral Commission, which implemented the shared policies of both Bilderberg and Trilateral through high appointive office.

A journalist asked about the Bilderbergers' Trilateral connections.

Scheel acknowledged some overlapping membership but denied any connection, saying there were "differences" because the Trilateralists "have more who attend all meetings," while the

Bilderbergers invite some participants who are one-time attendees.

The entire panel was challenged on this, with the observation
that the steering committee and advisory committee account for
44 permanent members, in addition to numerous members who
hold no Bilderberg office, but come every year, such as the
Rothschilds and Rockefellers, who jointly founded the Bilderberg
organization in 1954.

Eliot made the next mistake.

Objecting to characterizing Bilderberg meetings as "secret,"
while denying that this meeting had anything to do with the April
meeting of the Trilateral Commission in Rome or the upcoming
economic summit scheduled for May 28-30 in Williamsburg, Va.,
Eliot insisted on the term "private," rather than "secret."

Many meetings are being held "privately" on the subject of
world economics, he said, but the Bilderbergers tell everybody
about their meetings and do not deserve the "secret" label.

He was reminded that the Bilderbergers had denied their own
existence for more than a decade, and only went public after reading about themselves.

An awkward silence followed.

I asked, "considering that the president of the World Bank [A.
W. Clausen] and the chairman of the Federal Reserve Board [Paul
Volcker] are among numerous high officials and international financiers who will participate, do you expect to discuss the debt
problems of the Third-World and East-Bloc countries?"

"Well, anything can come up," Eliot responded.

"How can it not come up, when you are scheduled to discuss
'risks in banking and finance' and other issues on medium-term
prospects for growth in the world economy' and such?" I asked a
Bilderberg staffer later.

Still, Eliot refused to acknowledge that such a subject would
come up, although they all knew full well it would and did.

Scheel kept emphasizing that there was no joint communiqué.

Instead, he said, Bilderberg members would use the knowledge obtained at the meeting to press for various objectives, each in his "own sphere of influence."

"Under what terms have the chosen journalists been invited?" I asked. "Do they have an advantage in covering this meeting the rest of us are denied?"

"No" was the universal response. As are the rules of access for the Trilateralists' chosen journalists, the entire three days at a Bilderberg conclave is "off the record." Under the code of journalism, none of the press members attending the "private" meeting can report on what transpires behind the locked and guarded doors.

"They are journalist prostitutes," I said. "An event of significance to the whole world, and every taxpaying American, is taking place, and they are honor-bound not to tell the story."

The chosen journalists were headed by the permanent Bilderberger Henry Grunwald, head of *Time*. Others were Elizabeth Drew, widely known from the "Agronsky and Co." talk show, Lise Bissonette (editor of "*le Devoir*"), Bjorn Bjarnason, described as a "political journalist", William P. Bundy, editor of the Council on Foreign Relations' journal, *Foreign Affairs*, and a former Kennedy-era government official, Andrew Knight, editor of London's *Economist*, Neils Norlund, editor of *Berlingske Tidende*, and Theo Sommer, editor of the German publication *die Zeit*.

Pressed to tell more about what would take place, Eliot said that he always comes out of Bilderberg meetings with new "funny stories."

The pre-meeting press conference closed with the announcement that this year, unlike the recent past, there would be no post-meeting press conference.

Secluded Sweden ...

1984—Saltsjobaden, Sweden: My second year covering Bilderberg at the site of its annual gathering was at this four-star resort at Saltsjobaden, Sweden. That year, Bilderbergers called for increasing taxes in the United States to provide a safety net for the cabal of international financiers in the event that Third World and former communist countries default on risky loans made to them

CHAPTER THREE

1984

Saltsjobaden, Sweden

American Bilderberg watchers learned in 1984 that their taxes were to be increased in the years ahead, which, of course, came about.

he Bilderberg organization of international financiers and captive politicians planned to increase Americans' income taxes by $108 billion so there'll be plenty of money around when the time comes to again rescue them from bad loans to Third World and communist countries.

The proposal, presented at its annual closed-door meeting May 11-13, 1984, at Saltsjobaden, Sweden, called for tax increases that would immediately add $23 billion in revenue.

For fiscal year 1986, the hike would amount to $39 billion; in 1987, $61 billion; in 1988, $83 billion; reaching a total of $108 billion in new revenue by 1989.

The call for new tax increases came in a paper entitled "The Outlook for the Economy and Employment in the United States," presented by Alice M. Rivlin, director of the Economic Studies Program at the Brookings Institution.

Two other Brookings Institution officials who attended, Bruce K. MacLaury, president, and William B. Quandt, a senior fellow, declined comment. Miss Rivlin was also "not available," but I obtained a copy of her paper.

For no other country did the Bilderbergers presume to present a tax policy. But their strategy on behalf of the international bankers was well coordinated with that of their brother group, the Trilateral Commission.

As in the Trilateral meeting held in Washington, D.C., on March 31-April 3, 1984, the United States was blamed for the staggering debts of Third World and communist countries on grounds that the budget deficits generate inflation.

Enough pressure was exerted at both meetings to block a proposal to put a "cap" on interest rates on Third World debts, which then totaled $810 billion. Every time the privately owned and controlled Federal Reserve Board hikes the prime interest rate, it adds billions of dollars to the Third World's interest obligations. The Fed had hiked the rate by tightening the money supply since the Trilateral meeting in 1984, adding billions to the interest payments the debtor nations had to make to the big banks.

The proposal to ease the burden on the debtor nations by putting a limit on the interest charged was quickly rejected by Jacques de Larosiere, managing director of the International Monetary Fund (IMF), when IMF member-nations met in Philadelphia June 4 of that year.

"Capping [interest rates] would detract from the ability of central banks to facilitate" repayment of the debts, Larosiere said during the IMF's meeting.

According to three sources inside the Bilderberg meetings, the idea of limiting interest rates was effectively blocked while guilt was heaped on the United States as the culprit of the Third World's economic woes to set the mood for pressuring the United States for another bailout by the taxpayers.

"High interest rates in the United States lead to high interest rates around the world and greatly aggravate the precarious international debt situation," one paper delivered at the Bilderberg meeting said. "As interest rates rise, Third World countries find it increasingly difficult to meet the interest payments on their debt."

All blamed the interest rates on the U.S. budget deficits, setting the tone calling for higher U.S. taxes.

"It's a sham," I later told friends. "They demand higher taxes on Americans so funds will be available for the next bank bail-out while they influence the Fed to boost the prime rate—and their own profits by the corresponding billions—at a time when inflation is low."

During President Carter's time, bankers blamed high interest rates on double-digit inflation. When inflation was running at 14 percent annually, they pointed out that if they loaned $100 at 14 percent, they would lose because the $114 paid back after a year would be worth only $100.

Yet, with inflation down to a 3 to 5 percent annual rate, interest rates were kept high by the Fed. This made it more profitable to make loans to Third World and communist countries that are bad risks rather than to American farmers who offer their land and crops as collateral. American taxpayers, in effect, guaranteed the banks against losses to the Third World and communist countries. Meanwhile, thousands of American farmers lost their land every year because of the credit crunch.

On June 6 of that year, one day after I obtained a copy of her paper, Miss Rivlin presented the plan to a select group of establishment reporters as the Brookings Institution's proposal. The fact that it had emerged behind the locked doors of the Bilderberg meeting was not mentioned.

"The proposals for domestic spending and tax changes are in two stages," Miss Rivlin had told the approving Bilderbergers. "A short-run freeze on domestic spending to save money quickly would be followed by more basic restructuring of domestic programs. Similarly, tax changes designed to raise more revenue quickly through broadening the tax base and a surtax would be followed by a thorough reform of the federal system."

While the precise percentage of the proposed surtax was not mentioned, it would have to be enough to generate $23 billion more in revenues the first year and increase annually until it produced $108 billion more in 1989.

Perle of a Man ...

1985—Richard Perle, here appearing young, full of hair and not so corpulent as he is today, has regularly attended Bilderberg meetings since he first rose to power in the Reagan administration. In 1985, at the Arrowwood Resort, I pocketed Perle's nametag as proof that he was in attendance that year. Since its inception, Bilderberg has kept the list of its attendees from the public, including those U.S. officials who have attended on the American taxpayers' dime.

CHAPTER FOUR

1985

White Plains, New York

In 1985, I "crashed" the super-secret Bilderberg meeting at the exclusive Arrowwood Hotel in White Plains, N.Y., with the help of a number of local people, including an imaginative cab driver. For obvious reasons, the name of the cab driver is deleted.

"Your name is Mr. X" instead of Jim Tucker, the cab driver said.

"Fine," I responded. "I didn't think I could get away with being Henry Kissinger."

As the cab approached the plain-clothes guards who had road-blocked the entrance to the exclusive Arrowwood Hotel for the 33rd Bilderberg conference, I sat far to the right rear, hoping that my having made an earlier attempt to enter would not cause them to recognize me.

"Mr. X," the cab driver announced, and we were waved through. Obviously, it wasn't the name "X" that was used, but we had adopted a name that had a close resemblance to the name of a very real Bilderberg member who was registered for the meeting. I was posing as someone who very much had the right to be admitted and the ruse worked. (And this, of course, was in the earlier years when Bilderberg security was not quite as tight as it is today.)

A slight deception, of course, but well worth it for the sake of bringing much-needed news that Bilderberg would rather have had suppressed.

At the hotel, I was confronted by a smiling young lady in the lobby who was waiting to register me and tuck me into Bilderberg. Whoops!

I had nothing to identify me as Mr. X: in fact, I didn't even know whom "X" worked for or what magic the name would have. My peripheral vision showed that the Secret Service men had taken their eyes off me and were gazing in their assigned directions at the entrance to the lobby.

"Yes, yes, of course," I responded to her greeting. "But first," I said, showing great stress, "where's the men's room? Quick!"

"This way," she responded, and led me there right away.

I spent an hour in a place next to the restroom called the "Pub." I was the only customer, listening to the bartender and waitresses complain that they normally have at least 60 people at that time.

"Security has never been so tight," one said. "I had trouble coming to work."

"Who are all these big shots?" asked this journalist, playing innocent and ignorant.

"I don't know," the bartender replied. "A 'Bush' is coming, but they don't tell us anything."

"The vice president?"

"I don't know; all I know is that a Bush—one of them—is coming." Bush was neither on the list made available to reporters nor on the internal, slightly expanded list given to participants.

"But how can they close off a whole hotel for three days?" I asked. The bartender looked disturbed; he suddenly realized that, if I were not "one of them" I wasn't supposed to be here. And, if I were, why would I not know these things?

"It's some kind of diplomatic meeting," he said, still looking at me with uncertainty. "This bar, and the whole hotel, is only open to them. You, er, everybody, was checked out at the gate."

"Of course," I reassured him. "I'm only here to pick up something for somebody."

By now, there were more people milling about and it was easier to feign a benign Bilderberg look and move around. I checked one head table in a conference room and found only hotel brochures. I grabbed them anyway—in this business, you swipe first and examine later.

Checks of every restroom for discarded Bilderberg notes produced nothing.

In the main conference room, which looks like a small UN assembly chamber, hotel staffers were bringing in flowers.

"Hello," I smiled while striding past.

"Good evening, sir."

Posing as an aide to a Bilderberger, I made a leisurely search for nameplates, obviously trying to locate my boss's place so he could walk there with authority and no uncertainty.

"If I can't get something substantial, I'll at least get a souvenir," I thought. My eye fell upon a particular nameplate: "PERLE."

That would be for Richard Perle, assistant secretary of defense for international security policy. An old colleague, Andrew St. George, had long ago exposed Perle for advocating the interests of Israel over those of the United States, and his shocking stories were confirmed by the National Association of Arab Americans (NAAA), which used the Freedom of Information Act for much of the devastating evidence that the NAAA was pursuing in court.

So that would be one memento: the "PERLE" nameplate went into my pocket.

I found that the way to dismiss a challenge is with a question during my strolls; "The steering committee meeting is tonight, isn't it?"

I had been surreptitiously eyeballing a lineup of brown, stuffed portfolios in the lobby, presided over by two women and watched over by three Secret Service men. Of course, I wanted one, but it would be a chancy thing and timing would be essential. If I were caught, the notes I had taken, and the Perle nameplate, would be lost. I would probably go to jail. At least, the Secret Service would spend a lot of time shaking me down.

I remembered the name of a lesser-publicized Bilderberger who had probably not arrived. I then asked an attendant for a cab, explaining that I had left something at the airport. Of course, guests don't normally explain themselves to bellboys, but I wanted to reassure a Secret Service agent, who was listening while gazing in another direction.

I let two minutes expire, then approached the table loaded with portfolios.

"Do you have a portfolio for Sen. Charles Mathias?" I asked. "The senator needs a briefing." (This referred to then-Sen. Mathias of Maryland.)

The woman looked uncertain. "Your cab, sir!"

"Oh," I said, with understanding.

"Of course you want some identification," I said, partially exposing congressional press credentials. "I'm in a rush."

"Your cab, sir!"

"Coming," I shouted, grabbing the portfolio and thanking the distressed lady.

There was one more hurdle: the guards at the roadblock. Had the Secret Service radioed them to stop the cab? I had carried only notepaper in my pocket for such an eventuality. I put the portfolio on my right side, sitting against it and keeping it from view.

If challenged, my plan was to leap out, start arguing momentarily, then break for the adjacent golf course, head for the trees and lose myself on the campus of the State University of New York (SUNY) at Purchase.

Having enjoyed the challenge, I told myself how silly I was to feel a sense of disappointment when the "palace guard" waved me on with deference due royalty.

I didn't have to tell the cab driver to step on it; we had been collaborating since the guards had turned us away the first time I tried to enter earlier in the day. The hackie had expressed interest in the intrigues that had settled over this town and, when I had finished giving him a brief civics lesson and a fat tip, we had talked of ways

MARYLAND SEN. CHARLES MATHIAS, shown above in an undated photograph, was so upset that I had taken his Bilderberg meeting portfolio in 1985 that he demanded my press credentials in Congress be revoked. Like any good journalist worth his salt, I had used the information obtained in Mathias's packet to report in detail on the agenda of that year's secret confab. To this day, the bureaucrats in Congress—pawns of Bilderberg—have refused to restore my credentials.

to pierce the veil.

After the morning blockade, as he drove me back to my hotel, I had suggested entering the college and crossing the golf course under cover of darkness.

"Nah," he said, "The SS [Secret Service, not storm troopers] are expecting that; they know nobody plays golf at night. Better to jump over the fence about 4 p.m., when lots of golfers and kids are around."

We had ridden on in silence for a few minutes, then a thought popped into my head.

"Hey, you're likely to be taking others from the airport to the Arrowwood today, aren't you?" I asked. "They will have to give you a name to give the guards. Remember the name—not a famous name—then wait a couple of hours and use the same name for me.

"It's not a matter of calling up unless there is doubt. The guards have a list to check and, if the name's there, the car is waved through. For that kind of service, of course, a decent gratuity is in order" (sufficient to amount to a bribe, but cabbies are more comfortable with euphemisms).

So that's how I became Mr. X and assumed management of Sen. Charles Mathias's Bilderberg portfolio, containing all available documents, advance texts, the secret list of participants that goes beyond the "public list" and the means of waking up Kissinger in his hotel room, the list having conveniently provided the room numbers at the hotel of all of the listed participants.

Cars had been parked to block off the entrance to the plush Arrowwood a full day in advance of the Bilderberg meeting and only employees who had worked there for at least three months could report to work.

Arriving the first time 24 hours before the meeting, the cab had been challenged by efficient-looking young men in uniform blue blazers.

"Your name, please?"

"That's private property, sir," I had responded. "What's the problem?"

"The hotel is booked today for a private meeting."

"How could that be?" I inquired. "I called the hotel this morning. They told me that a bar inside the Arrowwood called 'the Pub' would be open at 11 a.m. and I'm supposed to meet someone there at noon."

"Who are you supposed to meet?"

"I'm not accustomed to explaining myself to bellboys and I don't intend to become accustomed to that," I responded.

By now, all three bright blazers surrounded my cab, letting certified Bilderbergers and fellow travelers wait. They did not relish the rank of "bellboy."

"I'm sorry, sir," he said. "If you could give me a name, I could check for a security clearance. But right now, the hotel is booked for a private party."

"What private party? Who are they?"

"I'm sorry, sir; I can't tell you, for security reasons."

"Whose security? Mine or theirs?"

The silence hung heavy. So, out of social kindness, I filled the embarrassing conversation gap:

"How long is the party booked—until 4 p.m.?"

"All day, sir."

"And tomorrow, too? When does the private party end?"

"I can't tell you. "

We turned away. As the guards looked at me, I could read their faces:

"He will be back."

They were right.

Stripped of Press Credentials

I was stripped of my credentials as a congressional correspondent, my pen name of "Harrison Horne" unveiled, and my income reduced several thousand dollars annually by Sen. Charles McC. Mathias (R-MD.)

Mathias was angry because I, posing as a member of his staff, had obtained the portfolio assigned to the senator at the Bilderberg meeting near White Plains, N.Y.

The portfolio contained texts of speeches, private telephone numbers and the confidential (as opposed to the public) list of participants. I had relied, in part, on the contents of the portfolio in revealing what had transpired among the Bilderbergers behind the locked and guarded doors of the Arrowwood Hotel. Other information in the stories was based on interviews inside the hotel when employees and Bilderbergers thought I was a member of the Bilderberg group.

At the time, I was an anti-establishment free-lance writer based in Washington. I had used the pen named "Harrison Horne" in order to confuse both the Bilderbergers and their brother group, the Trilateral Commission, about my identity.

Word that I had been found out and that my credentials as a member of the congressional press galleries would be revoked came in an angry phone call from Roy L. McGhee, superintendent of the Senate periodical press gallery on June 4 of that year.

McGhee said he was acting on a complaint by Charles Muller of New York, who heads the Bilderberg staff in the United States.

"They [Bilderbergers] have a right to a private meeting," McGhee had screamed. "None of the other papers carried anything."

"This was not a 'private meeting'," I countered. "It involves elected officials and other high officials of the State Department and other agencies."

"You took Sen. Mathias's property and did not return it?"

"Yes," I replied. "The public has an overriding right to know when public business is conducted behind closed doors."

However, McGhee—most likely under extreme pressure—refused to see the importance of exposing Bilderberg and threatened to lift the credentials of all the publications I free-lanced for unless I surrendered my credentials.

The congressional press galleries give credentials to publications, not individuals, so a writer serving several will be technically representing one.

I called my boss at the publication that had provided the credentials, asked to be fired and surrendered my credentials. My boss had received similar threats. Indirectly, I lost other clients and was economically punished in amounts of at least $10,000 annually.

I later called the press gallery and told the staff to expect the surrendered credentials by certified mail.

"If not offending a senator is a condition of carrying the card, I don't want it," I said. " I have a lot more senators to offend yet."

It is possible, but more difficult, to cover Congress without credentials. Sometimes witness lists and texts are in limited supply and provided only to those with credentials. Sometimes you sit on the floor instead of at a table if you are uncredentialed.

But the press galleries also amount to a huge taxpayer subsidy for many Washington journalists who are careful to avoid offending senators or congressmen. For many reporters, the galleries are a free office with telephone and various and sundry office supplies. Compare that to renting a small office for more than $1,000 monthly at the National Press Club, paying for telephones, furniture and supplies. The subsidy amounts to a huge payoff.

Journalists, explained a sympathetic colleague in the press galleries, are permitted credentials "at the sufferance of Congress."

The same colleague, who remains anonymous to protect his own green, plastic I.D. card, advised surrendering the card to avoid an intimidating, harassing investigation.

"They have an investigative staff with little to do, and they're eager to have somebody to investigate," he said.

As explained in detail earlier in this chapter, the incident that enraged the senator occurred after I had entered the Bilderbergers' hotel under a ruse and had spent time interviewing staff members and examining documents.

I saw the stack of simulated leather portfolios, each bearing the name of a participant, called a cab, explained that the senator needed a "briefing," showed my card and escaped with the property. Apparently, an alert Bilderberg staffer had spotted the name "Tucker" as my card was quickly flashed.

It is closed meetings of these types, Henry Kissinger and similar notables always attend, that McGhee defended, saying the elitists have a "right to a private meeting."

Fore... the Elites Only...

April 1986—Gleneagles, Scotland: Bilderbergers met this time in the secluded luxury resort and gold club in quiet Scottish town. Discussions that year focused on getting George H.W. Bush elected in 1988 and how to get more money for corrupt leaders and petty chieftains in Africa.

CHAPTER FIVE

1986

Gleneagles, Scotland

On the 1986 agenda for Bilderberg, was electing George H.W. Bush president, obtaining more money for Africa and bringing about an end to apartheid in South Africa. In fact, Bush was elected in 1988, taxpayers' dollars went to Africa and South Africa was turned over to a black government.

he world's shadow government, meeting in 1986 in Scotland and Spain, mapped out a campaign to escalate sagging oil prices, throw more American tax dollars to Third World and communist countries in Africa and pressure South Africa to end apartheid. The Trilateral-Bilderberg combine presented its subterranean proposals in a manner intended to convince the public the opposite was true.

Another priority agenda item—electing their own George Bush president—is so well on track, Bilderbergers said, that there was little to worry about.

What happened at the clandestine meetings of Bilderberg at the Gleneagles Golf Club in Scotland on April 24-27 and of its brother group, the Trilateral Commission, in Madrid, Spain May 17-19, was unearthed by subtlety.

One source, thinking he was talking to a Boston lawyer preparing a background paper for a participant, provided a verbal account of what transpired.

Another, trying to help a "graduate student" write on international affairs from an informed position, provided observations plus deep-background papers on condition that the words "Trilateral Commission" and "Bilderberg" not be used.

"We've got George in great shape; he's nominated and will probably be elected," said one, providing a press release from the Fund for America's Future, organized by Vice President George Bush as a vehicle for launching his 1988 White House campaign.

In less than a year, the document showed, Bush's committee had raised more than $6 million. It was founded in May 1986 after the Bilderberg meeting held near White Plains, N.Y. designated Bush for the GOP nomination. Bush is a longtime member of the brother group, the Trilateralists. The fund report noted that it contributed 27 percent of its receipts "directly to campaigns during the first quarter of this year" and, "This proves that Vice President Bush is the leader in the 1986 GOP effort to ensure Republican victories in November."

Bush had made 41 political appearances in 22 states, the fund reported. "He's collecting so many political IOUs with money and campaign appearances that he'll be impossible to catch in 1988," said the Bilderberg source.

The formal agenda, said the other source, was to "deal with the international economic problems—which means oil prices—and the financial distress of the African countries." Unbeknownst to him, he confirmed what the other source told me, that pressure on the government of South Africa would get much attention.

Both were asked if the Trilateral-Bilderberg coalition of international financiers and political leaders would similarly demonstrate their concerns for the human condition by pressuring the Soviet Union to abandon its policy of killing and enslaving political dissidents.

Both sources responded that, while Soviet repression is "not condoned," the situation in South Africa is now "critical" because of the "high public awareness" generated by people such as Sen.

April 1986—Washington, D.C.: Former Vice President Walter Mondale laughed when he was introduced to me. I introduced a friend as "an endangered species— one who voted for you" in the 1984 presidential campaign. However, Mondale's smile disappeared when questioned about his attendance, along with former President Jimmy Carter, at Trilateral meetings. "They do good work," he groused.

Ted Kennedy (D-Mass.), who travels there denouncing the segregation policies, and students boycotting firms doing business there.

"If they'd yell as much about atrocities in communist countries we would have to try to pacify them on that, too," said one source.

Noting that representatives of South Africa have attended Bilderberg and Trilateral meetings, this source said: "We were already making progress" on the issue before the meeting.

The next day, on April 18, South African President Pieter W. Botha announced that the "pass laws" would end within a few days on publication of a government white paper on urbanization. The pass laws restrict most blacks to their tribal homelands; those who wish to live outside must carry special permits.

A background paper on the Bilderberg-Trilateral program called for billions more in American tax dollars to be poured into the African continent. It was produced as a joint project of the Council on Foreign Relations (CFR) and the Overseas Development Council.

Endorsing the report calling for billions more for Africa from America were Rockefeller, John Temple Swing (CFR) and Robert McNamara, former president of Ford, secretary of defense under presidents John Kennedy and Lyndon Johnson, and a Trilateralist.

The report said, on page 20: "The United States should make a full contribution of $1.33 billion a year over the next three years to the eighth replenishment of the International Development Association, the 'soft loan' window of the World Bank, to ensure more adequate long-term multilateral finance for African development."

And, on page 21: "The United States should triple the long-term U.S. financing going to Africa, through a combination of bilateral and multilateral programs, to reach a new level of $3 billion per year."

The most difficult problem for the world shadow government remained the plunging oil prices. Oil is not only a direct source of megaprofits for these internationalists, but lower prices in the poorer debtor nations make it more difficult for them to repay their loans to the big banks.

Bush received so much political flak—from his recent statements that the prices must be propped up and hints that he would urge Saudi Arabia to reduce production—that he has been ordered into a low-key role.

President Ronald Reagan, who made the circle from Trilateral

2002—Chantilly, Virginia: In the above picture, I was photographed here attempting to get a reservation in the Marriott Hotel for the period of the Bilderberg meeting. I was told that all guests would be evicted from their rooms and the hotel would be closed for a special conference. Every year Bilderberg instructs all staff at the sites to keep mum about the meetings and threatens staff with dismissal if they divulge information to reporters.

critic in his 1980 campaign to Trilateral host at the White House in 1981, was ultimately back to his original balky self, opposing the internationalists' strange plea for "protectionist" import fees on oil.

Both the Trilateralists and Bilderbergers sent their political leaders home to campaign for production cutbacks to end the current oil glut and force prices upward. Since former heads of state and other high officials of many governments meet with the international financiers, much influence was directly applied to reduce production.

Americans were told to "welcome the stabilization" in oil prices as a matter of "national security" and to prevent new and harsher shortages in the years ahead.

"This is one of our more difficult periods," said one source, "but these things will come to pass. We have to do something about oil and Africa."

Presidential Pardon . . .

March 1991—Press Club, Washington, D.C: Former President Gerald Ford attended a Bilderberg meeting when he was House majority leader. When I questioned Ford in 1991 about the particulars of the meeting he said, fumbling over his words, "Pardon me, I really, uh, don't . . ." But before he could finish his statement, he was whisked off by his entourage. As you may remember, Ford was well known for stumbling over his words . . . and his own feet.

CHAPTER SIX

1987

Cernobbio, Italy

Bilderberg outfoxed us in 1987 and its secret meeting remained secret. But, with the help of crucial sources, it was possible to determine the scene of the crime and some of what transpired.

Bilderberg boys must have felt smug when they held a secret meeting April 24-26, 1987, at the Villa D'Este luxury resort here—no reporters or cameramen patrolled outside the gates.

That year Bilderberg succeeded in keeping its secret meeting secret, but continued pursuit, in collaboration with others, exposed much of what transpired behind the locked and guarded doors of the palatial resort.

It was subsequently learned that much of the Bilderberg discussion centered on the presidential election coming up a year later, in 1988. Since Vice President George Bush belongs to their junior varsity, the Trilateral Commission, Bilderberg used its immense influence to secure the Republican nomination for him. But, as mentioned, Bilderberg likes to own both horses in a two-horse race. So their choice for the Democratic nomination was Vice President Walter Mondale, who, like President Jimmy Carter, is a Trilateral veteran.

Most expected Bush to win because of the overwhelming popularity of his boss, President Reagan. But Bilderberg believes in taking no chances—in politics, anything can happen.

There was more discussion of the need to slow down production of oil to end the "glut" and generate higher prices. Many Bilderberg luminaries inherited their billions through the oil industry, most notably, Rockefeller.

Standard agenda items also received much attention: securing the European community as a single "super state," promoting "free" trade agreements that will result in an "American Union" with a single currency—the dollar. Similar to Europe, the "American Union" is to have a legislature and court superior to the U.S. Congress and Supreme Court. Every nation in the Western Hemisphere is to surrender national sovereignty to the "American Union."

2001—Gothenburg, Sweden: Police were busy arresting reporters and transporting them miles away from the Bilderberg meeting site. Above, a European journalist is loaded off a van in the middle of nowhere. The photo was snapped by AFP's Christopher Bollyn, who was on assignment with me that year. Bollyn was among those "dumped off" on the isolated roadway. It did not deter Bollyn, who hiked back to the meeting and promptly began snapping more photos.

2005—Rottach-Egern, Germany: Richard Holbrooke, a prominent U.S. diplomat and investment banker, takes a moment to communicate on his cellphone on the grounds of the meeting site in Germany. Holbrooke has been a regular at shadowy Bilderberg meetings since 1996, when he was President Bill Clinton's special envoy in Bosnia and Kosovo.

Kissinger's Lips Slip . . .

1988—Washington, D.C.: Longtime Bilderberg attendee and political powerbroker Henry Kissinger was so startled when I asked him about comments he made at a Bilderberg meeting in Telfs, Austria, he momentarily forgot he was supposed to have a thick German accent and said in perfect English: "That was a private meeting. . . ." Realizing his gaff, Kissinger immediately repeated the line to me in his trademark German affected accent.

CHAPTER SEVEN

1988

Innsbruck, Austria

Vice President George Bush knew, before he was elected, that he would break his famous "read my lips: no new taxes" pledge made during televised debates with Gov. Michael Dukakis of Massachusetts, the Democratic nominee. As president, Bush kept his word to Bilderberg but lost his re-election campaign in 1992.

s a summit in Moscow was ending, another meeting—this one of the world's clandestine leaders—was beginning. The results here had more impact on individual, taxpaying Americans. The Bilderberg group, meeting at a luxury resort atop a mountain nestled among the Alps, established its agenda for the years ahead:

• Impose higher taxes—in any form politically attainable—on Americans to increase war spending, using as an excuse the need for a stronger NATO force and the Strategic Defense Initiative (SDI). Part of the political argument to be set forth by the next president and new Congress is America's "deficit crisis," which would be blamed for the economic problems of an "interdependent world."

• Elect George Bush president. This was no tribute to Michael Dukakis, who was conceded to have the Democratic nomination locked up. Rather, Dukakis was an unknown candidate who might make drastic reductions in military spending, which would similarly reduce profits from the war industry, and might abolish "Star Wars," or SDI, in which the Bilderberg group was heavily involved.

Bush was one of their own, as a member of the Bilderberg's brother group, the Trilateral Commission. SDI had been on the Bilderberg agenda since Bush was elected vice president and from the moment President Reagan announced his space shield plan.

The new development in Bilderberg world policy, emerging from its meeting June 2-5, was the plan to spend more on NATO, also a richly profitable venture.

The Bilderbergers mapped out their strategy protected by armed guards who patrolled the only entrance to the Interalpen-Hotel Tyrol that sits above the tiny town of Telfs, 16 miles from Innsbruck.

Most, perhaps all, Bilderberg participants arrived by helicopter. The only other access is a two-lane road that circles the mountain to the top.

The road approach to the luxury resort, built two years previously, was marked by a little coffee shop. During the Bilderberg meeting, it was the only place in the entire complex where the unwashed multitude could enjoy refreshments.

From the site of the coffee shop, it was necessary to drive 300 more yards to the mountain peak, where the Interalpen was situated. There, armed guards patrolled the only entrance, which was fortified with a guardhouse.

The site selection was another manifestation of the Bilderbergers' determination to keep the fact of their meeting an absolute secret. Knowledge of their meeting was on a "need-to-know" basis, and these insiders were sworn to secrecy. Disinformation was also used as a secrecy weapon.

Reporter Cracks Security

"What do you want here?" the grim-faced, uniformed guard

asked, stepping outside his guardhouse.

"I've got an American tourist who wants to go to the bar," replied the driver. Both spoke in German; the driver translated for the "tourist."

The tourist, this writer, was identified as "Sam Davis."

"Just a moment; I have to ask," the guard replied. Stepping into his guardhouse, he picked up the phone and was engaged in heavy conversation for more than two minutes. Returning to the car, he spoke sternly:

"It's impossible until the fifth of June," he explained. "That's the date when the car can come back and you can have a look at anything."

The driver asked for "the sheriff [chief] of security."

"I haven't seen him yet," the guard responded, "but very important people are here and it's really impossible to go."

The driver had been hired, through a small hotel in Innsbruck the night before, for a morning venture on June 2, on condition that he spoke enough English to serve as translator.

On the trip from Innsbruck to the small village of Telfs a few miles away, the driver had confidently insisted that we would be admitted to the Interalpen-Hotel Tyrol, the new luxury resort atop the mountain. Many important meetings are held there, he explained, but he had driven many tourists there for an expensive drink and a breathtaking view of the Alps.

The driver, Paul Juttner, was shocked when admittance was refused. We drove back to the small restaurant or "coffee shop" a short distance down the road. There, Juttner told me that he wanted to collaborate in obtaining all information possible about the secret 1988 meeting of the Bilderberg group. The encounter with the guard had made him a believer in the conspiracy of international elitists.

The night before, Felix Zglincki, a German officer in World War II, had been discussing the case of one of his junior officers at a coffee shop in Innsbruck. Zglincki, a captain, was referring to Lt.

Kurt Waldheim, then president of Austria.

"I served in the German army and I'm proud of it," Zglincki said. "Waldheim was no criminal. He was my junior. He manned a desk."

After discussing Waldheim's being denied entry to the United States, and how unseen powers influence war and peace, Zglincki called "Andrea" (not her real name), a worker at the Interalpen Hotel, and asked her to cooperate with me the following day.

This set up my first interview with a hotel staffer. "Andrea" had been coached to listen to all she could hear, make discreet notes and lift any documents possible without risk to her own security.

What she and two others heard provided the meat of the Bilderberg story for 1988.

Juttner had a wide circle of friends in the tourist industry. Although the Interalpen, in an unusual policy, brings its staff in from all over Austria instead of hiring locally, Juttner was able to recruit two more staff informers.

All staffers had been admonished by the hotel management to remain silent on anything that transpired during the Bilderberg meeting. They would be summarily fired for the slightest violation.

One informer lived in the small village of Telfs at the bottom of the mountain. The other "commuted" the few miles from Innsbruck and was interviewed there.

In the Telfs interview, the informer sat in one room of a restaurant and was never seen by this reporter, who was in another room. Juttner relayed my questions to the informer, who not only responded but volunteered crucial information.

"If they learn of this," said the nervous owner of the restaurant, "I'll lose the shop."

He was reassured of confidentiality, and the interview continued.

The third informer was interviewed at Innsbruck. He provided his name and identified his job, trusting me not to expose him.

As this information was coming together over two days, two more attempts to penetrate the Bilderberg meeting were made.

Taking some Bilderberg memo paper obtained at the 1985 meeting near White Plains, N.Y., I scrawled:

"Admit Sam Davis and Aide—HK." The scrawled "HK" could have been "Henry Kissinger" or any of a number of people—the Bilderberg letterhead made it look official. The letterhead is not dated, merely labeled "Bilderberg Meetings."

This time, the guard was on the phone for an extended period, engaged in intense conversation. As he emerged he spoke in German to Juttner, who spun the car away.

"He was going to arrest you," Juttner explained.

Finally, after accepting the fact that I was unwelcome at the Bilderberg meeting, I still could not resist a final approach to the guard gate.

Juttner was afraid that I would be arrested this time so we agreed to make it fast. We drove to the gate, handed the guard a note written on the same Bilderberg memo paper, and fled down the mountain. The note was addressed to Muller, who handles Bilderberg's administrative affairs in the United States from his New York office.

Muller had worked feverishly to keep the meeting time and location secret. The note read:

"Dear Mr. Muller:

"Thank you for your generous hospitality and for providing me with such a wealth of information about the Bilderberg meeting this year. I have not enjoyed a Bilderberg meeting so much since White Plains.

"[Signed] James P. Tucker Jr."

Major Upheaval ...

1989—La Toja, Spain: Above, John Major became Bilderberg's man in 1989 when the secret group directed its powerful members to work to undermine Margaret Thatcher for her refusal to embrace the European Union. Thatcher had been denounced by globalists for her "provincialism" and "nationalism" for refusing to give up the country's sovereignty.

CHAPTER EIGHT

1989

La Toja, Spain

Bilderberg decided to use its immense influence to dethrone Margaret Thatcher as prime minister of Britain that year. They were angry that she resisted surrendering national sovereignty to the European Union. She was replaced by John Major of her own Conservative Party.

The Bilderberg group was discovered hiding out on this island off the Atlantic coast of Spain, near Pontevedra, during the weekend of May 11-14, plotting the political assassination of British Prime Minister Margaret Thatcher.

The meeting was confirmed by Miguel Garzon of the Spanish Embassy in Washington. Garzon said King Juan Carlos and Prime Minister Felipe Gonzalez of Spain would attend but would have nothing to say.

The meeting was also confirmed, in a negative way, by an associate of Kissinger who refused to deny that the secret meeting had taken place.

Kissinger, a top officer of both the Bilderberg Group and the Trilateral Commission, succeeded in maintaining an absolute news blackout. That year, a computer search for the word "Bilderberg" showed that it had not been used, during the first 15 days of May, by the Associated Press, United Press International, *The New York Times, Los Angeles Times, The Washington Post* or

PRESS RELEASE

BILDERBERG MEETINGS

31 May 2002

The 50th Bilderberg Meeting will be held in Chantilly, Virginia, U.S.A., 30 May-2 June 2002. Among other subjects the Conference will discuss Terrorism, Trade, Post Crisis Reconstruction, Middle East, Civil Liberties, US Foreign Policy, Extreme Right, World Economy, Corporate Governance. Approximately 120 participants from North America and Europe will attend the discussions. The meeting is private in order to encourage frank and open discussion.

Bilderberg takes its name from the hotel in Holland, where the first meeting took place in May 1954. That pioneering meeting grew out of the concern expressed by leading citizens on both sides of the Atlantic that Western Europe and North America were not working together as closely as they should on common problems of critical importance. It was felt that regular, off-the-record discussions would help create a better understanding of the complex forces and major trends affecting Western nations in the difficult postwar period. The Cold War has now ended. But in practically all respects there are more, not fewer, common problems - from trade to jobs, from monetary policy to investment, from ecological challenges to the task of promoting international security. It is hard to think of any major issue in either Europe or North America whose unilateral solution would not have repercussions for the other.
Thus the concept of a European-American forum has not been overtaken by time. The dialogue between these two regions is still - even increasingly - critical.

What is unique about Bilderberg as a forum is the broad cross-section of leading citizens that are assembled for nearly three days of informal discussion. The privacy of the meetings, which has no purpose other than to allow participants to speak their minds openly and freely.
In short, Bilderberg is a small, flexible, informal and off-the-record international forum in which different viewpoints can be expressed and mutual understanding enhanced.

Bilderberg's only activity is its annual Conference. At the meetings, no resolutions are proposed, no votes taken, and no policy statements issued. Since 1954, forty-nine conferences have been held. The names of the participants are made available to the press. Participants are chosen for their experience, their knowledge, and their standing; all participants attend Bilderberg in a private and not an official capacity.
There are usually about 120 participants of whom about two-thirds come from Europe and the balance from North America. About one-third are from government and politics, and two-thirds from finance, industry, labor, education, communications.

Participants have agreed not to give interviews to the press during the meeting. In contacts with the news media after the conference it is an established rule that no attribution should be made to individual participants of what was discussed during the meeting.

There will be no press conference. A list of participants is appended.

2002—Chantilly, Virginia: This official press release from Bilderberg is especially informative. It states that no interviews will be held during the conference and that no individuals shall be quoted directly by participants. It also says that Bilderberg is a private—not a public—meeting, meaning any U.S. elected or appointed official who attends is bound by the oath of his office to either pay for the trip with private funds, or divulge the happenings at the meeting if he is requested to do so by his constituents and those citizens he serves. This, however, never occurs. To do so would mean a "Bilderberg blackballing," and that official might never be invited again to the annual meetings.

any of the major news magazines.

The major newspapers in the United States have, over the years, had executives attend the secret sessions with the promise that nothing would be published.

Sources inside the secret society of international financiers and political leaders said their clandestine meeting this year emphasized the need to bring down Mrs. Thatcher because of her refusal to yield British sovereignty to the European super-state that was to emerge in 1992.

Mrs. Thatcher was denounced for her "provincialism" and "nationalism" for insisting that Britain would retain control over who enters the country instead of accepting passports of the super-state and not surrendering sovereignty over monetary policy and other issues to the super-government.

Political leaders in Britain who participated in the Bilderberg meeting were instructed to attack Mrs. Thatcher politically in an effort to bend the "Iron Lady's" will. It was suggested that enough public pressure could be generated to force her to yield her nation's sovereignty to save her own government.

The plan for a European super-state with no trade or travel barriers among the nations of Western Europe and Britain, and, ultimately, a common currency—the euro—had been on the Bilderberg agenda for years. It was viewed as a major step toward their goal of a world government and creates a favorable climate for the huge banks to consume the small ones and for huge, international conglomerates to absorb small firms.

Otherwise, the Bilderberg meeting followed, as is customary, the policies that were hammered out by the Trilateral Commission at its April meeting in Paris.

The Trilateral Commission had developed a plan whereby Mikhail Gorbachev and some East Bloc countries would initiate "reforms" demanded by the West in order to make it politically palatable for Americans to send tax dollars to prop up the communist system and save it from collapse.

In return, at least 17 multibillion-dollar "joint ventures" with the Soviet Union were under way, wherein western technology, managerial know-how and capital were used to finance, build and operate the plants. The Soviets provided the manpower and split the profits.

A week after the Trilateral Commission meeting in Paris, Bush promised a billion-dollar aid package to Poland as a reward for moving toward "freedom." The Kremlin was guaranteed control of the new national legislature that was to be "elected" in Poland.

This scheme was proposed by Rockefeller, Kissinger and other Bilderberg leaders to Gorbachev in January and to leaders in Poland and Hungary in March. It was given final approval at the Trilateral Commission's meeting in April.

The plan fit nicely with the European super-state program stressed by Bilderberg, because it would generate much trade among the conglomerates and new industries behind the Iron Curtain.

It was learned that former Sen. Charles Mathias (R-Md.), a regular, attended. Queen Beatrix of the Netherlands made her second Bilderberg meeting, having attended the session at Innsbruck, Austria, in 1988. Her husband, Prince Bernhard, was the first chairman of the Bilderberg group.

The sinister nature of these international schemers was demonstrated by the extravagant efforts to maintain absolute secrecy not only about their meetings but the very existence of the group.

A day after the Bilderberg meeting ended that year, on May 15, Muller, Bilderberg's administrative director in the United States, was telling Washington reporters he had no information.

Requests for information about the meeting from congressmen on behalf of constituents were repeatedly rejected as well.

Efforts to regain the total blackout that kept their existence in the 1950s and 1960s a secret were demonstrated by the fact that they rarely meet in North America now. Bilderberg used to meet

2004—Stresa, Italy—David Rockefeller, the "titan of the Western Hemisphere," was photographed by AFP's Christopher Bollyn while dining before the annual gathering of Bilderberg in 2004. One of its founding members, this global banker has been a regular attendee since 1954. Rockefeller has been characterized as the chief representative of the ruling class—those elites who work behind the scenes to shape and control the world's shadow

every third year either in the United States or Canada. Under their previous routine, they would have met in this country in 1998, instead of in Austria.

But since I penetrated the Bilderberg meeting near White Plains, N.Y., in May 1985, obtaining secret documents that revealed their plans, they have held most of their gatherings overseas.

Hunting Quayle ...

November 1990—Washington, D.C.: Bilderberg likes to own presidents—and vice presidents too. In 1990, Dan Quayle looked like a potential future president. Predictably, he was invited to a Bilderberg meeting. "They talked about a lot of important stuff," Quayle told me.

CHAPTER NINE

1990

Glen Cove, Long Island

In 1990, Bilderberg returned to the United States after an unprecedented five-year absence and again pressured President George H.W. Bush to break his pledge of "read my lips, no new taxes." He broke the pledge and lost the 1992 election.

Bilderberg again brought its considerable pressure to bear on President Bush to increase taxes. The group was confident he would comply—albeit with public expressions of reluctance.

Participants in the annual Bilderberg conference in 1990, hidden away under armed guard in the remote and posh Harrison Center, frequently expressed confidence that U.S. taxpayers would soon bear an increased tax burden, in one form or another.

From the moment they began gathering on May 9, a day before the official start of their three-day secret meeting, Bilderberg participants constantly talked of the urgency of increasing taxes to "reduce the deficit."

They also gave Vice President Dan Quayle tax-hike advice when he arrived on May 11 for his first-ever meeting with the Bilderberg wing of the world shadow government.

Asked to confirm what had already been learned from several Bilderberg participants, Kissinger was evasive: "anybody is free to raise the topic," he said by phone from his suite at the

Harrison Center at 7 a.m. on May 11.

And they did.

I penetrated the Harrison Conference Center three separate times, and the talk of raising taxes never ceased. The Bilderbergers claimed credit for Bush's recent agreement that, "Everything [would] be on the table" when the White House and congressional leaders met in a "budget summit" on May 15, 1990, two days after the close of the secret Bilderberg meeting.

They also talked of how the United States would be "chastised" at the economic summit of the seven leading industrialized nations in June of that year. There, all global economic problems were to be blamed on the U.S. budget deficit; and tax-hike calls were to be the centerpiece of international demands on the United States.

Bilderberg participants also spoke confidently about how the president would maintain expensive, long-range nuclear missiles and the highly profitable "Star Wars," during his summit in Washington with Soviet President Gorbachev in June of that year.

Like the Trilateral Commission, the Bilderberg Group discovered the issue of environmental deterioration. Bilderbergers embraced a report from the Trilateral Commission that year on the environment, because the potential profit in cleaning up the mess would be immense.

In fact, the White House chief of staff at the time, John Sununu, who was outspoken in his opposition to spending billions of tax dollars on overseas environmental projects, was summoned to his first-ever Bilderberg meeting for the express purpose of being pressured to change his position.

Rep. Tom Foley (D-Wash.), the House speaker in 1990, who also attended the Trilateral Commission meeting in Washington in early April, was summoned as well to the Bilderberg meeting to be briefed on strategies for raising taxes.

Bilderbergers strongly preferred a dramatic increase in the

federal income tax but recognized the "political difficulties" this would cause Bush, who, as a member of the Trilateral Commission, was one of their own.

"George will do all right on the environment—he has to buck a bit now for the sake of the right wing," said a tall, lean and gray-haired Bilderberg participant inside the Harrison Conference Center.

"Whether the money comes through the World Bank or otherwise, the United States will pay its share [for global environmental clean-up]," responded a dark-haired man of medium build of about 50 years.

Both men agreed that "Dick" goes along with "us" on getting as much for SDI and long-range missiles as possible. They were referring to the secretary of defense at the time, Richard Cheney, who had made such promises to the Trilateral Commission.

"And he will keep his troops in Europe—as many as he can," commented the dark-haired man.

"About a world war for the environment, George will have to do some grandstanding about U.S. spending money right now," said the gray-haired man. "And you know why, don't you?"

"Yes, he is going to raise taxes in some way—something we have wanted for a long time," said the dark-haired man. "He will have enough problems from the right on that. We've gotten the word on that."

On a subsequent penetration of the Bilderberg meeting, I managed to find a discarded note from one participant to another. It read: "We have to stress raising taxes."

The note, however, was confiscated by Bilderberg guards.

In conversations among themselves, Bilderberg members also took credit for the IMF raising its quotas on member nations by 50 percent on May 8, 1990—a day before the secret manipulators began gathering.

These international financiers, bankers, political leaders and

---

25-5-2001
BILDERBERG MEETINGS
Stenungsund, Sweden
24-27 May 2001

CONFIDENTIAL

REVISED AGENDA

SAT MAY 26

08.30 - 10.00	THE NEW US ADMINISTRATION	Conrad M. Black
		Christopher J. Dodd
		Jessica T. Mathews, moderator
10.00	Break	
10.30 - 11.30	EUROPEAN SECURITY DEFENCE IDENTITY AND	Richard N. Perle
	TRANSATLANTIC SECURITY - II	Marie-Josée Kravis, moderator
12:00 - 15.30	Luncheon boat excursion	
12.00 - 14.00	Buffet luncheon	
	FREE AFTERNOON	
16.15 - 17.45	THE RISE OF CHINA: ITS IMPACT ON ASIA AND	Kenneth S. Courtis
	THE WORLD	Henry A. Kissinger
		Franco Bernabè, moderator
17.45 -19.15	POLICIES FOR TRADE DEVELOPMENT AND	Pascal Lamy
	ECONOMIC GROWTH	Michael H. Moskow
		Etienne Davignon, moderator
19.30	Cocktails	
20.30	Buffet dinner	

SUN MAY 27

08.30 - 10.00	WHAT SHOULD GOVERNMENTS DO ABOUT FOOD	Franz Fischler
	QUALITY?	Dan Glickman
		Michael P. Pragnell
		Matthias Nass, moderator
10.00	Break	
10.30 - 11.30	ADDRESS AND QUESTIONS by the Prime Minister of Sweden Göran Persson	
12.00	Closing remarks	
	Buffet luncheon	

2001—Gothenburg, Sweden: Bilderberg is just a tea and crumpet party, or so they would like you to believe. In 2001, one of my high-level Bilderberg sources smuggled this out of an attendee's room. It is the official revised agenda for that year's meeting. Of note, neo-con warhawk Richard Perle was discussing trans-Atlantic security and Henry Kissinger, the world impact of the rise of China.

heads of multinational corporations have owned the IMF for years.

In their 1983 meeting near Montreal, Bilderbergers extracted a pledge of $50 billion from the Reagan administration to be paid out over his presumed eight years in office. This was confirmed to me by Pierre Trudeau, then prime minister of Canada, at the subsequent economic summit in Williamsburg, Va. As the years passed, Reagan more than made good on his commitment.

The IMF's quota increase meant the United States would pay 20 percent, or $12 billion. The 151 other member nations would make up the rest, spending pennies for every American dollar.

Bilderberg's discovery of the environment came as no surprise. The Trilateral Commission had issued the report mentioned earlier for members to use in pressuring their governments to spend huge allocations of taxpayers' funds on environmental projects worldwide. These projects would be profitable to the brokers, bankers and other financial manipulators who happen to compose the bulk of the secret groups' membership.

The Trilateral report called for members to use a wartime analogy in urging quick billions to be spent. When a nation's security is threatened militarily, it said, nations instantly marshal all their resources. The same should be done in a global fight to save the environment, according to the report.

That year, the news blackout on the entire affair was complete. As usual, *The Washington Post* and *The New York Times* were represented at the meetings by high officials of their respective publishing empires.

The only newspaper story about the meeting was composed of a few sweetheart paragraphs buried deep inside the local *Long Island Newsday*. The writer cheerfully quoted Muller as saying: "No statements will be issued or press conferences held."

Muller told *Newsday* that the site was selected for "security reasons."

Even as the secret meeting was in progress, the Bilderbergers' leading lackey papers were doing their jobs: Both *The New York Times* and *The Washington Post* were editorially calling for tax increases and denouncing the administration for refusing to immediately pledge billions to help the poor nations with environmental problems.

Despite the apparent obstinence of Bush and Sununu, the Bilderberg men remained complacent—even smug—in their confidence that the U.S. government would follow their dictates.

"I tell you, we do not have to worry about George, either on the environmental project or on the tax issue: he will do all he can in his own way," said a slightly built American, overheard while reassuring a man seated next to him during one of the meetings on May 12.

The American told his European colleague that "domestic politics" require Bush to do "certain things but "it will come out all right—you'll see."

The American made several references to "problems with the American right," a subject that was much on Bilderbergers' minds that year.

The presence of the vice president at the meeting was bad news for those who had been urging Bush to dump Quayle from the 1992 ticket. It meant that the international elite took seriously Bush's pledge to keep him on the ticket and the prospect that Quayle might be elected president in 1996.

Meanwhile, the global agenda of the Bilderberg group and the Trilateral Commission was clear.

Taxes, in some or many forms, were to be increased for Americans. The new revenues were to be justified by the "deficit." But never in history have tax increases actually been used to reduce deficits; because deficits mean profits for banks; without fail, such increases are used for new spending,meaning profits for international financiers and speculators. The new

2001—Gothenburg, Sweden: That year, Bilderberg security took the unusual step of erecting a massive steel fence around the entire meeting site. They believed these unprecedented measures would stop unwanted press coverage of the event. They were wrong. I was able to glean valuable information from staff and locals, who were irked that Bilderberg had gone to such great lengths to intimidate reporters and resort employees to keep its little meeting private.

revenues were to be used for the following purposes:

• To act as a safety net for international bankers by sending billions in taxpayer dollars to Third World countries so they can pay the interest on their bank debts;

• To send billions to struggling countries for new environmental projects from which the international financiers expect to reap huge new profits; and

• To send still more billions into the East-Bloc countries to help them recover economically from more than seven ruinous decades of communism. The internationalists would enjoy immense profits from the "joint ventures" already planned, and from buying up previously state-owned enterprises at bargain-basement prices.

Who Let This Guy in? ...

1991—WASHINGTON, D.C: Recognize that face on the left? As defense secretary under George Bush the Elder, Dick Cheney attended meetings of Bilderberg's brother group, the Trilateral Commission. "These things are supposed to be confidential," Cheney said to me in 1991. "When taxpayers pay the travel and personal expenses of federal officials, they are supposed to be open and a matter of public record," Cheney was told.

CHAPTER TEN

1991

Baden-Baden, Germany

Readers had advance knowledge in 1991 that the United States was going to war. It turned out to be the invasion of Yugoslavia under President Bill Clinton, who attended the 1991 Bilderberg meeting and was elected president in 1992.

he Bilderberg group planned another war within five years. This grim news came from a "main pipeline"—a high-ranking Bilderberg staffer who secretly cooperated with my investigation—behind the guarded walls of the Badischer Hof. At the time, he operated from inside with colleagues serving as "connecting pipelines."

The main pipeline met with me at least once daily, and sometimes twice a day, as the annual secret meeting of the world elite took place June 7-9, 1991, in this resort town.

While war plans were being outlined in "Bilderbergese," the air traffic controller at Baden-Baden's private airport reported numerous incoming flights from Brussels, where NATO headquarters are based and where the secretary of state at the time, James Baker, was at that moment promising aid to the Soviet Union.

Aboard one of those planes, en route to the Bilderberg meeting, was Manfred Woerner, NATO's general secretary in 1991.

It was repeatedly stated at the Bilderberg meeting that there would be "other Saddams" in the years ahead who must be dealt with swiftly and efficiently, referring to Saddam Hussein, the now deposed leader of oil-rich Iraq.

What the Bilderberg group intended was a global army at the disposal of the United Nations. In addition, it has been a long-standing goal of Bilderberg for the UN to become the world government to which all nations will be subservient.

Crucial to making the UN a strong world government, by "osmosis," in the words of some Bilderberg participants, was to bestow it with "enforcement powers."

"A UN army must be able to act immediately, anywhere in the world, without the delays involved in each country making its own decision whether to participate, based on parochial considerations," said Kissinger during one of the forums.

Kissinger and others expressed pleasure over the conduct of the Persian Gulf war, stressing that it had been sanctioned by the UN, at the request of Bush, before the issue was laid in front of Congress.

The fact that the president made his case to the UN first, when the Constitution empowers only Congress to declare war, was viewed as a significant step in "leading Americans away from nationalism."

If Americans can be persuaded to surrender war-making decisions to the UN, and let their young men die wearing a UN uniform, fighting under a UN flag, "parochial nationalism" in Britain, France and elsewhere would disappear, Bilderberg speakers said.

"The Persian Gulf venture has advanced the cause by years," one speaker said. Americans, so reluctant to commit their flag to foreign battlefields after 58,000 perished in the ill-fated Vietnam War, have had their attitude "completely turned around," he said.

It was "good psychology" for Bush to allow Congress and other leaders to express their fear of losing 20,000 to 40,000 Americans' lives, he said, when Bush knew the loss of life would be much lower.

When the allied casualty toll reached "only 378" and Americans read and heard of "only four" Americans dying in a week of ground war, it "was like nobody had died at all," one said, "and Americans enjoyed it like an international sporting match."

Such an adventure was essential to getting Americans into "the right frame of mind for the years ahead," said another.

In their circumspect way the Bilderberg participants claimed credit for influencing the president to go to war. And, they promised each other there will be "more incidents" for the UN to deal with in the years ahead. The Bilderberg group and the Trilateral Commission can set up "incidents" on schedule, they said, but in less direct words. The words "within five years" were heard repeatedly.

Another important step toward a strong, recognized and accepted world government is taxing power. The UN has always operated on "assessments" paid by each country. But that didn't stop the internationalists from proposing multiple schemes to tax Americans.

At its April 1991 meeting in Tokyo, the Trilateralists called for a UN levy of 10 cents per barrel of oil coming from the Persian Gulf. It was to be sold as "temporary," lasting only long enough to rebuild Kuwait and feed the Kurds until they are back on their feet.

The Bilderbergers approved of the move by their brother group. They knew that once people get used to a tax, it never is repealed. Ten cents a barrel would have a negligible effect on sales at the pump, and it could be extended worldwide "with appropriate increases" in the years ahead.

Part of the philosophy of a "direct" tax by the UN was already in effect, they had noted with satisfaction. At the time, the UN was demanding 30 percent of Iraq's oil profits from "reparations," and the United States had obligingly taken the position that it would be increased to 50 percent.

From the sum total of all things said, the Bilderberg strategy emerged: Start the tax by imposing it on a newly established "bad guy" who must suffer, and use the revenue for such humanitarian purposes as feeding the Kurds. Keep the initial tax so low that the public is unaware that it is levied. Then kick it up.

Under the secret Bilderberg plan discussed at this meeting, as the UN acquired its own global army and direct taxes as another source of revenue, the world could be divided into major "regions" for convenience of administration. Already Western Europe was preparing to be "without borders" in 1993. By 1996, it was to have a single currency. Eastern Europe and the Soviet Union would eventually be included. The Soviet Union was to remain intact and the Captive Nations were to remain forever subjugated. Dealing with 15 more small states would be too complicated.

Bilderberg pressure on Congress to pass the free trade treaty with Mexico was another step toward establishing the Western Hemisphere as one of the "regions." Free trade with Canada was the first step and Mexico the second. Thereafter, all Latin American nations were to be included.

In the years ahead, a one-currency movement for the Western Hemisphere was planned, identical to that of the European Economic Community and, ultimately, a world government with world currency.

Also, on the global economic front at the time, Bilderberg pressure on the Uruguay Round of talks on the General Agreement on Tariffs and Trade (GATT) was being felt. Even as Bilderberg was meeting with 120 of the world's leading financiers and political leaders, GATT negotiators announced a "new spirit of cooperation" and determination to reach an agreement.

Rockefeller and Kissinger praised actions by Gorbachev in 1991, whom they coached closely and to whom they had easy access.

In that year, Gorbachev had announced that he needed a $100 billion gift from the West—mostly from the United States—to survive. That, Bilderberg knew, gave Bush the room to posture for Americans by saying no, only $20 billion, and only if Gorbachev behaved.

Two days after the Bilderberg meeting, on June 11, Bush obligingly reversed himself—six weeks after curtsying to the "right wing" by proclaiming the Soviet Union "uncreditworthy"—and announced that the United States would guarantee $1.5 billion in loans for the communists to buy grain. A "loan guarantee" was almost synonymous with "gift."

Frank Murray, a journalist of stature long known to me from his years with the defunct *Washington Evening Star,* wrote in *The Washington Times* that it was the first "of what is expected to be a series of steps [to] ease trade and give economic aid to Moscow."

The White House also reiterated its opposition to moves in Congress to send any aid directly to the republics of the Captive Nations, thereby strengthening their bid for freedom without shoring up the crumbling walls of communism within the Soviet Union.

Billions of American tax dollars would be used, in the year ahead, to ensure the survival of the Soviet Union, with its domination of the Captive Nations perpetuated.

On June 8, 1991, the second day of the three-day Bilderberg meeting, Secretary of State Baker was in Geneva, promising American dollars to Gorbachev and reaffirming U.S. abandonment of the Captive Nations.

But while it was known that high officials of the State and Defense departments and the White House attended Bilderberg, it could not be learned if Baker was among the few arriving late, hidden behind a screen of guards.

The guards and other staff all had the same response to shouted inquiries about anyone's presence: "I don't know."

Gorbachev, of course, wanted to keep the Captive Nations enslaved as part of the Soviet Union. The United States was enabling him by taking the position that anticipated future billions of American tax dollars must go, through the World Bank and IMF, to the Kremlin to avoid the "complications" of dealing with 15 states that had regained their sovereignty.

The Bilderbergers endorsed this sellout just days before the United States' annual Captive Nations Week, once the occasion for tolling church bells and prayers for freedom of enslaved peoples.

Security Pierced

In 1991, penetrating the Bilderberg's annual meeting required new tactics. The first probe came in the early afternoon of June 5. The actual conference would not begin for two more days. But, as usual, an armada of advance men had been on hand to prepare.

To the cab driver, wanting to visit the Badischer Hof for lunch at Baden-Baden's most luxurious hotel in a city of expensive accommodations was not unusual. But what came next was almost routine to me. During the lengthy taxi ride from the modest accommodations at a hotel in Gaggenau, as in years past, my voiced doubts that the unwashed multitudes would be welcome at the Badischer Hof prompted reassurances from the cab driver.

Oh no, he said, many people go to the Badischer Hof to enjoy luxurious dining or the well-appointed cocktail lounges.

I said nothing. It would be more fun for him to learn for himself. Paying the driver, I asked him to wait a moment to make sure I gained entry. He nodded, humoring me. He never expected to see me again. But all of that changed with one step inside the glass doors of the lobby when several men in security uniforms confronted me.

"This is a public hotel. I just want lunch," I said.

"The hotel is closed down for a private meeting," I was told.

Over their shoulders, wearing his drivers-license-style Bilderberg ID name tag, I recognized my friend "Rog" from the Bilderberg meeting on Long Island a year ago, a young chap who was irritated by several in-house visits by me then.

I gave Rog a friendly nod and smile, but his face was frozen.

"See you later, Rog," I said with a wave as the Bilderberg guards escorted me out. Rog frowned.

1991—Baden-Baden, Germany: Bilderberg met this year in the scenic German town of Baden-Baden, plotting, among other things, more wars and a global tax to fund their drive for world government. Also on the agenda was the issue of burgeoning free trade with the development of the General Agreement of Tariffs and Trade.

The cabbie was still waiting, and I explained that I would not be admitted. He was outraged at the fact that I had been denied entrance to a public hotel, and he would have none of it.

He leapt from the cab and charged into the lobby, physically breaking through the security platoon and shouting at a clerk behind the desk. Shortly thereafter, he returned to the cab and said, with a bewildered expression: "That's a secret meeting."

The cab driver agreed to meet me outside the resort five hours later for the return to Stadhotel Gagenau.

After explaining more about the Bilderberg group, an English-speaking friend of the cab driver, a barmaid at the hotel, and two male customers said they could help me.

I was instructed, on the following evening, to sit at the bar on the first floor of the two-storied Westeiner Brasserie, a working-class restaurant a block from the Badischer Hof.

It should be noted that before I received any information from sources inside the meeting, there was much going on at that year's Bilderberg gathering from early morning to 9 p.m. as the world's elite began furtively entering the Badischer Hof.

There was efficient collaboration between the German press, television stations and the only American newspaper present, *The Spotlight*, which I reported for at the time. Among my collaborators were Dr. Hans-Ulrich Grimm, a reporter for *Der Spiegel*, and Jorge Briller, head of a five-man television team from Baden-Baden. There were many more, but getting their names was difficult as they were busy exchanging information in limited English. One whose name I never got served as a translator. He said he had worked for a German-language newspaper in Chicago for two years.

There were only two approaches to the Badischer Hof, at each end of a horseshoe driveway. Television crews guarded each entrance as Grimm and I patrolled both. Both entrances were guarded from mid-morning to 9 p.m. We took turns retiring to the brasserie to rest our feet, buy each other coffee and compare notes.

Ironically, the Bilderbergers had expected this meeting to be more secret than ever, yet not one of them got out of a limousine without seeing television cameras boring in on him. Many tried to mask their dismay with deadpan faces; few succeeded.

All of us print journalists and broadcasters found each other outside the Badischer Hof and immediately planned our collaboration. Most, except for Grimm and Briller, had little knowledge of the Bilderbergers but knew strange things were going on involving world figures. One was there because the air traffic controller at the private airport in Baden-Baden had tipped him off about planes arriving from Brussels, Belgium, bearing NATO leaders, and another from Sweden, with four bankers.

I had extra copies of the June 10, 1991, issue of *The Spotlight*, containing in-depth stories on the upcoming meeting, and passed them out. Two television stations covered the paper's articles at length, showing the reports on-screen. Their commentators would discuss the contents, and they would make tapes of me commenting on the meeting to air with translation. On returning to the hotel in Gaggenau late that night, I was informed that a woman from a French newspaper had called me eight times but left no message.

The efficient ladies at the reception desk had, on the first day, observed this former farm boy's habit of appearing in the dining room when it opened at 6:30 a.m. for the complimentary European breakfast, and had suggested that the reporter call me the following morning at 8. She did, and 8 a.m. became our regular time for my "fill-ins" for the duration of my stay.

Of course, on this first full day in Baden-Baden, and with the Bilderberg meeting starting early the next day, the guards who had stopped me inside the preceding day were outside, in large numbers, augmented by German police.

Despite the grimness of our mission, we were unable to escape a spirit of prankishness when I suggested a "surge" maneuver. When limousines approached at either end, often with police escorts, the other end would be alerted with shouts of "*Achtung*" ("Attention"). For about three seconds, we would remain on the sidewalk. Any closer was "trespassing" on this place of public accommodation. On a signal, we would all "surge" forward against shouts of police trying to push us back. To their credit, German police declined to bash heads. The huge contingent of Bilderberg guards, most in uniform, some in dress suits, and others dressed casually, attempting to be "undercover," were held in reserve.

By this method, we were able to identify many of the arrivals— Rockefeller early in the afternoon, Kissinger about 4 p.m., Queen Beatrix of the Netherlands at 6:40 p.m. etc.—and many were partially photographed as well as identified by sight.

It rained off and on, and a Bilderberg-owned guard started opening a huge umbrella when luminaries arrived and moved about to shield them from view. I took a photo of him using the

1991—Baden-Baden, Germany: Despite the large number of German police and private security at Bilderberg's gathering that year I still managed to get detailed information about the meeting. With the help of locals and a source inside, I was able to report in depth on the subjects discussed at the conference. And thanks to the German press, I was able to identify many of the attendees in 1991 as they arrived at the resort in limos and expensive cars.

umbrella in this fashion, and he looked embarrassed and put it away. They went back to the strategy of lining up to form a human wall to prevent observation.

By this method, we were able to identify many, but not all, of the arrivals. And we had fun adding to the discomfiture of the Bilderbergers.

Now, after knowing who was inside, the next goal was to learn what mischief they were undertaking.

On the second day, I visited my cab driver's friend, the barmaid at a hotel several blocks from the Badischer Hof. She again assured me help would be forthcoming from a source inside that year's Bilderberg meetings, and I should be, that evening, at the bar in the brasserie.

"Mr. Tucker?"

"Yes," I replied, rising from my stool at the bar.

"Shall we take a table?" a young man asked.

At a remote table in the huge restaurant, the young man said he had read the issue of *The Spotlight* I had left with the barmaid. But even before that, he told me he had felt instinctively that odd events were taking place. I would have his help, and the help of several colleagues whom I would never see. He had not told me his name or position and would not. If his collaboration were ever discovered he and many others would have been fired.

I told him if my friend up the street said his information was good, that satisfied me. To keep him more comfortable, I decided not to tell him that, from peering over high walls into the rear courtyard, I had already recognized him as a Bilderberg staffer of high rank.

We discussed how his collaborators inside the Badischer Hof could provide information and, without risk, procure documents. The young man then began to tell me what had already transpired.

Although the likelihood of being discovered at this working-class restaurant was remote, it was understood that if he concentrated on his own drink at a single table next to mine, I would become interested only in the newspaper in front of me. Not once, though, did we have to perform this charade.

Much of what I documented in that year behind the guarded doors of the Badischer Hof is a tribute to this young patriot's determination to expose the dark machinations of the Bilderbergers to public light.

One quote was embedded in my mind when he told me that a squat, gray-haired man in a black suit was heard telling Kissinger, dressed in gray, that: "You're not as [expletive]ing smart as you think."

Invading France ...

1992—Evian, France: That year, the world's most powerful powerbrokers, bankers and speculators invaded the sleepy town of Evian, France, much to the consternation of the local citizens who were not used to such a show of force.

CHAPTER ELEVEN

1992

Evian, France

Henry Kissinger boasted of great progress toward the Bilderberg goal of a world government in 1992. He laid out a scenario where foreigners would invade the United States and Americans would welcome a UN "rescue."

t the 1992 meeting in Evian, France, at the luxury resorts of the Royal and the Ermilar from May 21-24, the largest Bilderberg meeting in history—its size a direct result of its vain attempt to preserve the Soviet Union—celebrated what participants termed "remarkable progress" toward the group's goal of a world government by the year 2000.

The world, finally including even the balky American public, is "being rapidly educated into overcoming limited patriotism" and accepting "United Nations solutions to common global problems," Kissinger was overheard saying at the gathering that year.

Bilderberg participants expressed satisfaction with progress toward world government on two fronts:

• Establishing a UN tax to not only finance new global programs but to condition "citizens of the world" to the paying of tribute.

• Conditioning the public—again, especially "those stubborn Americans"—to accept the idea of a UN army that could impose its will by force on the internal affairs of any nation.

"Today, Americans would be outraged if UN forces entered Los Angeles to restore order; tomorrow, they will be grateful," Kissinger said.

Kissinger reported on a shocking speech made by the UN secretary general that year, Boutros-Boutros Ghali, to the American Association of Newspaper Publishers at UN headquarters in New York in early May. The publishers' newspapers covered up the story.

The UN Security Council must have a permanent force that can be deployed anywhere in the world, instantly, to "protect the peace" and "ensure human rights," the secretary general told the newspaper publishers.

This force must be allowed to intervene "at the local and community levels," the UN leader told the American publishers.

What is "especially gratifying," Kissinger said, is that the publishers showed no reservations about the prospects of UN forces landing in the United States and imposing the UN's will.

Members of the American Association of Newspaper Publishers are publishers of America's approximately 1,600 daily newspapers. (Today, there are only 1,200 daily papers.) The meetings of the trade group, however, are mostly attended by publishers of the large metropolitan newspapers. Few representatives of small dailies attend.

Normally, like most prosperous professional organizations, they meet in luxury hotels to "exchange ideas" between drinks. They are not known to have been previously summoned to UN headquarters.

At a speech a week later to working journalists at the National Press Club in Washington, the UN leader refrained from repeating his call for a UN military wing when I questioned him privately.

The UN tax would come in the form of a levy on oil to be imposed to finance a global "environmental" bureaucracy to transmit billions of dollars to Third World countries.

The European Community (EC) voted on May 13 to impose a $3 per barrel tax on crude oil beginning in 1993, increasing to $10 by 2000. But that is "conditional" on pending similar action by the United States and Japan. Subsequently, EC President Jacques Delors told the Bilderberg meeting, the tax revenues would be turned over to the UN to administer a "global energy policy."

A European leader—whom sources were unable to identify by name—reported on still more progress toward a world government made at the UN but which was kept from the public.

"Various ministers [at the opening of the 40th UN General Assembly session in September 1991] frontally challenged the concept that 'sovereignty' protects nations when they violate basic human rights," the Bilderberg participants were told.

"The right to intervene in the internal affairs of states to protect human rights was endorsed by foreign ministers of Germany, Canada, Italy and Austria," the speaker said.

He also revealed another previously unknown and startling development: At a meeting called the Stockholm Initiative in April 1991, 36 global leaders called for a "world summit on global governance . . . similar to the meetings in San Francisco [establishing the UN] and at Bretton Woods."

Half the signers were "incumbents, including prime ministers from Chile, Norway, Sweden and Jamaica," he said. Among the signers, he said, was former U.S. President Jimmy Carter.

He noted with approval UN resolutions that allow it "for the first time to enforce nuclear, biological and chemical disarmament in a 'sovereign' nation, Iraq," which he called a "significant precedent."

Another speaker at the brainwashing session—euphemistically known as an "Examination of Public Attitudes Toward the New World Order"—celebrated the growing acceptance of Americans being conditioned by the major media. The concept of a world government is widely accepted in Europe, so winning the support of Americans is high on the Bilderberg agenda.

The speaker cited numerous newspaper commentaries directly calling for a UN military that could intervene in a nation's internal affairs that "resulted in no objections, no angry letters to the editor nor any challenge from public figures."

"The Gulf War and its messy aftermath show the need to build a UN capability to deter potential aggressors with rapid deployment forces and protect peoples within national borders from internal aggression," wrote David Scheffer, senior associate of the Carnegie Endowment for International Peace, one of Bilderberg's many stepchildren, in *The Washington Post* on April 7 of that year.

"Internal conflicts can be a threat to international peace," Scheffer wrote. The American military must be available to the UN "on call," he said, and subject to the direction of the world government, rejecting the explicit constitutional provision that the president of the United States is commander-in-chief of the armed forces.

Washington Post columnist Jimmy Lee Hoagland's attendance at Trilateral meetings was kept secret, as are the many years of Bilderberg participation by the Washington Post Co. chairman at the time, Katharine Graham. Hoagland was praised for his efforts to persuade Americans to surrender national sovereignty to a world government.

Hoagland assailed "a prevailing view of national sovereignty" in *The Washington Post* on April 23, 1992.

"The United States today supports . . . the duty of the United Nations to intervene in what were once considered the internal affairs of member nations," Hoagland wrote approvingly. Hoagland praised Bush for his "willingness to help define an international right to intervene" in the affairs of a sovereign nation.

The fact that Sir Brian Urquhart, former UN undersecretary for "peacekeeping," was quoted in *The New York Times* calling for a new UN "police force" with no objections by American leaders was also noted.

"The unraveling of national sovereignty seems to be a feature of the post-Cold War period," Urquhart said approvingly.

Americans are also accepting the Bilderberg plan to divide the world into supranational regions for more efficient administration by the world government at the United Nations, the speaker said.

2004—Stresa, Italy: In this photograph, a group of European journalists bent on exposing Bilderberg to their readers interviewed me as I approached the gates to that year's meeting site. While the European press has seen the importance of reporting on the world shadow government, the mainstream media in the U.S. still keeps this important matter from the American public. Every year publishers, editors and reporters from the largest newspapers and magazines attend this gathering with the promise that their staff will report noth-

"The New World Order will be characterized by six major states (regions): the United States (Western Hemisphere), Europe (the European Community), China, Japan (Pacific Rim) and whatever emerges in the Soviet Union," Kissinger wrote in the *Post* on Dec. 3, 1991, the speaker reported.

The plan to turn the Western Hemisphere into a European Community-style "superstate" region was to be achieved through extending "free-trade" pacts to include all countries. At that time, the U.S. free-trade treaty with Canada was set. With Mexico, it was pending. And the White House announced May 13 that Chile was next.

Ex-USSR Republics Welcome

The Cold War was barely over in 1992 when Bilderberg boys planned to exploit the rich natural resources, cheap land, property and labor in the former Soviet Union.

For the first time, forces of the former Soviet Union had a major presence as the Bilderberg organization gathered in Evian for its annual secret meeting on global strategy.

The larger than usual number of attendees had caused the Bilderbergers to spill over into two hotels, the Royal and the Ermitage in this resort area. It also prompted the tightest security of any meeting so far.

There was some speculation Gorbachev, the former Soviet president, would make an appearance, although there were difficult logistic problems in secretly whisking him in and out without the world knowing.

In any event, the complicity of Gorbachev and other leaders of the former Soviet Union, and those from the former East Bloc nations, loomed large in Bilderberg's secret plans.

The international financiers and political leaders gathered in Evian to exploit the immense natural resources of the former communist bloc, which is why they were brought into the World Bank and IMF.

The World Bank and IMF not only send American tax dollars overseas to provide money for the former communist countries to buy goods produced by Western capitalists exploiting cheap labor there, but also are the means of controlling their new economies and old natural resources.

Right from the beginning, I saw early-arriving Bilderberg members and advance staff congratulating each other over Gorbachev's "cooperation."

This cooperation had been solid since the first known meeting in February 1989 between Gorbachev, Rockefeller, Kissinger and other leaders of Bilderberg and its brother group, the Trilateral Commission, which together make up the world shadow government.

Gorbachev called for a "stronger" United Nations, with the Security Council having its own forces. With contributions from all nations, it could use its army as it pleased.

On a speaking tour of the United States, Gorbachev's American audiences applauded this proposal to surrender more U.S. sovereignty to a world government and police force. It is exactly what the Trilateral Commission called for in 1991 in Tokyo and what Bilderberg sought in Baden-Baden, Germany, that same year. The fact that Bush first obtained UN permission to fight Iraq, then obtained Congress's concurrence without a declaration of war, was cited as a "real breakthrough" in overcoming "provincial nationalism," or "nativism."

Gorbachev's speeches could have been dictated by Kissinger after being drafted by Rockefeller, which was exactly what happened so far as content was concerned. Gorbachev held out the Bilderberg-Trilateral vision of a UN military force that could invade once-sovereign nations to enforce "human rights."

"The New World Order means a new kind of civilization," Gorbachev told the Chicago CFR on May 8, 1991. Gorbachev also denounced "unlimited patriotism" of the kind manifested by "nationalists" in a clear call for Americans to put loyalty to the UN ahead of fidelity to the United States.

"Everything is still ahead of us," Gorbachev told the CFR, referring to the world government, which Bilderberg, during its Baden-Baden meeting in June 1991, was determined to have in place by the year 2000.

It's All Greek . . .

1993—Vouliagmeni, Greece: With one of their boys firmly in place in the White House in Washington, Bilderbergers met in this beautiful resort town to discuss ways in which they could solidify their power and increase their profits from the growing calls for a cleaner environment.

CHAPTER TWELVE

1993

Vouliagmeni, Greece

In 1993 Bilderberg celebrated the collaboration of one of its own members, President Bill Clinton, in helping elevate the United Nations into a world government.

Behind the guarded walls of the elite Nafsika Astir Palace Hotel, situated high on a hill a few miles south of Athens, the secret Bilderberg group once again plotted to exploit the rich natural resources of the former Soviet Union and Indochina.

Also high on the Bilderberg agenda was establishment of a new, huge United Nations bureaucracy on the environment, so the industrialists can reap immense profits from new technology to clean the world's air and water.

Bilderbergers also celebrated the collaboration of one of their own, President Bill Clinton.

"It's really a direct message to us through the newspapers," said Bilderberger Dwayne Andreas, the chairman of billion-dollar agrigiant Archer-Daniels-Midland Company at the time, referring to reports that Clinton promised to sign the Rio Treaty, which calls for billions of American tax dollars to be circulated around the world in the name of a "clean environment."

"Yes, and he's doing it early in his first term," said Andreas's companion. "George [Bush] wanted to wait until his second term to make a few changes to pacify the American right. Bill seems to understand that if certain things go undone in a first term, there may be no second term."

It was the first indication that there may have been a Bilderberg "tilt" toward Clinton to punish Bush for stalling on the Rio Treaty and resisting more new taxes after his broken pledge of 1990 on taxes turned into political suicide.

Bush had been a longtime member of the Trilateral Commission, which has interlocking leadership with Bilderberg. Clinton had been a Trilateralist for seven years and was promoted to the Bilderberg in 1991. Thus, the world shadow government owned both presidential candidates in a typical win-win race.

"If George [had had] a second term, he [might] have moved on health care and new taxes, since he would not have been worried about reelection. And he certainly would have signed the Rio Treaty, possibly with a little political posturing by insisting on nit-picking changes," Andreas said.

"But we would not have fast action, as with Clinton," said the other.

The Rio Treaty calls for establishing a UN commission on the environment. Americans will pay most of a multibillion-dollar program to clean the air and water, preserve topsoil and prevent erosion in undeveloped countries. The rationale is that Americans consume and pollute more than the rest of the world.

Adding a new UN agency to police the environment among once-sovereign nations also advances the Bilderberg goal of turning the UN into a *de facto* world government. Thus, Bilderberg also celebrated public acceptance of a permanent UN army, in which Americans would fight under a foreign commander who would be accountable only to the Security Council, not the president or Congress. They found it significant that Americans remaining in Somalia were serving under a Turkish general under UN command. Contrary to the Constitution, the president was not their commander in chief.

There will be "more and more Somalias to help the world become accustomed to UN supremacy," said one. "There must be at least five places on Earth so full of misery that we can break American hearts whenever we choose."

2003—Versailles, France: Security was tight as usual at this Bilderberg meeting. That year, we photographed police on motorcycles escorting visiting dignitaries *en route* to the Bilderberg meeting at the Trianon Palace near Versailles.

There was much discussion of the fighting in Bosnia, but most Europeans urged Americans to shun air strikes and simply enforce the economic embargo.

"It would not be like Somalia, with few casualties and pictures of soldiers feeding starving children," one said. "Planes will be shot down; airmen will die. And if you get into ground action, there will be many casualties."

"You can't compare it to the Persian Gulf, either, where the terrain made it easy to deploy an overwhelming force, bomb Iraq into rubble, take few casualties and proclaim a great victory," said another. "Your people will not see this as some sort of sporting contest."

Nevertheless, Bilderberg sources said Americans from the State and Defense departments joined the NATO secretary general at the time, Woerner, in calling for the UN to authorize air strikes.

"There will be much for the UN forces to do in the years ahead, things of the type that will gain public acceptance for its role anywhere in the world," said another. "UN troops could go into Sudan with food supplies if we made an issue of the people starving there and spread films of misery on the network news."

Bilderberg men expressed some nervousness about getting all West European states to surrender their national sovereignty to a European super state under the terms of the Maastricht Treaty but were confident the North American Free Trade Agreement would be ratified. This too was important to the Bilderberg goal of a world government.

A third "regional government" is to be formed in the Pacific Rim, and the UN is to be the seat of the world government.

To exploit the natural resources of the former Soviet Union and in Indochina, Bilderberg agreed to establish a "High Council" of 12 members. A committee was named to select the 12.

Members must be "of such status that they have instant access to heads of state and parliamentary leaders throughout the world," a Bilderberg speaker said. The 12 will pressure Western nations to send more and more billions to the former Soviet Union. They will claim credit for this help in talking with the leaders of the former Soviet republics.

The 12 will then demand of the republics the right, at an absurdly low price, to extract oil, gold and other precious metals. "The gold in the ground, the oil undrilled, do you no good," the 12 will argue. "Cooperating on this will mean that we continue to use our influence to get more financial assistance from the West."

It was a typical Bilderberg project: Use public funds—the lion's share coming from American taxpayers—to "pay" for the right to extract oil and precious metals from the former Soviet Union and reap immense profits.

At that time, the only barrier to exploiting the resources in Indochina was America's refusal to "normalize" relations with

2001—Gothenburg, Sweden: Swedish Security forces were out in great numbers patrolling the woods around the Bilderberg conference site making sure reporters and other independent investigators were kept at bay. The police were accompanied by guard dogs. AFP's Christopher Bollyn took this photograph shortly before he was picked up and forcibly taken miles away by local authorities.

Vietnam until the POW-MIA issue is resolved.

The Bilderbergers were considering urging the Vietnamese government to take a dramatic step: Admit that some communist troops held some Americans after the war ended and claim they shot them all a few months later. Hanoi was to say, under this scenario, that the officers who ordered the executions were shot as punishment, that the executions were done against orders from the communist regime, and that Vietnam apologizes and wants normal relations.

"It may take something dramatic like this," one said. "Otherwise, the issue may never go away."

The Bilderberg group's concern was oil, not American soldiers being held as slaves in filthy prison camps.

Not Buying it ...

2004—Stresa, Italy: That year a large contingency of Bilderberg security had been given photos of me and knew in advance I was not "Etienne Davignon" as I had wryly told them at the front gate of the meeting site. I promptly turned around and formulated another plan of attack, inevitably gathering vital information about the meeting from sources inside Bilderberg he has been courting over the years.

CHAPTER THIRTEEN

1994

Helsinki, Finland

In 1994 Bilderberg was gloomy over some resistance to the European Union's evolving into a superstate and concerned about "stability" in Japan amidst an economic depression in Asia.

International financiers should claim "equity of expertise—in exploiting the former Soviet Union because seven decades of communism made it impossible to conduct "business as usual," several speakers said during the June 2-5, 1994, meeting of the Bilderberg Group here.

The Bilderbergers also named a joint committee, including some members of the Trilateral Commission, to seek "political stability" in Japan.

The faces gathering at the sealed-off, exclusive compound of plush buildings known as the Kalastajatorppa Hotel were unusually gloomy, partly because of an unprecedented blizzard of local publicity generated by this paperboy.

Bilderberg leaders were concerned about growing resistance of some European nations to the surrender of their sovereignty to the European Union, the continuing political chaos in Japan, (their Trilateral brethren engineered the downfall of the premier while meeting in Tokyo last April) and of the deepening economic chaos in the former USSR.

Several sources from inside the locked and guarded doors of the Bilderberg meeting, and Bilderberg documents I acquired, painted a portrait of gloom for the globalists, which was good news for the forces of nationalism and self-determination.

Rockefeller and Kissinger were among members of the "task force" charged with helping Japan find a prime minister who will lead the nation into a Pacific Union.

The Bilderberg, through its Trilateral proxy, had ousted Japanese Prime Minister Morihiro Hosokawa in April 1994 for his reluctance to surrender sovereignty to the planned Pacific Union.

"Now, none of us knows who will lead Japan tomorrow or next week," complained one Bilderberg member.

In addition to Rockefeller and Kissinger, other familiar faces appeared, including: Lord Peter Carrington, Queen Beatrix of Holland, NATO chief Woerner, President Ahtisaari and Prime Minister Esko Aho of Finland, German Chancellor Helmut Kohl, German central banker Hans-Otto Pohl and Atos Erkko, a well-known Finnish publisher.

Also: Franz Vranitsky, president of Austria; Percy Barnevik, president of ABB (Asea Brown Boveri Ltd.) of Sweden; Giovanni Agnelli, head of the giant Fiat firm in Italy; Max Jacobson and Jaakko Illoniemi of Finland; Rozanne Ridgway, assistant director of the White House Office of Management and Budget; and Volker Ruhe of Germany.

Also: Katharine Graham, owner of the Washington Post Co.: Louis Gerstner of IBM; Thomas Pickering, U.S. ambassador to Russia; Brent Scowcroft, adviser to Bush; Paul Allaire of Xerox, Peter Sutherland of Britain; Queen Sofia of Spain; Rudd Lubbers, David Oddson and Willy Claes of Belgium; Jose Manuel Durao Harroso of Portugal; Andrzej Olechowski of Poland; Thirvald Stoltenberg and Bright Breuel.

Problems with Japan and new resistance to a "European super-state" alarmed the Bilderberg group because of the threat they posed to its Orwellian program of dividing the world into three great regions for the administrative convenience of the emerging world government.

2000—Brussels, Belgium: The world press is starting to catch on, even if the U.S. media still plays lapdog for Bilderberg. Above, journalists from across Europe, including Tony Gosling of Britain, met with me at a local pub to discuss strategy. The help of independent journalists in exposing Bilderberg cannot be overestimated. With their Bilderberg coverage, enough pressure may be brought to bear on the U.S. media to force them to report on the meetings.

While Bilderberg members displayed dismay over political developments in 1994, it was the deepening economic crisis in Russia and the Baltic states that caused the most distress. The Bilderbergers had decided to exploit the rich resources of the former Soviet Union while meeting at Evian, France, in 1992.

But, after using their immense influence to transfer countless billions to Russia so the cheap labor of inhabitants and the rich natural resources could be exploited, the results of "shock therapy economics" had been disastrous.

"Western nations, and especially mine, should be made to understand that aid to the former Soviet republics must be extensive and continuing," an American said.

Much more was said about sending mostly American tax dollars to the former communists when, to general approval, a speaker said Western investors must make claims on Russian property—"land structures, resources"—as "a price for our expertise."

"You negotiate with the Russians and they say, 'profit? What's profit?' No Russian alive today has lived in a free market economy after seven decades of communism. If the biggest gold mine in the world was discovered beneath a potato patch, they would still grow potatoes so they could make vodka," one speaker said.

"In developing natural resources, a proportionate amount must be demanded by the Western investor because of his valuable contribution of expertise," said the speaker.

The text of a Bilderberg presentation I acquired elaborated on this position. The paper's author was apparently European. He was literate but made spelling errors unlikely from one whose first language is English. It was apparently a rough draft, discarded after being retyped, but with the name blacked out as an extra precaution.

"Mentality differences complicate the problems in stability, lack of individual effort or initiative, fear of responsibility, complicated decision-making secretiveness and carelessness," the author said of the former Soviet Union.

"These are very dominant natures of the business-making in those countries—to change the mentality by Western business people will take several years," he said.

Kissinger, in a major speech, reported that the world's leading industrial nations were complying with Bilderberg requests to reschedule much of Russia's debt for 1994. The agreement was reached in Paris on June 4, while the Bilderberg group was still meeting. Russia owed about $80 billion to Western governments and banks, much of it inherited when the Soviet Union collapsed in 1991. Kissinger told his colleagues that the rescheduling agreement would save Russia $7 billion in interest payments this year. But, Kissinger said, Russia must have a longer-term, more comprehensive debt rescheduling in addition to more outright aid.

Russia now pays more in interest on old debts than it receives in Western aid, he said. Thus, Kissinger and the Bilderbergers were calling for more American aid to Russia so that it can pay interest on loans from the international financial cartel, while the economic props will also make the beleaguered nation more vulnerable to exploitation and "equity expertise."

At Bilderberg that year, a U.S. State Department official reported that Clinton's reversal of his campaign position in extending Most Favored Nation status to China—and disconnecting the issue from human rights—reflected Clinton's commitment to promoting the Pacific Union.

He cited a speech by his boss—the secretary of state at the time, Warren Christopher, to the Asia Society in New York on May 27, 1994.

Continuing Most Favored Nation status "encourages Chinese cooperation in building a new regional and international order," Christopher had said.

"The president's position could not be more clearly expressed," the State Department official said. Clinton was a longtime Trilateral member who was summoned to his first Bilderberg meeting at Baden-Baden, Germany in 1991.

Woerner tried to cheer his colleagues by reporting that the formation of the UN's standing world army is progressing nicely. The precedent of American pilots bombing targets in Bosnia under orders of a British general accountable to the UN Security Council—not Congress or the president—was cited to general approval. Similarly, the precedent of American soldiers serving in the field under a Turkish general in Somalia—again accountable only to the UN—was noted.

"And we heard no great protests from the Americans," one said.

"They're asleep," said another.

Secluded Mountain Paradise ...

1995—Burgenstock, Switzerland: That year, Bilderbergers returned to scenic chalet in this mountain town. Increasingly, the world shadow government has been choosing sites that facilitate security, making it more difficult for us to infiltrate their gatherings. Undaunted, the sources I have been courting over the years have come through for me, providing vital information that has appeared in no other U.S. publication.

CHAPTER FOURTEEN

1995

Burgenstock, Switzerland

Bilderberg boys were gloomy when they gathered in Switzerland in 1995 after perceiving a demand by American voters for an America first approach to both domestic and foreign affairs.

he Bilderberg group gathered here in a beautiful mountain setting but with ugly hearts. They were high on a hilltop but down in the dumps. David Rockefeller limped in, having fractured a leg on the sidewalks of Tokyo after voters broke his heart in November 1994 with a rousing demand for a Japan first approach to both domestic and foreign affairs.

At age 80, and staring eternity in the face, Rockefeller yearned to see his dream of a world government well launched, and already the deadline of the year 2000 had been shoved back.

Like its junior varsity, the Trilateral Commission, which met in April in Copenhagen, Denmark, Bilderberg members were depressed by the mood of America, which was "nationalistic"—a profane word in their circles. Add coverage by the Swiss media, and you can understand the somber mood.

Many of the 73 freshman Republicans elected in November, when they took control of both houses of Congress for the first time in 40 years, were young businessmen—not lawyers or bankers, Bilderberg operatives noted sadly.

The eagerness to balance the budget, reduce spending and the size of government and abolish foreign aid scared the Bilderberg boys. Many freshman Republicans campaigned against pork in their own districts—asking voters to reject federal money for courthouses, post offices and bridges—and were elected by wide margins.

The Bilderberg boys were deathly afraid that Pat Buchanan's run for the Republican nomination would pull the candidates toward more nationalistic, patriotic and noninterventionist positions. They were even afraid that Buchanan might be nominated and elected president. The Bilderberg pain can best be understood by recalling recent history. They are unaccustomed to having to worry about who is president. They are accustomed to owning the president— whoever he is and whatever party is in control of the White House.

A look back: Clinton, Trilateral and Bilderberg; Bush, Trilateral; Reagan, received the Trilateralists at the White House and had his vice president (Bush) address their meeting; Carter and his vice president, Walter Mondale, both Trilateralists; Jerry Ford and his vice president, Nelson Rockefeller, both Bilderberg; and Richard Nixon, banished from the White House for bucking Bilderberg.

So while the Bilderberg-Trilateral arms of the world government are used to owning both horses in a two-horse race, the presidential election of 1996 had them nervous.

If Clinton were nominated—and they were working feverishly to make sure he was unchallenged within his own party (even though Sen. Bill Bradley [D-N.J.] belonged to Bilderberg, too)—they will own one candidate.

But would they own the Republican? The leading contenders, Sen. Bob Dole (R-Kan.) and Sen. Phil Gramm (R-Texas), had never been known to participate in Trilateral or Bilderberg.

World Leaders Follow Orders; Bow to Bilderberg

Two goals of the Bilderberg group, decided at the internationalists' latest meeting in Burgenstock, Switzerland, were:

• Establishment of a world superfund to remove economic risks to international financiers who invest in poor countries to profit from slave wages, the absence of government-imposed fringe benefits and cheap real estate; and

• Getting British Prime Minister John Major out of office or back in line—fully supporting complete political integration of Europe.

World leaders at the economic summit of the seven industrialized nations, or G-7, were responding directly to instructions from Bilderberg when the group called—in a communiqué written before the leaders even gathered in Halifax, Canada—for an "emergency financing mechanism."

The "mechanism" would double poor nations' borrowing power from the IMF to $50 billion. The collapse of the Mexican peso in 1994 was the oft-cited reason for the international bankruptcy fund.

Bilderberg's demands, as called for in the G-7 communiqué, were officially adopted when the IMF's 178 member states met in Washington in September.

Clinton insisted to the U.S. public that the action would not touch American taxpayers. But the United States guarantees 20 percent of what member states take out in "special drawing rights" and the other 177 nations put up the rest.

Using the IMF has an historic ring. In May 1983, meeting in Montebello, Quebec, Bilderberg extracted a secret pledge from Reagan for $50 billion to be sent to Third World and communist countries over eight years.

That pledge was more than kept. It became known to the public as the "Brady Plan." Then, as now, the IMF was the conduit for shipping American tax dollars to uncreditworthy nations to protect the immensely profitable risk-free investments of international financiers.

The Bilderberg problem with Major had not only an historical ring but a paradox. Bilderberg engineered the downfall of Thatcher in 1989 because she resisted totally surrendering British sovereignty to the European Union. In 1995, Major was in the gun sights for the same reason.

June 26, 1995—Press Club Private Meeting: Lady Margaret Thatcher, known to some as the "Iron Lady," said she considered it a "tribute" to be denounced by Bilderberg at the 1989 meeting in Spain, assailing those who would surrender national sovereignty to international institutions. Bilderberg engineered her downfall when she resisted the euro as the common currency for Great Britain and bucked other European Union demands. She was replaced by her own Conservative Party with a political trapeze artist, John Major.

Up until that point, Major performed as a Bilderberg lapdog. He couldn't move Britain into the European Union far enough and fast enough. Establishing a European Union, American Union (NAFTA) and an Asian-Pacific Union is critical to the Bilderberg goal of dividing the world into three great regions.

But the rising tide of nationalism in the United States had crossed the Atlantic and patriots in Britain opposed further entanglement with the European Union, specifically, the proposed common currency. Backbenchers shouted their disapproval. Under this pressure, Major, chosen by Bilderberg to champion the surrender of Britain into the superstate, backed up. He said Britain may never agree to a common currency, which would surrender an important symbol of sovereignty.

So the Bilderberg that made Major became the Bilderberg that unmade him. History often repeats itself, but mankind rarely learns from it.

Thatcher Trashes Bilderberg: 'Global Plantation Will Fail'

Lady Thatcher both denounced and ridiculed Bilderberg in a private talk with me at the end of June in 1995.

"It is an honor to be denounced by Bilderberg," Lady Thatcher said. "Anyone who would surrender the sovereignty of their country . . ." her voice trailed off as she shook her head in disgust.

"They are a stuck-up set," Lady Thatcher added.

She appeared optimistic, however, that Bilderberg would fail in its goal of establishing a world government by 2002.

"They said 'nationhood should be suppressed,' but there will never be a new world order," Lady Thatcher said.

Lady Thatcher's comments were made privately to me and another guest at a reception prior to a speech to a full house at the National Press Club in Washington on June 26, 1995.

In her formal address, Lady Thatcher denounced the European Union (EU) as a "superstate."

"I reject the notion that we should effectively cease to govern ourselves," Lady Thatcher said.

She denounced the proposed common currency even as EU leaders were meeting in Cannes, France, to set up a 1999 deadline for monetary integration. In Cannes, they decided that each nation would call the new currency by its traditional name with the prefix "euro"—europound, eurofranc, etc.

Lady Thatcher warned against "passing on more powers to a Brussels bureaucracy" and a European court that "can overrule our country" and those who would "destroy nationhood and national sovereignty."

It is wrong to "create one nation from 15 countries speaking 13 languages," Lady Thatcher said. "The European superstate is an empire, and empires collapse."

Unforgiving Internationalists Show Clout

When Major resigned as head of the Conservative Party, placing himself in position to be ousted as prime minister of Britain on July 4, 1995, it stunned the world but came as no surprise to Bilderberg—or me. Bilderberg had called for Major's political scalp less than two weeks earlier in Burgenstock, Switzerland, because he appeared to be growing soft in his commitment to surrendering all British sovereignty to the European Union.

Paradoxically, Major had succeeded Lady Thatcher when Bilderberg called for her ouster as prime minister for the same reason: Resisting subjugation into the European Union. For years, Major was Bilderberg's tool and fool. Britain could not be swallowed into the European Union fast enough. But the new wave of nationalism that swept the United States in this past year crossed the Atlantic, and many in parliament became "Euro-rebels."

Under pressure from British patriots, including many in parliament and Lady Thatcher, Major tried to walk a tightrope—satisfying Bilderberg while pacifying supporters who wanted to retain sovereignty. The rope broke.

Even as Bilderberg was gathering atop Burgenstock Mountain, Major was saying that Britain was unprepared to join in the European common currency by the year 2000 and that "the time may never be right."

This position brought some applause by "Euro-rebels," because abandoning national currency in exchange for a new European Union currency is one of the last great acts of surrendering national sovereignty. That was enough for Bilderberg. The world shadow government cut his political tightrope, and Major was tumbling down.

Major tried to grab the dangling rope and climb back into Bilderberg's arms when Lady Thatcher and other Conservative Party "Euro-rebels" pressured him for a declaration that Britain would never adopt the common currency. He refused.

Bilderberg threw the rope back, and Major was bound for oblivion. Bilderberg made him and, despite his years as a faithful lap dog, Bilderberg unmade him.

But the world shadow government was forced to forgive him, given the other choice to lead the party. The only challenger to emerge had been John Redwood, a Thatcherite who bitterly opposed surrendering British sovereignty to the European Union. Consequently, the Bilderberg group was forced to embrace its Prodigal Son again.

There was still more bad news for Bilderberg: Redwood's 89 votes, and 12 ballots, caused more trouble for Bilderberg. Major's 218 votes fell far short of the 230 British politicians he needed to be secure at 10 Downing Street. One-third of his own Tory members of Parliament opposed him and a merger with the European Union.

Elections would be held by April 1997 despite the fact that the Conservative Party was 30 points behind Labor in the polls. Many Labor Party leaders also opposed closer ties with the European Union.

This, too, was bad news for Bilderberg, which wanted world government to be achieved while people are sleeping, not debating the issue. Bilderberg can't win a battle of ideas by democratic means.

But in that same year, another Bilderberg goal was achieved when Vice President Al Gore and Russian Prime Minister Viktor Chernomyrdin signed a $15 billion oil exploration deal in Moscow.

Oil fields will be developed off Sakhalin Island, which had been stolen from the Japanese following World War II, in Russia's Far East. Exxon invested as much as $15 billion and Japanese firms also shared in the deal.

Exploiting Russia's natural resources and slave-wage labor has been high on the Bilderberg agenda since the Berlin Wall tumbled.

Creative Editing by CBS on Trilats

I never expected CBS to give me 20 minutes—about the length of the interview—on its nightly network newscast on May 2, 1995, but I had hoped for more than one sentence:

"The conspiracy is to have a global government in which the elite will control the entire world and the unwashed multitudes will have a higher loyalty to the world government than to their own provinces such as the United States."

CBS's Anthony Mason had asked about the Trilateral Commission.

But all of that fell on the cutting room floor. This was not live, but taped in advance. Might CBS have chosen some more interesting sentences?

Mason had seemed particularly interested in the interlocking leadership of the Trilateralists and Bilderbergers, which I doubt he had ever heard about. The role of Rockefeller, Kissinger and others in both groups was explained.

The participation of the major newspapers—*Washington Post, New York Times, Los Angeles Times* and others—in both groups, on vows of secrecy, was explained. I referred Mason to Graham, boss of *The Washington Post,* who participates in both groups, for further information.

From the Trilateralists' own reports, I read Mason quotes in which the United States is denounced as an "individualistic" society where it is difficult to "groom the elite" for leadership roles.

While the Trilateralists seem worried about their "elite's" ability to be elected in the new mood of populism in America, I pointed out to Mason that they have had success with their own members in the past.

Presidents Carter, Bush and Clinton were all Trilateralists and members also fill high posts in every administration regardless of party, Mason was told.

But all of that remained on the cutting room floor.

Big Wig of Bilderberg Left Speechless

Outsiders are not supposed to know what gets said at secret Bilderberg meetings, as this June 1995 confrontation I had with Kissinger shows.

"Dr. Kissinger, I attended the last Bilderberg meeting when a white-haired European told you, forcefully, that Americans must understand that foreign aid was in their own interest," I said.

Kissinger almost dropped his scotch and water, and his mouth fell open, speechless probably for the first time in his life. Other journalists, who had covered Kissinger over the years, later said they had never before seen him lose his poise.

Kissinger, who came to this country as a young boy but has always affected a heavy German accent, finally found his voice, but he momentarily forgot his accent.

In plain English, Kissinger said: "I'm not saying it didn't happen; so much is said at these meetings. . . ." His voice trailed off, and apprehension filled his eyes.

I gave him more information about what had transpired within the Bilderberg meeting as Kissinger squirmed uncomfortably, his eyes alternately bulging and contracting.

"Actually, Bilderberg is not as gracious to me as they are to you, Dr. Kissinger," I said. "They don't invite me and sometimes they are somewhat inhospitable."

"I know," Kissinger murmured, having recovered his German accent but still looking furtive.

"I will be with you at Bilderberg again this year, as usual," I said.

"I know," Kissinger murmured.

But he seemed less than enthusiastic.

Truth Eludes Major Media

Over the years, the mainstream media's cover-up of Bilderberg has always had me asking: Are the members of the Establishment media simply stupid and incompetent, or are they part of the conspiracy?

On Monday, May 22, 1995, I sent a news release to all of the major media in the United States informing them of one of the most important meetings of the year—the secret annual Bilderberg session. Not that they didn't know about it already.

In 1995, the Bilderberg group met at Burgenstock, Switzerland, June 8-11. Among the attendees were representatives of the Establishment media. Said media did not report on what was said in the secret session. That year, as in years past, one of America's most powerful media moguls—Katharine Graham of the Washington Post Co.—attended. So did I. Mrs. Graham was invited; I was not.

So along with the press release sent to *The Washington Post,* I asked Mrs. Graham to consent to an interview on the subject of the Bilderberg group.

The following is the text of my letter.

May 22, 1995
Katharine Graham
Chairman, Executive Committee
The Washington Post Co.
Washington, D.C.

Dear Mrs. Graham:

I have attended Trilateral Commission and Bilderberg meetings with you for more than 10 years and yet I have never read about Bilderberg meetings in *The Washington Post* while stories about the Trilateralists are subject to their approval. (You were invited; I most definitely was not.)

Having spent 20 years with daily newspapers—the *Washington Daily News, Richmond Times-Dispatch* and *Akron Beacon Journal,* among others—I cannot reconcile the *Post's* cover-up of the Bilderberg group by any standards of journalism I ever learned at the slot-man's knee.

Can the fact that you, and high officials of *The New York Times, Los Angeles Times,* the news magazines and others in journalism, attend the meetings on a vow of silence—a pledge to reveal nothing—be defined as anything but a conspiracy? Is not such a promise journalistic prostitution, not unlike a reporter having the mayor approve of his city council story before submitting it to the city desk?

If you choose to believe that the Bilderberg group and Trilateral Commission are benevolent organizations helping solve the world's problems—and we of the unwashed multitudes should be grateful—how would that change anything?

Certainly, if 120 of the world's top film stars or football players or citizens' militia leaders met secretly for three days behind locked and guarded doors, the *Post* and other newspapers would make energetic efforts to report what was happening.

How, then, is there no curiosity at all when 120 of the world's most powerful financiers and political leaders meet secretly behind guarded doors? You know as well as I that the decisions they make affect all Americans and most of the world.

The taxpayers heavily subsidize these meetings, paying enormous travel costs of high officials of the White House and government departments who attend. (I have seen their travel vouchers and they don't fly coach or stay at the YMCA.)

For 20 years, I spent my life pawing through Associated Press, United Press International, *The New York Times* and *Los Angeles Times* wires. Yet, I never knew the Bilderbergers existed until I joined Liberty Lobby and *The Spotlight* in May 1975. I just did not believe such events could transpire in a complete news blackout.

What else is this but a media conspiracy to silence the truth? It virtually makes one retch to confront your hypocrisy and intellectual dishonesty, your callous and corrupt cover-up of one of the most important stories of our lifetimes.

I would like to interview you next week and discuss your part in this conspiracy and will call your secretary to arrange an appointment.

Cordially,
(Signed)
James P. Tucker Jr.
Spotlight Correspondent

Are you surprised to learn my letter was not answered?

Swiss Media Spotlights Bilderberg; We Told The Story

The Swiss media has proven it has more guts than the Establishment media in the U.S.

On May 22, 1995, I had press releases sent to the major media outlets in the United States announcing this year's secret meeting of the Bilderberg group. I said I had details I was willing to share. I got no response.

I also sent the release to major European media, particularly newspapers in Switzerland where the Bilderbergers were meeting. The Swiss responded, reporting the facts for their readers and in at least one instance, crediting me for the tip that led to their investigation.

Following are translated excerpts from the Swiss press.

From the Friday May 26 edition of *Tagesschau*, a Swiss newspaper: The headlines read: "Secret Conference on Burgenstock Mountain," "Burgenstock Will Be the Mecca of the Elite in Politics and Finance in June."

And, "The Swiss Military to Protect International and Leading Economists and Statesmen."

The following is the translation of the story:

> Prominent leaders from the world of politics and economics will be meeting at Nidwalden, on Mt. Burgenstock, Switzerland, for the very secretive Bilderberg conference. About 100 participants are expected from June 8 to 11; among the participants are leading bankers, politicians and industrialists from Europe and North America.
>
> Isolated from world news media, the attendees will be discussing current topics of world politics. The substance of the discussion remains secret; only topics and participants are being announced.
>
> The first conference was held in 1954 at the Bilderberg Hotel near Oosterbeek in Holland. This is the third time the luxury Resort Palace Hotel on Burgenstock has been used for the meetings.
>
> The luminaries from the 1995 meeting include Kurt Furgler, Walter Scheel, Henry Kissinger, Helmut Kohl, Fiat Chairman Giovanni Agnelli, shipping magnate Stavos Niarchos, David Rockefeller and Prince Claus of the Netherlands. This year's conference organizer is David de Pury, the CEO of the powerful conglomerate Asea Braun Bovere (ABB) of Switzerland.

According to the *Luzerner Zeitung* of May 26:

> Local police have asked the Swiss Army to guard the hotel and protect the participants of the meeting. For the most important participants, a special helicopter is being used to bring them to the hotel. Only participants

of the meeting will have access to the hotels; anyone accompanying the participants (including their body-guards) will have to stay at the Park or Grand Hotel near-by.

Extra telephone lines will be installed to provide instant communications with governments and corporate headquarters anywhere in the world. At the last meeting, Swissair even went so far as to install special ticket counters for participants of the meeting.

The May 26 *Luzerner Zeitung* reported: "The time when it takes place was revealed in *The Spotlight,* an American weekly, and confirmed by the Swiss government."

From the *Bunder Zeitung:*

The Secret World Government Is Meeting
Wherever the international elite meets for visits of state of conferences they are always chased down by the media. However, when the so-designated "secret world government" Bilderberg conference meets it's dead air in the media. This Thursday, here we go again. It is estimated that 100 important people from Europe and the U.S.A. will meet for four days to discuss important economic and political problems.

It is the first time this group is meeting at the same place twice. They also met at the Burgenstock in 1981. [Actually it was 1960—Ed.] Burgenstock is an ideal location for the meetings since it is situated where access to it can be easily controlled. Indeed, the picture the public has regarding the Bilderberg conference seems to rest mostly in the secrecy of the meeting. These get-togethers are truly secretive and therefore many rumors and much speculation surround this exclusive club meeting behind closed doors. Neither a list of participants is provided nor any news releases . . . very little substantive information reaches the public. At best the media will be given a promise of a closing statement and, even if representatives of the media are included in this exclusive club, such as the boss of *The Washington Post* for example, Katharine Graham, they too keep the code of silence. From the *Post Schweiz,* June 6.

Timetable for World Government

As reported in the U.S. newspaper, *The Spotlight,* this year's Bilderberg conference will take up the issues, "the dangerous new populism in the U.S., the western world's investment in the former U.S.S.R. and the issue of NATO expansion into Eastern Europe." Furthermore in view of the coming world order, *The Spotlight* writes of a timetable for the world government by 2002. This year's meeting was to be held for four days instead of the usual three.

From the *Sonntags Zeitung* of June 11:

Burgenstock: The Fortress of Power

There are speculations about a world shadow government because of the importance of the participants of this conference. The U.S. paper *The Spotlight* of Washington, D.C. claims that there is already a schedule for the foundation of a world government. This paper has occupied itself for years with the subject of the Bilderbergers. "The political opening of the East and the demise of Margaret Thatcher of Great Britain are results of the Bilderbergers" strategies," said *Spotlight* correspondent James Tucker. Tucker is not present at the conference, which is generally inaccessible. Instead he is sitting on the terrace, which is as close as he can get to the meeting. The conference itself is closed to the public, and security is tight. The local police from Lucerne are there with dogs.

People Shouldn't Know ...

December 1995—Washington, D.C.: Former House Speaker Tom Foley attended both Trilateral and Bilderberg meetings. "People shouldn't know about Bilderberg or the Trilateral Commission," he fumed as he got a similar remedial civics lesson like that given Dick Cheney in 1991.

CHAPTER FIFTEEN

1996

King City, Ontario

Growing nationalism in 1996 forced the Bilderberg group to revise its strategy for global domination.

unkering down in an unwelcome blizzard of publicity, Bilderberg developed a new strategy for achieving its goal of a world government. Behind lines of mostly invisible security at the Canadian Imperial Bank of Commerce Leadership Center, Bilderberg set forth its plans during its annual gathering from May 30 to June 1 in 1996.

For openers, the Global Plantation wanted to employ new propaganda techniques to counter surging patriotism in the West.

New "scientific studies" warned of impending world disasters: Refugees fleeing farms for lack of "sustainable growth" would lead to famine in cities. Also, hysteria over water and air pollution was to be generated.

One speaker said:

"People of the world, but especially stubborn Americans, who want to cling to every last shred of sovereignty, must be made to understand that we all breathe the polluted air and drink the foul water; the air and waterways know no borders and have no loyalties.

"To say that a supranational agency under the UN must address this problem is stating the obvious," he added. "It is equally obvious that the UN must have final arbitration over immigration issues as the refugees grow in number."

And another:

"Since we last met [in Burgenstock, Switzerland] we have seen the problem of nationalism increase, not abate, in Europe but more so in the United States. If reforms are to succeed, we must convince the middle class that supporting new powers for the UN is a patriotic duty, to save his country from natural disasters."

Also listening and promising to report nothing were these journalistic prostitutes: Conrad Black, who owns more than half of Canada's newspapers; conservative leader William F. Buckley, Jr., editor-at-large of *National Review*; Paul Gigot, *The Wall Street Journal*; Margarida Marante, identified as a "TV journalist"; Peter Job of Britain, who heads Reuters; Andrew Knight of Britain, who heads Zionist billionaire Rupert Murdoch's media conglomerate, News Corporation; Norman Podhoretz, editor of *Commentary*, the "neo-conservative" voice of the New York chapter of the American Jewish Committee; Toger Seidenfaden of Denmark, editor of *Politiken A/S*; and Walter Veltroni of Ireland, editor of *L'Unita*.

The presence of two leading "conservative" voices within the ranks of the plutocracy, the aforementioned Buckley and Podhoretz, indicates that Bilderberg intends to continue flexing its influence over the "loyal opposition" in the ranks of the so-called "Republican right" and the "conservative movement." Buckley and Podhoretz are charged with suppressing populist and nationalist grass-roots rebellion within the GOP as represented by Buchanan's maverick presidential candidacy. At last year's Bilderberg confab in Burgenstock, Switzerland, the official "guest conservative" was Buchanan's leading critic, William Kristol, publisher of Murdoch's *Weekly Standard*.

The gathering of the international elite heard more:

"Make [the masses] understand that, if we fail to have a strong global government, empowered to act effectively, quickly and decisively, the disaster that will eventually strike this Earth will impact them, too, and waving a flag will be meaningless. What is the value

HAIL CANADA: In 1996, this group of patriotic Canadian citizens gathered outside the Bilderberg meeting site in King City, Ontario, to protest the secrecy surrounding the Bilderberg confab. Since that meeting Canada has moved closer to a model police state, clamping down on free speech for controversial topics.

of the nation-state if it cannot meet these challenges?"

In that year, the general feeling imparted by Bilderberg was: Brace for propaganda designed to make you feel unpatriotic unless you support massive transfers of American tax dollars overseas.

"We must promote a 'Lincolnesque' view . . . the world cannot long endure half-poor and half-rich . . . hunger in Africa and poverty in Russia are as important a problem for America and other industrialized nations as highways and bridges."

Unless wealthy nations acted, the propaganda line went, they would be overwhelmed with floods of refugees that could not be stopped.

"Is it not better to surrender a significant amount of sovereignty so world problems can be addressed on a global level than be so overwhelmed later that our precious borders are meaningless?"

one asked.

"We cannot let America or any other country arbitrarily close its borders so the refugee burden falls more heavily on others," one said. "Still, establishing a supranational UN agency to arbitrate these matters will be as difficult to sell as it is necessary to be done."

Despite their dejection over the increase in "provincialism" and "nationalism," Bilderberg had something to celebrate. "We have now established NATO as an instrument of the UN, and there has been little adverse reaction other than the far-right wing," one said. He predicted that NATO would change its charter to allow ventures outside Europe—anywhere in the world.

"The European experiment has succeeded," he announced. He was referring to the fact that NATO intervened in former Yugoslavia under direction of the UN Security Council. Americans served under a foreign commander; the president and Congress had no voice in the matter, despite the Constitution.

The U.S. defense secretary that year, William Perry, who once assured this writer that he opposed a UN standing army, is not known to have objected to these comments, although he was present.

"Even American 'conservatives' welcome NAFTA and call for expansion, so the only problem we must deal with is super patriots and nationalists of the right-wing," one Bilderberg was overheard saying.

The plutocrats agreed that the program to establish Europe as a superstate with a common currency is on track and the Asian-Pacific Economic Community is evolving, at a satisfying pace, into the Pacific Union.

"Our biggest problem is America," one said, in an unintended tribute to the United States. "Where once we could make significant progress undisturbed, every year we are having more problems with American nationalism, making some things politically difficult."

One of the final goals of the Global Plantation has been to expand the European Union to include Poland and eventually other former Warsaw Pact countries and, then the former Soviet states, making the entity continent-wide. Similarly, one-world leaders wanted to press the expansion of NAFTA to include all nations in the Western Hemisphere, essentially laying the groundwork for the hemispheric unit to ultimately have a governing "parliament" for an "American Union." The final step would be the creation of the "Pacific Union," thus dividing the world into three great regions as George Orwell predicted in his book *1984*.

Establishment Acts on Bilderberg Orders

A few days after the 1996 Bilderberg meeting ended in Canada, one-worlders quickly put together plans to strengthen the Global Plantation. What a coincidence.

Moving swiftly to advance the Bilderberg agenda unveiled in King City, Ontario, international manipulators moved to make housing and food an "international right" and expand NATO as the UN's standing army.

Ultimately, these two moves were to merge into a situation where the UN would have final authority—enforced by a world army—which would allow it to enter the United States or any nation, and whereby it could arbitrarily ship taxpayer funds from the Western nations to poor countries.

These mutual missions have the weight of the White House behind them. Clinton had sent his senior advisor George Stephanopoulos to the secret meeting in Canada to receive his orders.

Even as the UN-sponsored Habitat II conference in Istanbul, Turkey, was deciding that housing is a "right" for all people, UN functionaries were calling for a "food summit" in Rome in November 1995 to proclaim a full stomach a world "right."

Once it was decided that adequate housing and food are the

rights of every world citizen, it would become the proclaimed "duty" of the United States and other industrialized nations to implement these "rights."

While these dual campaigns would advance the visionaries' dream of a world government, there were immediate and immense profits in store for the Rockefellers, Rothschilds and other international financiers involved in these secret sessions.

While American taxpayers and those of other Western nations provide housing and food, these international entrepreneurs would be hailed as statesmen for "helping" the poor countries as they build factories and other enterprises.

As your tax dollars provide food and shelter, the rich get richer by paying slave wages in poor countries that are unencumbered by such "fringes" as pensions, paid vacations and health insurance provided by many domestic companies.

The Food and Agricultural Organization, a UN agency, would work toward achieving a "food for all" goal in November, it said in a statement.

"Support from the United States has been extremely important" for both food and housing "rights," said Hilmi Toros, who was participating in the Istanbul summit. "They have given us their full support."

Agreement on the housing "right" in Istanbul was applauded by the United States. "For the first time [the agreement] translates [housing rights] to the common level," said Michael Stegman, assistant secretary of Housing and Urban Development and alternate head of the U.S. delegation.

Participants weren't timid about demanding the resources of the United States and other Western nations. Wealthy nations should not only make housing a "right," but should pay the costs, said Fernando Berrocal Soto, a Costa Rican delegate and representative of the "Group of 77" poor countries.

"Substantial financial resources should be mobilized by the international community with a view to address the issue of human

March 1995—Washington, D.C.: When he was speaker of the House, Rep. Newt Gingrich (R-Ga.) said he never had and never would attend a meeting of either the Trilateral Commission or the Bilderberg Group. As far as can be determined, he spoke truthfully. However, he is a proud member of the Council on Foreign Relations. His name has never been found on the participants list of either organization, although he is a proponent of American military aggression around the world. This chat came in March 1995, when Gingrich had only been the speaker since January.

settlements," he added.

Meanwhile, NATO was being revised to enhance its emerging role as the UN's world army. Meeting in Berlin, NATO bureaucrats agreed to be "more flexible" and to continue working "outside the alliance," as it is now in Bosnia, where troops will remain beyond the one-year commitment.

NATO also agreed to bring in Poland first, then Hungary and the Czech Republic. Ultimately, all European countries, including Russia, would be part of this continental army.

When Life Gives You Lemons ...

1996—Lake Lanier, Georgia: This year, several good-natured supporters brought me a large glass and a pitcher of lemonade. The temperature was near 100 degrees and the humidity around 90 percent that year, making Bilderberg hunting extremely uncomfortable even for this southern gentleman. The guards were amenable to a cool drink, but would not let me past the gates of the venue site. I still got my story, working sources inside the hotel and amongst the personal staff of the attendees.

CHAPTER SIXTEEN

1997

Lake Lanier, Georgia

"Racial and cultural differences are to blissfully blur," Bilderberg promised in 1997, in a new "world without borders."

ilderberg celebrated what participants called significant progress toward world government while meeting behind locked doors and armed guards at the remote but posh Renaissance Pine Isle Resort 50 miles from Atlanta from June 12-15 in 1997.

Leaders called for a new push for "racial harmony" in the United States as an important step in cultivating the public mind to accept "a world without borders."

To patrol this world government, new accords calling for the expansion of NATO and giving Russia a voice meant that the troops could operate outside of Europe, Kissinger was overheard saying at Bilderberg that year.

NATO had earlier become, effectively, the United Nations world army, Kissinger said, referring to earlier Bilderberg meetings. This was achieved when American troops wore blue helmets in Bosnia, serving under a European commander who reported to the UN Security Council, with the Congress and president having no voice.

Now another major step had been accomplished, with UN expansion and a Russian role allowing NATO to send troops anywhere in the world.

It is "likely" that NATO's first venture outside Europe would be an African "hot spot," perhaps the Congo, Kissinger said at the time. "This would cause less consternation among nationalists than if NATO jumped into some Central American country."

Another speaker praised Clinton for extolling the virtues of racial harmony "as we speak." In 1997, Clinton had named a panel on "race relations" and, on June 14, 1997, he had delivered a commencement speech at the University of California, San Diego, extolling "brotherhood," telling Americans to prepare for America being a nation with a non-white majority. Clinton also talked of a formal congressional "apology" for slavery as Bilderberg was meeting.

At the Bilderberg conference, a speaker who was an American with dark hair and complexion, and who appeared to be in his 50s, likewise hailed the new world order: "In the years ahead as white Americans, African-Americans and Asian-Americans marry and bear children, racial and cultural distinctions will blissfully blur," he predicted.

"As this biological process proceeds, the public will come to more and more accept a world without borders, a world where the nation-state is a relic of history," he said.

These words keyed into the subject of world ecology, a popular cause in recent years with Bilderberg and the Trilateral Commission.

Dirty water and dirty air know no borders, and people everywhere are growing to accept the fact that a supranational agency under the UN is "a necessary tool to preserve spaceship Earth," he said.

Another speaker, a European in his 60s, also took up the racial banner, citing a recent Gallup Poll showing a high acceptance of integration in the United States. The poll found 61 percent of white Americans favor intermarriage with blacks. In 1958, only 4 percent of whites favored intermarriage with blacks, and the figure grew to 45 percent in 1994. In the latest poll, 93 percent of whites said they would vote for a black for president, up from 35 percent in 1958 and

77 percent in 1987, Gallup found.

Despite voicing this in the poll, many middle class white Americans would most likely neither marry a black person nor vote for a black man for president, another speculated during a discussion period. "But it is tremendous progress that so many whites feel compelled to say so, anyway, and American public opinion is moving swiftly away from the nationalist mentality," he said.

"Let them spend their lives watching television and eating French fries—we'll make them visionaries in spite of themselves," said another, to approving laughs and smirks.

To help promote the dual goals of internationalism and the establishment of NATO as the UN's world army to be deployed anywhere on Earth, Gen. Colin Powell, the only black man to serve as chairman of the Joint Chiefs of Staff, was recruited into Bilderberg ranks at this meeting and attended as a "star guest" at the Renaissance Pine Isle Resort.

Thanks to constant major media promotion and attention, Powell's popularity among Americans has remained in the astounding 90 percent range since he became a public figure during the Persian Gulf War.

"The [first] Gulf War was worthwhile just to create Powell," a Bilderberg participant said.

Powell's marriage to Bilderberg is a natural. Years ago, when he was still chairman of the Joint Chiefs, I had confronted Powell on the issue of American soldiers serving under foreign commanders. Powell also describes himself as a "Rockefeller Republican." He defended the unconstitutional practice.

Powell told his new Bilderberg colleagues that he would strive for world "harmony" and "a strong UN and NATO."

"Colin Powell will be of great value in helping 'fringe' Americans overcome their obsession with national sovereignty and to accept the world as it is going to be," said Stephanopoulos, who was attending a Bilderberg meeting for the second time.

Some concerns were expressed about supporters of America-first advocate Pat Buchanan and France-first champion Jean-Marie Le Pen in France. The presence of *Spotlight* readers and "right-wing extremists" picketing outside the gates of their gathering place also unnerved the Bilderbergers.

"These pockets of resistance to social justice are a problem and must be dealt with seriously," said one, who spoke in a low voice believed by inside sources to belong to Rockefeller. "But they can be isolated and contained; a whole new generation is emerging that is immersed in the vision of a world with peace and prosperity for all."

Historically, the generations of Rockefeller and his nephew Sen. John D. Rockefeller IV (D-W.Va.), who also attended, have a special definition of "prosperity for all."

It means lowering the American standard of living while lifting that of poor nations until the world economy is leveled off—while increasing Rockefeller power and fortune.

Others stressed the need for more immigration to the United States from poor Latin nations to both relieve their economic pressures while supplying cheap labor to American industry. For this, NAFTA was toasted and the call of their Trilateral brothers for a UN agency to arbitrate immigration issues was endorsed. Under such a "supranational" agency, America could be compelled to accept an undesirable immigrant.

"Some of us will be surprised at further progress we find next year," an American said.

Bilderberg Charade Proves Transparent

Clinton followed the Bilderberg script in 1997 by promising the United Nations to seek binding international agreements to reduce carbon dioxide and other "greenhouse" emissions.

The ultimate goal is a new "supranational" UN bureaucracy that could patrol the United States and other countries to enforce

2004—Stresa, Italy: Under Secretary of Defense for Policy Douglas Feith was at this meeting, pushing for more war in the Middle East. In 2004, Feith was called "the dumbest [expletive] guy on the planet," by a prominent U.S. gener-

such commitments as part of the overall scheme to establish a world government.

The president had earlier pledged to "convince the American people and the Congress that the climate change problem is real and imminent." But, as scripted, he had stopped short of publicly committing to specific targets at the economic summit in Denver as a political gesture to Americans who enjoy frying hamburgers in their back yards or using power mowers.

Scientists who cite studies showing there is no "global warming" and economists who warn that American jobs will head south NAFTA-style under such agreements were also targets of Clinton's pose as a reluctant damsel.

Because "poor nations" were exempted from the immensely expensive burden of reducing emissions by 15 percent by 2010, economists warned, many thousands of American jobs would disappear as industries fled the country to avoid the costs.

In an unlikely alliance, the National Association of Manufacturers (NAM) and the AFL-CIO warned that exempting China, Korea and other "developing nations" would lead to a flight of U.S. jobs. Many NAM members are small businessmen, not to be confused with international corporations represented in Bilderberg.

"Millions of Americans would lose their jobs and American manufacturers would take a severe hit in the world marketplace," NAM President Jerry Jasinowski told a Senate Finance subcommittee June 26.

Clinton had promised the UN a specific commitment in time for a December 1997 meeting on global warming in Kyoto, Japan.

The president also embraced the guilt complex imposed on the United States by the UN, acknowledging that this country has 4 percent of the world's population but produces more than one-fifth of all greenhouse gases.

Using an unprecedented scare tactic, the president argued that if the United States fails to act, 9,000 square miles of Florida and Louisiana will disappear, agriculture will be crippled, multitudes will die of heat stress and infectious diseases will ravage the land.

"That was a blatant attempt to scare Americans into surrendering their national sovereignty," an anonymous State Department official told this reporter later that year.

Tucker Receives Special Attention in Georgia

This year, Bilderberg's security team ran out of patience with me, and ran out of southern hospitality, where I was involved.

I called him "My Shadow," not only because of the nursery jingle about a child's companion, but also because a dog named Shadow brightened my morning breakfast. And, the Bilderberg Shadow and the dog Shadow look alike.

Wherever I roamed the Renaissance Pine Isle Resort, Shadow (the Bilderberg kind) was discreetly in evidence. It was kind of fun. I would take an elevator to the fifth floor where the Murden Co. of New York is situated (they handle Bilderberg logistics when it meets in North America) and where they had quarters for the advance staff.

I had made many "fly-bys" in the search for information. Knowing Shadow would be up on the next elevator, instead of getting off, I would go back down to the lobby, wait a moment and make another fifth-floor fly-by without Shadow.

I couldn't help teasing Shadow. While having lunch, or coffee, I would stick my nose in my bag as if I were making a phone call. I knew Shadow was listening.

"Listen carefully, Shadow," I would say, "in a moment, I'm going to say something profound and you don't want to miss it."

This always brought a frozen moment. Once, while turning a page in *The Atlanta Constitution*, which he was supposed to be reading, Shadow forgot to finish turning the page for a long moment. Another time, his arm was suspended from hanging up a public phone. Another time, for a long moment, Shadow forgot to finish bending over to pick up some papers off a table in the lobby.

I enjoyed transfixing Shadow.

Shadow was effective at scaring sources, who had been responsive on my first day at the Renaissance. In separate conversations, three told me they had been forced to sign waivers and undergo background checks. They also told me that any employee with less than a full year's service could not work during the Bilderberg days. This is a tribute to those who had the courage to meet with me in person and by phone daily during the Bilderberg meeting, serving as my eyes and ears.

As I approached one who was alone on Day Three of this year's Bilderberg meetings, I was greeted with these words, spoken loudly:

"I will not tell you a thing!"

Then, bending close and speaking softly, the employee said, "I will meet you at the time and place and help you all I can."

This source also knew the walls had ears. Whether he knew it or not, Shadow and his accomplices were successful in scaring away some—but not all—Bilderberg sources.

Bilderberg took the direct approach on the same evening.

"Mr. Tucker, may I have a word with you?"

We sat together on a bench outside the resort's main restaurant.

"My name is Jim Penn, head of hotel security," said the man, who was of average build with dark hair and appeared to be in his 30s.

"I'm sure you are doing a good job," I said affably.

"Bilderberg is very unhappy that you are here," Penn said.

"That's no surprise," I replied. "I've chased these kids all over Europe and North America for many years and they never warmly welcome me."

"I understand your mission, but my employees are very upset that you ask them to observe Bilderberg and pick up papers sometimes out of a trash can," Penn said. "And you promise them rewards for spying."

"Look, Mr. Penn," I said. "I would never forgive myself if I were the reason Bilderberg ruined an employee. But the 'rewards' you refer to are nothing more than refreshments—perhaps a sandwich and Pepsi—which is a courtesy newspapermen often give informants."

"They are very upset; they are simple, hardworking people who are dazed by what is going on," Penn said.

"I'm sure they are," I agreed. "Bilderberg never met here before and never will again, at least for 30 years when a whole new generation of employees will be on hand."

"I must ask you to stop approaching my employees and asking them to get information," Penn said.

"I would never ask them to do anything but be vigilant and exercise their First Amendment rights," I said.

"I must ask you to stop," Penn said.

"I will take your words to heart," I responded, pointedly not promising to stop.

Penn seemed edgy and glad to conclude the conversation.

"Thank you, Mr. Tucker."

"Good night, Mr. Penn."

In reviewing events in my mind there was only one of the numerous employees I had tried to develop as sources where I had suggested checking papers in a trash can. With others, I mentioned that papers may be left on tables or on a bar. I knew who had tipped off Penn. I briefly thought of retribution by profusely thanking the employee for his promises of help within earshot of Shadow, but quickly abandoned the idea as not Christian.

The next day, I let Shadow report that I was being good by talking to employees, nodding my head and jotting a note. When Shadow would trot up to them, they could accurately say that I was asking directions to here or there, not discussing Bilderberg. It was nice to let Shadow feel that he had finally won a few. In the meantime, I developed two more sources.

I psyched myself to awaken about 3 a.m. on the fourth day, the day the remnants of the unwashed multitudes (us non-Bilderbergers) had to be out of the hotel by noon. I dared not leave a wake-up call for fear of awakening Shadow, too. I had left a wake-up call for 5 a.m. as usual. I left my room in shirtsleeves and open collar, as one unable to fall asleep. Shadow was nowhere in sight. I never saw that chap again, despite our closeness.

Roaming through a reception area outside the offices of the Bilderberg advance team, I encountered a security guard. We agreed that neither of us could sleep. Not a piece of paper was in sight; even the trash cans had been completely emptied. I wandered aimlessly into the large Bilderberg meeting room, where microphones and translator devices were set up, when he called me back out.

"Something big must be going on," I said, leaving the forbidden area.

"Yes, something big," he concurred.

I encountered Shadow No. 2 on leaving my room about 6, to go to the bottom floor gift shop for *The Atlanta Constitution*, the only paper on sale. The new Shadow made little attempt at discretion; he trailed me to the gift shop and back to the elevator, hitting the button for the fifth floor—Bilderberg's floor. I hit No. 3 for the lobby and restaurant floor.

Shadow 2 followed me into the restaurant and was seated several tables away, joined by a man in a dark suit whom I had casually talked to the day before.

"Good morning, Mr. Tucker," said the man in the dark suit.

"Good morning," I responded. Double confirmation for Shadow 2: Shadow 2 was on the elevator as I returned to my room, getting off at the same floor. A few moments later, I swung my door open and saw Shadow 2 leaning against the wall, 30 feet to my left.

"Am I paranoid or could you be following me?" I inquired.

"Yes," he answered.

"I'm checking out soon, and as you know, I'll be checking into the Hilton," I said. "Will you be joining me there?"

"I might."

"Well, bear with me a few minutes," I told Shadow 2. "As soon as I pack, we'll go to the front desk and check out."

Shadow 2 looked a bit confused, but nodded.

"Come on," I told Shadow 2 as I emerged with suitcase and typewriter. "No thanks," I told him, "I'll carry my own stuff because an old man like you must be tired from all your standing." That was, of course, a response to an offer that Shadow 2 never made, but it was fun to keep him edgy.

"Those Bilderberg kids take themselves seriously," I said, continuing the affable tone. Shadow 2, a thin man in his 60s, remained silent. But those pompous asses hate to be referred to as "Bilderberg kids" so I helped him make his report interesting.

"Come on, now we have to go over to the bellhops," I told Shadow after checking out. Bellhops arranged free transportation to the Hilton, a mile away. I sat down on the bench outside, awaiting the shuttle.

"Won't you sit down here, Shadow?" I asked. "Surely an old man like you is tired from all that standing." Shadow, still looking bewildered, shook his head.

"Christians are always concerned about people's well-being," I explained in a tender, loving voice, "even scum."

"Good bye and get some rest," I said, boarding the shuttle.

As the bus pulled away, Shadow 2 was reporting my departure on a portable phone. Bilderberg and I maintained our close relationship at the Hilton. Several Georgia cops in short pants and guns were on patrol. Some chased about on bicycles. And the following morning, the patriot who dug the bug out of my sofa called.

My Hilton phone was also bugged, he advised.

It was a former federal intelligence official, who obviously must remain nameless, who had volunteered to help me by meeting my plane in Atlanta and driving me to the luxury resort. Within a moment after checking into my room—on my first day at the Bilderberg hotel—the phone rang and the front desk advised that I could remain until Wednesday noon as originally requested—instead of Tuesday noon—if I would take the same-type room a few doors down the hall.

The moment we entered the second room, the intelligence officer started walking about with a small device that made interesting sounds. He turned the couch over, slashed the bottom with a pocket knife and handed me the "bug" as a trophy. He also advised me that the telephone was bugged.

So sources, collaborators and *The Spotlight* were made aware that when we talk from my hotel room phone, Bilderberg operatives were listening. We had some fun, saying outlandish things that hot-eyed Bilderberg boys would take seriously.

Clinton Acts Quickly on Bilderberg Agenda

Following that year's Bilderberg meetings, I wondered if Clinton's rush to carry out the agenda of the shadowy globalist group was just coincidence—or was it a conspiracy?

In 1997, the Clinton administration had acted speedily on the dual goals outlined at the latest Bilderberg meeting: eliminating racial and ethnic distinctions and letting NATO forces patrol the world as the UN army.

Just days after a Bilderberg participant said intermarrying means "racial and cultural distinctions will blissfully blur"—leading Americans to accept a "world without borders," Clinton picked up the theme from the oval office. "We want to become a multiracial, multiethnic society," Clinton told a group of black journalists.

"This will arguably be the third great revolution—to prove we literally can live without having a dominant European culture," Clinton said.

Clinton then went to California to celebrate because the state was about to lose its majority-white status.

"Within the next three years here in California, no single race or ethnic group will make up a majority of the state's population," Clinton said. "A half century from now, there will be no majority race in America."

Bilderberg orders to Clinton had been transmitted officially by Samuel Berger, the assistant to the president for national security affairs at the time, who represented the White House at the secret meeting of the world's elite.

Clinton was also given unofficial fill-ins by his wife Hillary, the only first lady to ever attend a Bilderberg meeting, and Stephanopoulos.

Mrs. Clinton's presence was kept off even Bilderberg's own "confidential, not for circulation" list of participants. But her presence was confirmed by me at the Lake Lanier Islands, Ga., meeting site. In Washington, the White House reluctantly confirmed her presence, although the mainstream press obeyed orders not to report the fact.

While no previous president has uttered such radical comments, the campaign to deny America her heritage and culture is well entrenched in the educational system.

Under threat of withholding federal tax dollars, states had been bullied through "Goals 2000" and other programs to adopt textbooks and courses that denounce American settlers for "genocide" against Indians and in many ways demean the Founders.

Clinton had named a panel of left-wingers to a race "commission" even as Bilderberg was meeting. Its chairman, historian John Hope Franklin, since spoke to students at Duke University.

Similarly, the secretary of state at the time, Madeleine Albright, was quick to begin conditioning the public mind to accept the Bilderberg claim that, under agreements allowing its expansion, NATO was no longer confined to defending Europe but could patrol the Earth as the UN's standing army.

In a guest "global viewpoint" commentary for the Los Angeles Times Syndicate (whose executives participate in and cover up Bilderberg), the secretary of state wrote of NATO's "quest for stability in Europe—and beyond."

That one little word "beyond" has great significance for the United States and the world.

Rothschilds Attend ...

1998—Turnberry, Scotland: Evelyn de Rothschild, chairman of NM Rothschild and Sons, attended that year's meeting. A member of the prominent banking family is always present at the secret meeting of Bilderberg.

CHAPTER SEVENTEEN

1998

Turnberry, Scotland

In 1998, the world's most exclusive club sought supremacy in the judicial and economic fields.

lthough moderately distracted by the new nuclear arms race between India and Pakistan, Bilderberg concentrated on meeting goals it set on the road to world government:

• Establishing a global court that would be superior to the U.S. Supreme Court and to the top courts of all nations;

• Pressing British Prime Minister Tony Blair to have the political courage to drag his country into the European common currency, the euro;

• Pressuring Congress into approving $18 billion to make interest payments to international banks that made bad loans to uncreditworthy countries on the assurance that taxpayers would make them good.

At this year's Bilderberg meetings, the British prime minister had been summoned to shuttle back and forth from the summit of the eight industrialized countries held 450 miles away in Birmingham, England, at the same time—by design.

Blair was hardly treated as a head of state. He was lectured severely for failing to bring Britain into the common currency, which was phased in beginning Jan. 1 of that year. Blair assured Bilderberg that Britain would join, but he had to revolve "political problems" because "there is a surge of nationalism at home."

"You're a Maggie Thatcher in long pants," a German told Blair.

This was a crude reminder that Lady Thatcher had been dumped as head of state by her own Conservative Party—on Bilderberg orders—and replaced with trapeze artist John Major, for the same reason.

"Helmut Kohl [the German head of state at the time] never flinched" in pressing his country to join the common currency, the German told Blair. "He may lose this election because of this. You know Germany has a problem with nationalism. But Helmut stood firm."

Blair turned and walked away.

There was much discussion and optimism among Bilderberg participants about a June meeting of the UN in Rome, to draft a treaty establishing a permanent International Criminal Court (ICC). Unlike the present World Court, the ICC would have enforcement power and could impose its decisions globally.

"Will America's nationalists give us trouble about the court treaty?" asked one.

"I think not," replied an American believed to be—but not positively identified as—Casimer Yost, director of the Institute for the Study of Diplomacy, School of Foreign Service, at Georgetown University in Washington.

The American pointed out that in 1994, the U.S. Senate voted 55-45 to encourage establishment of the International Criminal Court (ICC) under the UN. The Senate did so, he said, with the full knowledge that the global court, with judges from communist China or other rogue nations, may pass judgment on the United States and individual citizens.

"There was some objection by the American public, but not much," the American said. "Most of them know nothing about it and probably won't."

"Unless one of them is sent to jail by the ICC," interjected another.

"Yeah, then they will notice," the American said.

The latter exchange was jocular and scornful.

On expanding NATO, Bilderberg participants were impatient.

"The shortest path to permanent peace is to bring everybody in—including Russia—as fast as practical," said one speaker whose comment met with general approval.

A question was raised about costs.

"Costs, you ask?" the speaker responded. "How much did two world wars, Korea, Vietnam and the [first] Gulf War cost Americans? Peace is far less expensive."

To ensure "permanent peace throughout the world requires a strong enforcement mechanism, which means keeping the expanding NATO intact but under UN direction, for which there is a precedent to which none except rabid nationalists objected," the speaker said.

The "precedent" referred to was UN forces in Bosnia, where American soldiers were issued the UN uniform and served under a foreign commander who reported directly to the Security Council.

Bilderberg participants were again stating that the UN was to emerge as a world government with its own army patrolling the globe, enforcing its will.

Bilderberg luminaries expressed outrage that Congress did not approve the $18 billion for the IMF to bail out the big banks a year ago.

"How could you let your Congress get so out of control?" asked a Frenchman of an American during informal glass-tinkling. "It was never a problem before."

"Our Congress has a problem we call voters," came the answer.

"That's because we have less direct communication," the Frenchman said. "Leaders of your Congress no longer accept our invitations to attend Bilderberg."

"Again, the problem is voters," the American explained. "For years and years, we enjoyed almost total privacy. Now, right-wing extremists stir the voters up and congressmen have too many questions asked of them."

For decades, such congressional leaders as former House Speaker Tom Foley (D-Wash.), former Senate Banking Chairman Lloyd Bentsen (D-Texas) and others attended Bilderberg. Bentsen continued as Clinton's treasury secretary, but was not listed among this year's participants.

For the past several years, the only legislators to attend were Sen. Sam Nunn (D-Ga.) and a House member—but only after each had announced his retirement.

"We need them back, as the IMF problem shows," the Frenchman said.

"But how?" asked the American. "Congressmen now consider attending Bilderberg to be political suicide."

Bilderberg regulars were all accounted for, including Rockefeller, Kissinger and Evelyn de Rothschild, chairman of N.M. Rothschild & Sons of Britain and Europe.

Clinton had sent his usual assortment of administration officials: Marc Grossman, assistant secretary of state; Vernon Jordan Jr., a top unpaid advisor who will report Bilderberg demands directly to the president; Lawrence Summers, deputy secretary of Treasury; and Christine Todd Whitman (R), governor of New Jersey. This was Mrs. Whitman's first Bilderberg meeting, which meant they had plans for her.

Other old-time luminaries present included Chairman Peter Carrington, former secretary-general of NATO; Paul Allaire, onetime chairman of Xerox Corp., and Conrad Black, the now disgraced former chairman of a vast newspaper chain, among other global interests.

Lots of Fun Trying to Penetrate Bilderberg

I got the idea that Bilderberg didn't want me at its 1998 meeting. But as usual, I still managed to find sources inside the group's annual secret gathering.

Unlike in years past, in 1998, I failed to penetrate the meeting, but not for lack of trying. A volunteer, who can be no further identified for the sake of his physical and economic safety, had driven me to the rear of this palatial resort at 2 a.m. on May 15. I had scouted out the rear end of Turnberry on the previous day.

The hotel is hundreds of yards away from the back entrance, with a straight road leading to the gate. But it had a waist-high hedgerow parallel to the road. At the time, I decided that my mission should be to use this hedgerow as cover to approach Turnberry. My driver parked about 100 yards up the road with lights out.

I got over the wall apparently unobserved. But by the time I had hunkered my way 50 yards up a path, lights began to flash and motors roared. I made no further attempts at concealment and ran for the wall. My driver, still with headlights out, quietly pulled the car up to me, and I leaped in. Still without headlights, he took off. His lights came on after we were out of sight. By pre-arrangement, we entered a small restaurant and bar, a long walk but short ride from Turnberry. Knowing this was where the Turnberry staff took refuge, I had spent considerable time there earlier that week, developing sources.

My penetration effort had been such a failure we had to wait almost an hour—to 3 a.m.—for the appointment. Right on time, "The Source" appeared.

Actually, "The Source" represented several brave Scots who had, for months, known something sinister was about to happen at Turnberry. They deserve the gratitude of their countrymen and the world. Much of what you read about Bilderberg's 1998 confab came from "The Source"—our eyes and ears inside Turnberry.

Security Blanket Ripped From Bilderberg

Bilderberg security has always rivaled that of a head of state, but this year, paranoia about secrecy reached new heights. Despite this, all of the security in the world couldn't keep word of the 1998 Bilderbergers from leaking out to the general public.

For at least the past 15 years, when this paperboy chased them all over North America and Europe, Bilderbergers began the shutdown of their hiding place on Wednesday of the week they met.

Previously, all other guests had been told they must check out Wednesday morning. By Wednesday night, the resort would be emptied of all but Bilderberg and staff. During these Wednesdays, much could be learned and developed as Bilderberg's advance staff arrived and began setting up.

I arrived at the Turnberry at 11:05, Wednesday, May 13, expecting to spend several hours before checking into the Glendrishag Guest House in nearby Girvan. I was driven by Matthew Browning, editor and publisher of the journal *Wake Up.*

We were surprised to be greeted at the entrance by two uniformed police officers, who explained that the Turnberry was now closed to the public because of a "private meeting."

"Oh? Is Bilderberg meeting here?" I asked.

"Yes," the officer replied smiling.

They asked for identification "for the record."

I started to respond, but the officer interrupted: "We only need to identify the driver; we know who you are."

As the officer was checking Browning's drivers license, noting the details on a clipboard, I asked him: "Who am I?"

He smiled.

"My name is Jim Tucker."

"Yes, from *The Spotlight*," the officer said. "I understand you have been coming to Bilderberg meetings for years."

"Yes, but their welcome is less than warm."

At this he laughed and said something to the effect that he was following orders. I had the impression that he knew—and regretted—what he was doing: protecting a bunch of internationalists who would usurp the sovereignty of his country.

As we took our enforced leave, I said, "give my regards to David

Rockefeller, Henry Kissinger and Tony Blair—he'll be here, too."

The officer smiled and waved good-bye.

Checking into the Glendrishag House, we found an astounding coincidence. Glendrishag is one of hundreds of economical, bed-and-breakfast establishments in the area (no phone in your room; bathroom across the hall).

We were told by the proprietors, Kate and Findlay MacIntosh, that one Richard Greave, a lawyer and subscriber to the now defunct *Spotlight* newspaper, had been their guest the previous night and had gone to Turnberry to pass out literature criticizing Bilderberg.

Police had seized Greave, the MacIntoshes said, searched him and his car and demanded to know where he was staying. Greave returned to the Glendrishag, visibly shaken, and related the events.

I had never heard of Greave, and it was only by a miracle of chance that we both checked into the Glendrishag in pursuit of Bilderberg. Later, Greave confirmed the MacIntoshes' account. But the MacIntoshes were afraid Bilderberg would see a "conspiracy."

Findlay MacIntosh knew a joiner (construction specialist) who had spent the previous six months "sealing off entrances" that were not to be used during the Bilderberg meeting, among other "security precautions."

On Friday, May 15, while the Bilderberg meeting was taking place, police grabbed Campbell Thomas, who was covering the event for the Scottish *Daily Mail*. He was roughed up, handcuffed and held for eight hours.

Escape for Royalty ...

1999—Sintra, Portugal: Bilderberg met in beautiful Sintra, Portugal in 1999. Above is the Palacio de Peña, one of several grand palaces in the Sintra area. Sintra was the summer spot for Portuguese royalty looking to escape the heat and humidity of Lisbon. And royalty of sorts was again in Sintra, with the world's most rich and powerful meeting in the historic city for the annual Bilderberg meeting.

CHAPTER EIGHTEEN

1999

Sintra, Portugal

The global elite in 1999 announced plans for a new economic world order. Of course, the blueprints had been on the drawing board for years.

inning the war on Yugoslavia at any price was high on the Bilderberg agenda, as was establishing an "international financial architecture." While the Bilderberg luminaries were behind the locked and guarded entrances to the Caesar Park Penha Longa, in Portugal, from June 3-6 in 1999, the Yugoslav embassy issued a statement saying Bilderberg was behind the unprovoked attack on its country. The statement relied on these facts as I reported in *The Spotlight* on May 10, 1999:

• NATO defied its own self-defined role as a defensive organization by attacking a nation that posed no threat.

• At its most recent summit in Washington, NATO announced that it could now act anywhere in the world, specifically mentioning the Middle East.

• At the summit, French President Jacques Chirac said NATO would only go to war on instructions of the UN Security Council.

Taken together, this clearly states that NATO is now the UN's world army. But for credibility, NATO must win its war on Yugoslavia, Bilderberg luminaries were telling each other. At the same time, Clinton was conferring with U.S. military leaders on plans for a ground war. Clinton and Bilderberg were only a phone call away.

On the same day that the president of Yugoslavia at the time, Slobodan Milosevic, accepted NATO's surrender demand to prevent more spilled blood, including hundreds of civilians bombed in shopping malls and hospitals, NATO continued its air campaign.

Calls were placed from the Bilderberg resort to Moscow and Belgrade. Bilderberg had won the war it had started through its proxies, the UN and its world army, NATO.

The Yugoslav news agency Tanjug said the war in the Balkans was drawn up by Bilderberg in 1996 and updated and finalized last year when it met in Scotland. It cited the Yugoslav edition of the newspaper *Vojska.*

Vojska said an "independent" American journalist had exposed the group and identified its leaders.

Under Bilderberg's original war plan, it said, the first move was to arrest "war criminals from among the Serbs," provoking a strong reaction that would be used to justify going to war. Unable to provoke a hostile reaction, NATO attacked anyway.

Kenneth Clarke, a member of the British parliament (MP) and former chancellor for the exchequer, had called for a new "international financial architecture" at the 1999 meeting of Bilderberg.

The world should have three major regional currencies, Clarke told his Bilderberg colleagues. The first is already on the world scene: The European euro. And Britain will join in the European common currency, he said. Clarke said he would like to see the pound grow weaker to facilitate Britain's entry into the common currency. Clarke is a Conservative opposition member of Parliament who joined the Labor Party's Tony Blair, prime minister and fellow Bilderberg member, in calling for the further surrender of British sovereignty to the European Union.

The next step is toward a second great regional currency in the Western Hemisphere, Clarke said. The "amerijo" will come about by the "dollarization" of Latin America. Panama had already abandoned its currency for the dollar in 1994. Argentina and Brazil are considering a unilateral adoption of the dollar currency, although there are talks with the Federal Reserve Board. At the time, Clarke said he believed the common currency of the Western Hemisphere would become a reality "soon." He added that a common currency for the Asian-Pacific region must emerge.

Clarke told Bilderberg that a generation from now people will find it hard believe that the world once had so many currencies, with each nation being identified by its own.

Part of Clarke's "new architecture" involved establishing "supra-national agencies" to handle the ebb-and-flow of the three major currencies of the world. He called for a sort of "world finance minister" at the UN.

Bilderberg colleagues agreed that the emerging regional currencies, which will be identified with no specific country, will do much to eliminate "nationalism" and the "antiquated notions of sovereignty."

Much of this talk came during agenda discussions of "the New Economy" and "Emerging Markets" at the meetings. Other formal agenda items included the "Atlantic Relationship During a Time of Change," "European Politics" and "U.S. Politics."

For the first time, Russia had two representatives: Lilia Sheviso and Dmitri Trenin, both of the Carnegie Foundation's Moscow Center. The U.S.-based Carnegie Foundation and offshoots have long been an arm of Bilderberg. Jessica Mathews, president of the Carnegie Endowment for International Peace, returned to this Bilderberg meeting.

The Russians were assured that more (mostly American) dollars would flow into their wrecked economy through such conduits as the IMF and the World Bank. Stanley Fischer, first deputy managing director of the IMF at the time, and James Wolfensohn, president of the World Bank, were there to confirm the promise.

Rockefeller and numerous financiers were also in Sintra to hear that interest payments on their bad loans to poor credit risk nations would be backed by U.S. taxpayers.

During the discussion of "U.S. Politics," Bilderberg leaders expressed confidence in retaining control of the White House. They noted that the likely Republican nominee, Gov. George W. Bush of Texas, was the son of former president and Trilateralist George H. W. Bush. "His father has talked to him," one said.

But what about Vice President Al Gore, the likely Democrat nominee? "*His* father [Clinton] has talked to him," the Bilderberg man repeated with a confident chuckle.

In fact, Bilderberg has had a direct influence on the White House since President Dwight Eisenhower's years. Most presidents have been members of at least one of the two groups, and all have had representatives attend Bilderberg meetings to receive their orders.

Bilderberg to Establish 'Financial Architecture'

Bilderberg will be working in 1999 to establish the "world's financial architecture," said British member of Parliament Kenneth Clarke.

In the presence of five reporters in Washington, Clarke was surprisingly forthright in speaking of the secret Bilderberg group just before the group met behind closed doors and armed guards in Sintra.

Bilderberg drew "political and business leaders" for "informal, off-the-record talks," Clarke said. "There is much talk about improving the world's financial architecture."

One topic, which Clarke said would be discussed, is "dollarization," whereby Argentina and other South American countries would abandon their own currencies in favor of the American dollar. Does this mean the beginning of a common currency for the Western Hemisphere and then the world?

"It's an idea whose time has come," Clarke responded. "I think it will come in the near future. I feel in my bones something like this is going to happen."

2001—Gothenburg, Sweden: Penetrating Bilderberg was tough that year as the organizers packed the attendees onto a boat and sailed them around their private island resort. However, AFP's Christopher Bollyn still managed to snap this photo perched in a tree near the dock. Of note, in this photo is David Rockefeller (left, light shirt) chit-chatting with Susan Eisenhower (center, dark hair, large sunglasses), President Dwight Eisenhower's daughter.

Americans should not be "fearful" of the dollar becoming the common currency of the hemisphere, Clarke said, because Panama has already embraced the dollar and "there are more dollars outside the United States than inside."

Eliminating national currencies has long been a goal of both Bilderberg and the Trilateral Commission, because it not only destroys a major symbol of sovereignty and paves the road toward their dream of a world government, but because the dollar is issued on taxpayer debt by the privately owned Federal Reserve, it is extremely profitable for the Fed's owners.

"Our grandchildren will look back and find it comical that the world had so many national currencies," Clarke said. "Obviously, something will be on the agenda" at the Bilderberg meeting addressing the elimination of national currencies.

Clarke said Britain will abandon the pound in favor of the European common currency, the "euro."

The "euro is a done deal," Clarke said. The MP added he hopes the pound gets "weaker" to make the transition more politically palatable.

Clarke described himself as "leading the pro-European Union faction in the Commons."

Bilderberg Flack Leads Cheers for New World Order

In 1999, Clinton boldly pushed the Bilderberg doctrine, which calls for the United Nations to become a world government with a global army to enforce its decrees. It appeared in the daily newspapers for all to read, but too many sleep. Until Clinton, public leaders were circumspect in calling for world government. But, mostly unchallenged, the president spoke boldly.

In Europe, shortly after the latest Bilderberg meeting, Clinton had addressed a NATO meeting on June 22, 1999. "Whether you live in Africa, or Central Europe, or any place, if somebody comes after innocent citizens and tries to kill them en masse because of their race, their ethnic background or their religion, and if it's within our power to stop it, we will stop it," he promised.

This follows the public pattern established at the NATO summit in Washington in April 1999 and pursued when Bilderberg met in Sintra, Portugal, in June of that year. NATO celebrated the fact that it defied its own stated mission as a defensive organization and, in its only act of war during 50 years, invaded the sovereign nation of Yugoslavia, which posed no threat.

At that major summit meeting, NATO leaders said they were now empowered to patrol the world—but only on directions of the UN Security Council. This was amplified and celebrated at Bilderberg, where NATO was ordered to ease its demands and end the war, which had become an embarrassment.

These developments were celebrated by *The Washington Post's*

Bilderberg representative Jimmy Lee Hoagland in a column on June 27, 1999.

"The president promises a future in which Americans stand ready to intervene militarily if they can stop wholesale racial or ethnic slaughter 'within or beyond other nations' borders,' " Hoagland wrote.

"He sees a future in which the United States actively works with the United Nations and other international bodies to thwart and punish political mass murderers . . . he promises a new world order," Hoagland wrote approvingly.

"The president has acted boldly as well as spoken ambitiously," Hoagland wrote. The war on Yugoslavia, he said, "has dismantled borders as a barrier to military action." This merits the support of Congress and the public," Hoagland said.

Meanwhile, another part of the Bilderberg agenda was moving forward. As promised at Sintra, the IMF agreed to give $4.5 billion to Russia over the next 18 months. The deal was announced by the Russian prime minister at the time, Sergei Stepashin, in Moscow on June 30.

Teamwork Breaks Bilderberg Barrier

Teamwork broke the barricade of Bilderberg in this scenic, mountainous area 40 miles from Lisbon. A two-man television crew from Lisbon drove me to and from the hotel we shared and the Caesar Park Penha Longa, where Bilderberg was entrenched, every day.

The trio also traveled back to Lisbon to meet with Paul Luckman, who gave heavy coverage of Bilderberg in the English-language weekly, *The News*.

Originally, a British TV crew, who had spent a day with me in Washington to learn about Bilderberg, agreed to have their names and television outlet—which is seen all over their country—published. But because they hoped to get interviews with Bilderberg

2001—Gothenburg, Sweden: Above, Etienne Davignon, high-level Flemish banker arrives at the Quality Hotel Stenungsund, the site of the 2001 meeting. Davignon is a Bilderberg regular and sports his trademark pipe. Davignon has attended numerous Bilderberg meetings, identifying him as a "mover and shaker" in European financial circles and one of the leading forces behind the euro.

luminaries in the months ahead, they had second thoughts and asked to be known only as "John" and "Mike." Now, I can tell you the name of the broadcaster: John Ronson.

The British crew was working on an 18-month project to create a six-hour special on the "New World Order." Ronson also was writing an unflattering book, called *Them,* containing several chapters about Bilderberg and me that was replete with errors and personal invectives.

Mike also expressed concern that Bilderberg power might cause them to be banned from the United States if their collaboration was known.

After trying for three days to find out where Bilderberg hotel staff relaxed, I later found them under my feet.

The clerk in the hotel lobby said he knew people who work there and would bring them in.

I gave them advanced assurances they would not be identified, fired or blackballed. After that, they were most helpful.

Attempts at penetrating the meetings failed, however, because Bilderberg was able to intimidate people with nonsense about guards being given "shoot-to-kill" and "use all necessary force" orders. These warnings came from a number of sources.

I had made arrangements to meet a man who would drive me to the Bilderberg scene and escort me over the wall and through the woods. In other years, I had contracted only a driver, who would wait outside the grounds. But the terrain at the Penha Longa and the patrolling cops required an escort.

After detailed arrangements were made, the escort backed out. Rumors of "shoot-to-kill" orders apparently made him change his mind.

Were "shoot-to-kill" orders a bluff?

Herndan De Beer of *The News* was patrolling the Bilderberg gate on June 5 and remarked to one of the cops how lightly the place was guarded.

Not so, the cop replied.

Pointing to boulders adorning hilltops, the cop said snipers were deployed along the perimeter.

"When you cross the line, they will know—you're Jim Tucker's people," the cop said.

Bilderberg Sets A Trap

Once again, the Bilderberg elite's protection service made sure I was never alone during my "vacation" in Portugal. But that didn't stop me from getting inside information from sources within the heavily guarded walls of the confab.

Reporters from London who were collaborating with me were surprised when a lone guard at the gate allowed us to enter the mostly empty Caesar Park Penha Longa on June 1. The broadcasters, Ronson and Mike, and I had expected the usual huge deployment of police, military men and private security forces to be surrounding all entrances. We had lunch at the pool-side, but the grim-faced personnel "had no knowledge of a big meeting." Mystified, we departed.

Soon, the mystery was solved as a black car started following us.

Mike, who was driving, suddenly stopped at the roadside and the car sped by. Just after that, another black car also stopped on the road, about 300 yards back. Mike started driving and the other car started, too. Mike again pulled off the road and the other car did, too, about 100 yards ahead. Mike spun around, driving in the opposite direction and the car followed.

On the right side was a wall surrounding the Caesar Park plantation. Mike stopped and the other car stopped.

Mike took some footage of Caesar Park from long range. I was photographing the chaser car. Then, on camera, Ronson continued his marathon interview with me that had begun in Washington. Mike also filmed the chaser car.

The chaser followed for several miles into downtown Sintra when the reporters stopped, parking illegally in front of a median strip—ready to pursue in either direction. A city policeman approached the chaser, gesturing for him to move on. The chaser talked to the officer and was allowed to remain.

The pursued trio approached the chase car, noting the license number: 53-02-IZ. The window was up and doors were locked. Ronson displayed his credentials and shouted through the closed window that he was British television and wanted to know why they were being pursued. The chaser gestured wildly but said nothing.

The chaser continued the pursuit for five more miles as the trio approached their hotel. Ronson got out to check on whether the room had been ransacked as Mike and I went weaving about town, chaser in tow, back to the hotel.

The chaser parked on the street beside the hotel and he stood on the sidewalk. He had a dark complexion and seemed to be about 30 years old.

I climbed the several steps to the lobby level, crossed the swimming pool area on the right and poked my camera between tree branches. The chaser ran behind a tree, and we played "peek-a-boo."

"Come on, smile pretty," I ordered, waving the camera. The man struggled against it, but for a brief moment, his grim expression turned to an involuntary grin, then was reset.

When hours later, by pre-arrangement, I went to another hotel cafe a block away, the chaser's car was gone.

When Ronson and Mike joined me, they reported two new stalkers in the hotel lobby. How did they know the two men were stalking? "You can tell by their demeanor," Mike explained.

We left, one by one, Ronson, then Mike, then me. I never gave them a direct glance, but peripheral vision showed one to be an older man and the other dark-haired and about 30—but he was not the original chaser.

Without looking back, I walked a block to a cafe next to the home hotel. Suppressing superstition, I took a table near the rear of the establishment, sitting with my back to the door. After five minutes, I suddenly looked to my rear to find the younger of the replacement stalkers sitting several tables back.

I smiled and gave the stalker a friendly wave. The stalker remained grim-faced. Stalkers are not very polite.

On the Taxpayers' Dole ...

2000—Brussels, Belgium: The shadowy cabal known as Bilderberg gathered this year at the scenic resort, Chateau du Lac, 20 minutes outside of Brussels, Belgium. A coterie of the world's power elite and high-ranking officials attended the annual meeting, including the director of the WTO, the head of the World Bank, the president of the New York Federal Reserve and a former CIA director. Sen. Chuck Hagel (R-Neb.) is pictured above removing his coat upon his arrival at the hotel on the first day of the meetings. That was Hagel's second consecutive Bilderberg meeting. Does Bilderberg have high hopes for this outspoken senator?

CHAPTER NINETEEN

2000

Brussels, Belgium

Bilderberg demonstrated its tough discipline by banning Jimmy Lee Hoagland of The Washington Post *this year. Bilderberg has, on rare occasions, cast aside members who become a liability, as in the case of its first chairman, Prince Bernhard of the Netherlands, who in the 1950s was caught up in a corruption scandal involving the airliner maker Lockheed.*

t this year's Bilderberg meeting at the Chateau du Lac near Brussels, Belgium, sources said part of the thinning of their ranks this year was the efficiency of being "less conspicuous" but a significant part was discipline—as in the case of Jimmy Lee Hoagland of *The Washington Post.*

Hoagland, associate editor of the *Post*, was a committed Bilderberg regular. He had been holding Donald Graham's hand at Bilderberg meetings since his now deceased mother, Katharine, had stepped aside for him as *Post* publisher. Now, at the annual gathering, Hoagland was conspicuously absent over the course of the weekend from June 1 to June 3, 2000.

Hoagland had faithfully echoed Bilderberg policies in his opinion column. He had dutifully written columns advocating NAFTA, the World Trade Organization and NATO's invasion of Yugoslavia to demonstrate that it had become the UN's army and would patrol the world and other positions secretly dictated by Bilderberg.

Early in 2000, Hoagland's staff had said he would not be attending Bilderberg that year. But on May 21, according to Bilderberg sources, the reason became known in a column published in the *Post.*

Bilderberg had long called for Congress to approve permanent normal trading relations (PNTR) with communist China, as an important step toward its entry into the WTO and in the creation of a world government. But, on May 21, when he already knew he would not be attending Bilderberg this year, Hoagland broke ranks and questioned whether Congress should approve PNTR now or wait a bit.

Bilderberg did not want to wait.

Hoagland first made the point that PNTR "is not a vote about how China's government treats its own citizens." This defies the argument by globalists that trade with China will somehow make its government kinder to its people and that another nation's domestic policies are somehow the business of the United States.

Hoagland also bucked global elitist ideology by being concerned that China is a military menace determined "to maintain Beijing's ability to hit American cities with nuclear missiles." The Bilderberg-globalist doctrine is to pretend China is no threat and to have no concern about international corporations selling computers and other devices that have military applications to the communists.

"Using the national security standard, the House should force the administration to pull this legislation back to avoid defeat and to work to get the strategic context right, as well as the trade details," Hoagland wrote.

While Hoagland stopped short of saying there should never be a China trade deal, his call for a delay and his consideration of the military implications is insubordination by Bilderberg standards.

"It's impossible to say whether Bilderberg bounced Hoagland because they knew the position he was going to take or whether he

2000—Brussels, Belgium: This group of supporters arrived to help me (pictured at far left) welcome the Bilderberg Group to the grounds of the Chateau du Lac. The sign in the background reads in part: "Welcome Bilderbergs. • One world government. • One world religion. • One military under UN." At least some citizens of the world (and AFP readers in America) understand that what goes on at Bilderberg meetings is newsworthy.

---

wrote what was really on his mind after the fact," one source said, "because he knew he would not be in Brussels for several days before he wrote that column."

But top people among the major newspapers—the *Post, The New York Times, The Los Angeles Times*, the news weeklies and broadcast networks—attend these meetings after taking vows of secrecy, he pointed out. They never write the term "Bilderberg" or admit it exists, he said, but they are expected to fully advocate the right positions.

Hoagland's raising the issue of the military impact of the China deal and calling for a delay of the legislation is the first time since

1954 that the *Post* has made the slightest deviation from Bilderberg policy.

European Banks Leap to Bilderberg Bidding

Just days after Bilderberg ordered interest rates increased worldwide in 2000, the European Central Bank (ECB) responded like a dog to the whistle. The ECB increased its benchmark rate by half a point on June 8, 2000, in what the Bilderberg-controlled *Washington Post* approvingly described as "an unexpectedly bold move." It had been ordered just five days earlier by Bilderberg. Analysts said the increase to 4.25 percent on interest on loans to commercial banks was unexpectedly high but might help the sagging European currency, the euro.

Bilderberg demanded the increase to enhance profits for financial institutions and to increase unemployment by reducing job-creating capital ventures. Higher unemployment means lower wages.

Announcement of the rate increase came with a technical change in how the ECB conducts business. Instead of fixing the rate it charges member banks to borrow, the ECB will set a minimum rate and loan to banks that pay the highest rate.

In announcing the rate increase and minimum-rate policy, ECB President Willem Duisenberg called the actions "accommodative," which, in bank double-speak, indicates more rate increases, according to analysts.

But, in saying that the technical change "clears the horizon," Duisenberg was indicating that if member banks offered to pay enough above the new minimum, future formal increases could be avoided, analysts said.

Either way, bank profits would go up as employment went down.

Thomas Mayer of the Goldman Sachs Group in Frankfurt, Germany, hailed the ECB action as "a bold move."

Goldman Sachs is always represented at Bilderberg. In 2000,

John Thornton, its president, and Tommaso Padoa-Schioppa, a member of the ECB's executive board, also attended.

"If it works, price stability and the euro should benefit," Mayer said. "The risk is that they lose control of interest rates."

The variable-rate system will help the ECB control interest rates, analysts said. The ECB routinely receives bids from banks for more than 100 times the amount of money it wants to disperse into the system as a means of controlling interest rates.

Under the new system, more like the Federal Reserve System, they said, successful bidders will have to pay more than the 4.25 percent minimum, forcing the costs of borrowing still higher for businesses and consumers.

"This will permit Bilderberg, through its control of the ECB and ability to manipulate interest rates, to dictate economic conditions in Europe—whether there shall be high employment and prosperity, or economic slow downs and resulting unemployment—whatever suits the selfish motives of international financiers," said a high official of the State Department and long-time reliable source.

He predicted similar actions in the United States and Canada and—through the Trilateral Commission—in Japan and other Asian nations.

"It's about global control," he said.

Bilderberg Loses Blackout Battle

Despite choosing a site where the state subsidizes the press; where reporters and the public are intimidated; and where a massive campaign of disinformation was easily conducted, we made a significant dent in Bilderberg's blackout attempts in 2000.

Victory came when a Brussels, Belgium paper, *DeMorgen*, carried a major page one story about Bilderberg hiding out behind armed guards at the Chateau du Lac. Inside, on page 7, another detailed story and a photo of two Bilderberg participants strolling past the lake was published.

DeMorgen reporter Sue Somers had heard about the dramatic sealing off of the five-star Chateau du Lac and appeared because she thought it had something to do with the world soccer championships, which had Europe and the United Kingdom in the grip of great excitement.

My colleague, reporter Christopher Bollyn, who is fluent in French and several other languages, explained the situation to Miss Somers, giving her a copy of a special supplement put together by *The Spotlight* titled, "Who's Hiding Inside the Chateau du Lac?" This feature was so in demand that the hundreds of copies available were exhausted and supporters had to make photocopies.

Miss Somers and her colleague, Walter DeBock, called their newspaper and remained at the chateau, working on the Bilderberg story. Their work appeared the following day. Meanwhile, other reporters from Britain, who had collaborated with me at earlier Bilderberg sessions, appeared again in Brussels, assuring further exposure.

But it was the toughest fight ever as Bilderberg went even beyond its usual extreme efforts at secrecy.

It began in Washington as Bilderberg tried to divert reporters to the wrong country. *The Washington Post* reported the meeting would be in France. *Post* Publisher Graham knew this was a lie because he attended the meeting near Brussels.

Bilderberg knew *The Spotlight* would be on hand when facts about the meeting were released on May 18, said an angry policeman who was harassing and searching Herbots Didier, who was caught passing out issues of *The Spotlight* to an eager public.

Knowing that they had been uncovered, Bilderberg tried to divert all reporters and supporters to the NATO headquarters in downtown Brussels. They came dangerously close to succeeding.

I arrived in Brussels on May 29 for advance scouting. On May 30, I was led into conversation by a friendly, middle-aged man in a Bilderberg "uniform"—a pin-striped suit—at the Hilton International, where he was quartered.

Yes, some Bilderberg people will be at the chateau, the man said, but others will be staying elsewhere because of the limited (121 rooms) space. They would be shuttled each day to NATO headquarters, where they would do business.

"NATO headquarters is your target," he added, "and good luck."

I've had much experience with liars, having covered the Internal Revenue Service, and broken bread with liberals, but this expert seemed believable.

Another attempt to hide was by not taking over the hotel as an organization called "Bilderberg." When I called to make reservations and was told the chateau was completely filled up, I said that I was to attend a meeting of a group called Bilderberg. No such group had made reservations, the hotel said.

Later, when Bilderberg shut the place down, they called themselves Bilderberg. And when I—posing as a friendly trooper—asked if the place had been secured for Bilderberg, plainclothesmen said, "yes."

My first visit to the Chateau du Lac was as a casual but thirsty tourist. There, an employee explained that she would have to stop working after Wednesday but those who remained on the job were required to wear photo-ID badges. This sounded like a traditional Bilderberg shutdown. Also it was learned that the chateau had several villas to accommodate more staff and participants.

By prearrangement, Bollyn had been able to check into the chateau on Wednesday, May 31, but had to check out by noon the next day on June 1. Bollyn called me at the Hilton to say the guards were being deployed and a tent was set up to hide the participants as they entered the chateau.

But this is neither where efforts to suppress the news began nor ended.

Mark Delcour of Brussels had been in extensive contact with me for a month, starting when it was only known that "all planes are flying to Brussels" while the site was still unknown. The moment Delcour was called with the information, he alerted the Brussels media. Between them, Delcour and Didier had advised 60 others who normally would want to appear.

"They are intimidated," Delcour explained. "The press and the people are afraid of losing jobs and other forms of punishment. With the government subsidizing the press, they can stop the story."

Damien Mears, a freelance writer from London who had collaborated with me in 1998 at the Turnberry in Scotland, arrived and started calling reporters he knew at local newspapers.

At first, Mears said, they all seemed excited about Bilderberg. But when he would call back an hour later, all explained they had been forbidden to cover Bilderberg.

Earlier in the day, Mears had been threatened with arrest by the police if he did not leave even though he was on public property. He didn't and they didn't.

But Bollyn had a close call. Security men were at his side for hours as he photographed luminaries with a long-range lens.

"These two thugs were shadowing me," Bollyn said. "Whenever I tried to take a picture, they would get in the way but I was usually able to outrun them."

Bollyn, outrunning the "thugs," aimed his camera at George Soros and Carl Bildt.

"Then, the head of Belgian security came to me and said: 'If you keep running behind people, I'll jump on you,' " Bollyn added.

Bollyn avoided being taken by outracing the cops to a small restaurant on the edge of the compound. There, he waited for a cab that took him to the train station.

Didier was followed by guards armed with machine guns, he said. When stopped, the guards were told by radio to ask him certain questions. That's when he learned that *The Spotlight*'s web site had alerted Bilderberg.

They demanded Didier's identification. He gave them three cards—all with different addresses. They painstakingly recorded it all.

Also present were people from the National Front in France and nationalists from Hungary and other countries.

Stalking began on May 29 when I first began scouting the chateau. There was always one, but most often two, hotel personnel at my side as I roamed public areas as a tourist.

The "lead stalker" was later identified as Christophe Voet, the hotel's banquet and conference manager. Another was Alain Vanbinst, the food and beverage manager.

Later, it was Vanbinst who helped Bilderberg security harass Bollyn on the morning he was checking out.

The hotel had angered the few remaining guests, who loudly protested as they checked out that the noisy Bilderberg security setup had kept them up all night. One man refused to pay his bill for lodging because he was unable to sleep.

As Bollyn roamed the hotel on the morning he was to check out, he was constantly shadowed. Staff urged him to hurry up and check out. Bollyn pointed out that checkout time was noon, not 11 a.m. Hotel employees told him to stay in his room but Bollyn refused.

When checking out as his deadline approached, Bollyn strongly protested his treatment. Hotel personnel apologized profusely. By that time, they were much experienced at apologizing.

But despite all the disinformation, intimidation and threats, Bilderberg was covered and photographed.

More newspapermen from around Europe came streaming into Brussels after the DeMorgen story broke and pressure was brought on Bilderberg to open up. There was also a lengthy look at Bilderberg arrivals on a French TV station.

A source in the European Union provided me with the list of participants. Then the Bilderberg staff hastily prepared its standard bland "press release," explaining they are nobodies doing nothing, with the list of participants dutifully attached.

A Well Deserved Break ...

2001—Gothenburg, Sweden: At that year's Bilderberg meeting, I took a moment to enjoy the sights and sounds of the city of Gothenburg, Sweden. The gathering of the world's most rich and powerful people was being held on a fjord just off the coast, making penetrating this Bilderberg meeting especially tough.

CHAPTER TWENTY

2001

Gothenburg, Sweden

In response to unwelcome media attention, Bilderberg took unprecedented steps in 2001 to ensure its cryptic parley is hidden behind closed doors near Gothenburg, Sweden. They hid out at the Quality Hotel Stenungsund, located on an island near Gothenburg.

In 2001, Bilderberg took dramatic action to keep its program for a world government from possible collapse while planning some kind of intervention in the Middle East. While Bilderberg has always held its secret sessions behind heavy security and armed guards, this year a SWAT team joined in patrolling the grounds of the Quality Hotel Stenungsbaden while the world's shadow government met from May 24-27 near Gothenburg, Sweden.

Christopher Bollyn, who was reporting for *The Spotlight* at the time, was seized on private property by Swedish police, driven six miles into the wilderness and dumped. A European reporter was held for several hours.

Tensions among Bilderberg and its armada of police, private security and personal bodyguards were high because of extensive coverage by Swedish media generated by my early advisories.

I spent hours being interviewed by newspapers, magazines and broadcasters throughout Bilderberg's sessions.

Local coverage was persistent, day by day. The large number of reporters collaborated to keep the gates guarded virtually 24 hours a day. Bilderberg refused, even under the pressure of hostile coverage by major newspapers, to yield up its list of participants and the agenda. However, participants were identified by sight.

Sources inside Bilderberg and people who move in Bilderberg circles back in Washington, D.C. provided more names and information on what transpired behind the guarded gates. From inside the resort, a source was finally able to provide me with a hand-copied list of names and the agenda—at great personal risk.

Notably absent was Carl Bildt that year, United Nations envoy to the Balkans and host country Sweden's former prime minister. A long-time Bilderberg luminary, Bildt was attending a meeting of the Aspen Society—an arm of Bilderberg—in Brussels.

Notably present was Mohammed Nashashibi, finance minister in Yasser Arafat's Palestinian Authority. He was identified by Roland Rossier of l'Hebdo magazine. Following the meetings, Rossier did an in-depth story of Liberty Lobby and The Spotlight's pursuit of Bilderberg over the years.

In 2001, Bilderberg was fearful that the European Union might be coming apart. They had expected Britain to be a full partner and embrace the euro by 2001. A new leader in Italy who planned dramatic tax cuts that would confound the euro troubled them.

Further depressing Bilderberg was fear that "right-wing nationalists" in the United States would, with help from such countries as Brazil, block President Bush's Free Trade Area of the Americas from emerging as scheduled in 2005.

In a panic, Bilderberg ordered Europhiles in Britain's Conservative Party to bring participation in the common currency to the top of the list of priorities as soon as the expected Labor Party victory in the June 7 elections is official. At the time, it was already being privately discussed with Labor Party leaders.

The orders were transmitted by Kenneth Clarke, the Conservative member of Parliament and former chancellor of the exchequer who regularly appeared at Bilderberg. Clarke has been dedicated to Bilderberg's campaign for a world government.

It was what one called "Maggie's revenge" that prompted the Bilderberg panic. While Bilderberg was hiding here, Margaret Thatcher, the former prime minister, was speaking to a Conservative Party rally.

"The greatest issue in this election, indeed the greatest issue before our country, is whether Britain is to remain a free, independent nation state or whether we are to be dissolved into a federal Europe. There are no half-measures, no third ways and no second chances," Thatcher said at that year's rally.

The Conservative Party and its candidate for prime minister, William Hague, had made a deal with the Labor Party to keep the issue of joining the common currency out of the campaign debate. However, at the time, the Conservatives would publicly rule out the euro only for the duration of the next Parliament. This was acceptable for the Labor Party and Europhiles in the Conservative Party who were committed to a federal Europe because polls then showed that two-thirds of the British people were opposed to giving up the pound or surrendering more sovereignty to the EU. The internationalists wanted more time to condition the British mind to accept the superstate and the euro.

Lady Thatcher's outspoken opposition, in spite of her own party's admonition, forced Bilderberg to issue orders for Conservative and Labor Party leaders to bring the euro to the top of the priority list immediately after the election. They didn't want to press the issue early in the face of popular opposition but felt their hand was forced.

Bilderberg referred to Lady Thatcher's intervention as "Maggie's revenge" because the world's shadow government had manipulated her downfall as prime minister. She had opposed surrendering sovereignty to the EU and joining the common currency.

However, the effects of Lady Thatcher's strong, unscripted speech took a comical turn. Tony Blair, Labor's prime minister, felt compelled to argue that it is "patriotic " to "share sovereignty" with the EU and "patriotic" to give up the pound, a symbol of sovereignty, in favor of the euro.

Conservative candidate Hague had been hammering the Labor Party over its support of EU plans to "harmonize" taxes among the EU states. The Tory leader said the EU planned to "harmonize" taxes such as VAT, (value-added tax) and broaden it to include books, transport and clothing.

"More and more of the rights and powers of the British people are being signed away," Hague said at campaign rallies.

Labor and Liberal Party functionaries rushed out to denounce Hague's "scare mongering" and deny there was a plan to harmonize taxes. EU officials also issued denials.

Hague produced a "leaked document" from the EU that *The Guardian* of London described as "a document on tax priorities which did, as the Tories alleged, envisage harmonization of some taxes, including those governing transferable pensions and environmental taxes."

In 2001, Bilderberg was fearful that Italy would rip another seam in the EU because of the election of Silvio Berlusconi and his conservative coalition.

The Bilderberg-controlled *Washington Post* called him "the biggest challenge yet to the young euro currency" on May 18, 2001.

Post Publisher Graham had again attended the Bilderberg meeting that year.

Berlusconi, though a multi-millionaire, is far removed from Bilderberg and its agenda. He has pledged dramatic tax cuts which, Bilderberg participants said, undermine the euro. He was also denounced by Bilderberg for "anti-immigration views."

Bilderberg was already concerned that "provincial nationalism" on the part of Americans would ultimately block the emergence of the "American Union" when the stunning news arrived that the defection of Sen. James Jeffords (Vt.) from the Republican Party would put Democrats in control of the Senate.

"Now we have to worry about those [Pat] Buchanan bastards ganging up with the labor unions to stop the FTAA in a Democratic

Senate," said one Bilderberger.

On the formal agenda, Sen. Christopher Dodd (D-Conn.) and newspaper tycoon Conrad Black led a 90-minute discussion on "the New U.S. Administration" at 8:30 on Saturday, May 26.

President Bush was given high marks for promoting the FTAA, but all speakers expressed disappointment that he rejected the Kyoto Treaty, one of the building blocks of Bilderberg's world government campaign.

They also expressed confidence that Bush could be pressed into backing some kind of "global warming" pact that would enhance UN control of the world.

Richard Perle, assistant secretary of defense, then led a discussion called "European Security Defense Identity and Transatlantic Security." Perle had attended Bilderberg meetings on behalf of President Reagan in the 1980s. In 2001, there was debate, but no consensus, on President Bush's plan for a missile shield.

Bilderberg participants then boarded the cruise ship Erik—which had a big "B" painted on a smokestack—for lunch and non-agenda deal-making.

In the afternoon, Kissinger presided over a discussion of "The Rise of China: Its Impact on Asia and the World." Kissinger, through his international consulting firm, Kissinger Associates, has extensive financial interests in communist China. It was universally agreed that the United States must "remain engaged" in China and "not be distracted" by such incidents as crashing American planes in international air space. The importance of "opening Chinese markets" and smoothing its path into the World Trade Organization was stressed. It is important, Bilderberg stressed, especially for the benefit of Dodd and Sen. Chuck Hagel (R-Neb.), that Congress erect "no barriers" to China's entry into the globalist group, the World Trade Organization, because of "petty reactions to some incidents."

Both Dodd, 57, and Hagel, 55, participated for the third time. They were regarded by Bilderberg colleagues as potential presidents. They are from opposite parties and Bilderberg likes to own both horses in a two-horse race.

The closing session on Sunday, May 27, addressed the subject: "What Should Governments Do About Food Quality?" It was led by Franz Fischler, who represented Austria in the European Union.

The conclusion was predictable: a UN bureaucracy must be established to make certain the global population has a healthy diet.

"Bilderberg is really dazed," said an inside source. "They thought by now the EU would be a full super-state with nation-states obsolete. Now they are afraid the whole agenda could unravel."

With the U.S. Senate "turned upside down, they are afraid Big Labor will help stop the FTAA and the 'American Union' will never happen," the Bilderberg source said.

Bilderberg Takes to the Sea for Security

Fearful that someone would somehow slip through the barricades and peek up their ideological skirts and view their dirty underpinnings, Bilderberg took to the high seas at noon on Saturday, May 26, 2001.

As each member of Bilderberg and staff boarded the ship, name tags were observed by security men—one photo badge in one color for actual Bilderberg participants, another color background photo badge for Bilderberg staff and still another for employees of the island resort, Quality Hotel Stenungsbaden. It was the first time in nearly half-a-century of such secret meetings of the world's most powerful men of international finance and politics that they became so paranoid they took their plotting to sea.

Earlier, Bilderberg leaders had ordered a very willing Kenneth Clarke to bring the issue of Britain joining the common currency and otherwise surrendering sovereignty to the European Union to the top of the list of Conservative Party priorities.

Clarke, a Conservative member of Parliament and former chancellor of the exchequer, is a long-time Bilderberg stalwart who is committed to the European Union and world government.

The world government wing of the Conservative Party has been muted during the current campaign as former Prime Minister Margaret Thatcher has spoken loudly against embracing the euro and surrendering British sovereignty to the EU.

Bilderberg men, including Clarke, hope and expect the Conservatives to lose in a landslide to Prime Minister Tony Blair's Labor Party in the June 7 elections. Blair is himself a Bilderberger who fervently yearns for the euro, a single European state and world government.

Politically, Britain has been forced to do what most of the EU former nation-states refused to do, have a popular referendum on whether to embrace the common currency.

While all major polls point to a big victory for Labor, many in Britain are angry at losing sovereignty to the EU and the euro is in peril when put to a popular vote.

That's why Bilderberg gave orders to Clarke, which he was glad to receive: visit Blair and urge him to bring the issue up immediately, promising strong support from Conservative Party Europhiles.

Two years previously, the British were outraged to learn that the European Court had nullified two acts of Parliament. This year, they were outraged when small merchants were tried, fined and threatened with prison for selling products using Britain's traditional weights and measures instead of the EU-imposed imposed metric system.

Even as Bilderberg was gathering in Sweden, Lady Thatcher was speaking against embracing the euro and the European Union, warning that it cost Britain the sovereignty they had "fought and died for."

Blair felt compelled to respond to Lady Thatcher by proclaiming that it is patriotic to embrace the euro and "share sovereignty" with the EU. It was in this atmosphere that Bilderberg ordered Lady Thatcher's own Conservative Party to make embracing the euro a priority.

Upper Crust Only . . .

2002—Chantilly, Virginia: This sign was posted at the entry drive to the Westfield Marriott Conference Center. Translation: "No peons allowed." The sign didn't stop me from my annual attempt to bring America the truth about what was going on behind closed doors at yet another secret Bilderberg meeting.

CHAPTER TWENTY-ONE

2002

Chantilly, Virginia

In 2002, Bilderberg was hiding out in the posh Westfields near Dulles Airport in a Virginia suburb of Washington. This time it was less of a love-fest, with deep divisions among Americans and the European elite.

he issue of American aggression against Iraq was delayed, with the White House agreeing to wait at least until 2003, instead of late summer or early fall of 2002, but many issues simmered at this year's secret Bilderberg meeting held at the luxurious Westfields Marriott from May 30 to June 2.

President Bush lied when he said there were no plans for war on Iraq or anywhere else "on his desk" in 2002—the plans were piled high. But military brass in the Pentagon warned the president that the United States is unprepared for war. European leaders were opposed. Only civilians at Defense and State wanted war.

The role of peacemaker is new to Europe. At the Bilderberg meeting in Baden-Baden, Germany, in June 1991, the Persian Gulf war was celebrated and enthusiastic calls for more military action "in five years" were heard. It was at Baden-Baden that Clinton attended his first Bilderberg meeting. The next year, he was elected president and the United States went to war in 16 countries, euphemistically termed United Nations "peace-keeping missions."

But the warmongers fought to the end. In the May 29 *Wall Street*

Journal, Michael O'Hanlon, a senior fellow at the Brookings Institution, made a strong plea for an invasion of Iraq in a commentary that amounted to an in-house memo.

Brookings is one of numerous Bilderberg torch-carriers. The "conservative" *Journal* is always represented at Bilderberg meetings and its editorial policy is subservient to the globalist agenda. This war cry came just one day before Bilderberg formally gathered for its annual secret session.

With the war issue momentarily delayed, other fights were emerging in probably the most divisive Bilderberg meeting ever. On the basic agenda, the unity that has prevailed for nearly half a century remains intact: Creating a world government in which this international elite will dominate.

Bilderberg boys from the European Union were outraged that Bush protected the domestic steel industry from overseas dumping. They are equally angry over the farm bills, which significantly increased agricultural subsidies. "Family farmers" who benefit include Bilderberg luminaries David Rockefeller and Dwayne Andreas of Archer Daniels Midland.

European Bilderberg members—with many "Americans" agreeing—want the United States to change her tax laws to suit their pocketbooks. They call it "tax equity." Bilderberg also clings to its long-held commitment to create a global tax payable by "world citizens" directly to the United Nations.

The paradoxes would be amusing if not so damaging to U.S. interests. Farm subsidies are necessary for real family farmers—not to be confused with Bilderberg boys, TV mogul Ted Turner or millionaire basketball players—because of what Bilderberg hath wrought: NAFTA and other "free trade laws" as opposed to "fair trade."

The European Union countries also subsidize agriculture and other exports but object to America's protecting her domestic economy.

Europeans are also angry at the United States for rejecting the

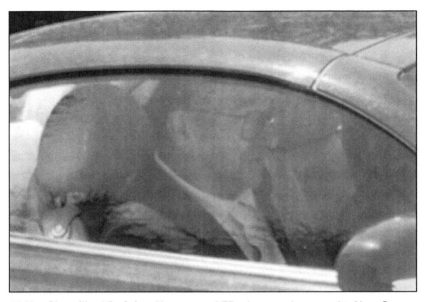

2002—**Chantilly, Virginia:** Above, an AFP photographer caught Alan Greenspan—the supposed wizard who controls the U.S. economy—and his wife, NBC correspondent Andrea Mitchell, arriving at the "wedding" at the Westfields Marriott. Mitchell was later photographed leaving Westfields on her way out. NBC neglected to report on Bilderberg, let alone Greenspan's attendance.

International Criminal Court and the Kyoto Treaty on global climate control, which economists warn would generate skyrocketing inflation here while requiring nothing of 60 percent of the world. Another point of sharp disagreement is U.S. Middle East policy. Many Europeans object to America's abject pro-Israel policy. This is in large part because the European media has far more balanced coverage of the turmoil there than the one-sided U.S. press.

As grim-faced armed guards and plainclothes security agents began encircling Westfields, they were awaiting Bilderberg luminaries who also looked glum. One of the longest faces belonged to Kenneth Dam, deputy secretary of the Treasury Department, who faced a grim grilling from his European counterparts.

Never has Bilderberg met this close to Washington. In 1962, Bilderberg took over all of Colonial Williamsburg—built by

Rockefeller money—located several miles south of Richmond, Va.

Security experts have explained why: Bilderberg boys were afraid of Middle Eastern terrorists. Dulles and Washington Reagan National Airport are the most secure in the United States because of their heavy traffic in congressmen and high administration officials.

One security man was overheard telling his counterpart: "If terrorists could bag a Rockefeller, that would be one hell of a trophy."

Westfields is situated seven miles south of Dulles Airport. When sealed off at the entrance, Westfields is out of sight. Luminaries can take short helicopter trips from either airport to Westfields's private heliport. Nevertheless, many of the pompous chose long black limos, complete with police escorts and screaming sirens.

Westfields had enough of its own black limos to provide these parades. To make sure everything was in order, a black car with State Department tags was parked outside Westfields five days in advance—on May 26.

Bilderberg Bashes U.S. on Middle East, War

Bilderberg luminaries battered their American counterparts over U.S Middle East policy. They blamed Americans' one-sided support of Israel for causing the need for a "war on terrorism" which could lead to bloody military misadventures.

However, most Bilderberg boys from both sides of the Atlantic were, for some reason, confident there would be no war between Pakistan and India. At that moment, both nations were on the brink of a nuclear holocaust.

It could have had something to do with the appearance of Defense Secretary Donald Rumsfeld, who was hastily summoned to appear on Saturday, June 1. Rumsfeld had attended a Bilderberg meeting in 1975 at Cemse, Turkey, as an assistant to President Jerry Ford. Ford had attended Bilderberg as speaker of the House.

Rumsfeld is known to have been summoned to reassure the

Europeans there would be "no immediate" U.S. invasion of Iraq as had been planned by the White House. He was pressed, but refused to say, that the United States had no plans for future wars.

Whether Rumsfeld also helped reassure Bilderberg there would be no war between Pakistan and India could not be determined.

But, even as Rumsfeld was assuring Bilderberg of at least a momentary delay in launching a new war, President Bush was rattling sabers in a commencement address at West Point.

"Pre-emptive strikes" will be used against nations or groups that threaten the United States, Bush told the newly minted Army officers. He vowed to "take the battle to the enemy, disrupt its plans and confront the worst threats before they emerge."

Besides Rumsfeld, Deputy Treasury Secretary Kenneth Dam had long been scheduled to attend—and did.

But unity was expressed with kind words, smiles, handshakes and embraces on Bilderberg's long-term agenda:

• Empowering the United Nations until it becomes a *de jure*, as well as *de facto*, world government.

• Advancing this goal by creating a direct UN tax on "world citizens," expanding NAFTA throughout the Western Hemisphere as a prelude to creating an "American Union" similar to the European Union and empowering international bodies to further erode the sovereignty of nations. Further establishing NATO as the UN's world army was also discussed.

There was much hand-wringing over "rising nationalism" in Europe, as demonstrated by the electoral successes of Jean-Marie Le Pen in France and by a populist "resurgence" in The Netherlands and Denmark. Americans agreed to pursue a "world without borders."

But on the issues of war and America's Middle East policy, Americans faced three days of chastisement, both in formal sessions and during glass-tinkling between sessions. A grim-faced Kissinger and others had to take it as Europeans denounced U.S. policy.

It reached the point that Europeans were praising their detested press, which has showered them with unwanted publicity in recent years. This is a close paraphrase of the angry words Americans heard:

"In Europe, you would be unable to conduct such a one-sided policy in the Middle East. Europeans know, because of heavy press coverage, of Israel's wars of expansion and brutal occupation of Palestinian lands. They are aware of the cruelty inflicted on civilians, including women and children, for no military objective at all.

"Europeans know that Israel's military machine is financed by the United States. They know that the planes, tanks and weapons attacking innocent citizens are provided by the United States. While there is no justification for the attacks in New York and Washington on Sept. 11, Europeans know that Palestinians will resist in any way they can.

"Because of the unfair Middle East policy of the United States, we Europeans now must be your allies in your war on terrorism."

Americans responded to this with grim faces and shrugs.

The administration had anticipated this barrage and tried to soften it with a peace plan that included an independent Palestinian state. This goes beyond previous U.S. positions, Americans reassured the Europeans, which merely called for Palestinian statehood.

The plan was still being drafted as Bilderberg met but they were assured it would be publicly unveiled in July.

Bilderberg celebrated the fact that a global UN tax is "part of the public dialogue" without a public outcry by "nationalists." I had first reported this years ago. Alan Keyes, as President Ronald Reagan's UN ambassador, denounced the proposed tax and it has been widely discussed since.

Bilderberg has offered several variations of the world tax. First, it suggested a 10-cent tax on oil at the barrel head, meaning citizens would pay a direct tax to the UN when gassing up their cars or using oil in any way. A surcharge on international travel by air or sea and a tax on international financial transfers were also proposed.

Like the federal income tax, a UN levy would be so small at the outset the consumer would hardly notice. But establishing the principle that the UN can directly tax citizens of the world is important to Bilderberg. It is another giant step toward world government. It is openly discussed with little public notice or objection "except for the Ron Pauls in Congress" and in "nationalist" publications, Bilderberg boys assured themselves. The references were to populist Rep. Ron Paul (R-Tex.) and *American Free Press*, which began publication in 2001 after *The Spotlight* and its publisher, Liberty Lobby, were judicially assassinated

There were also demands for "tax equity"—meaning that the United States must revise her tax laws to more evenly reflect the high-tax, socialistic societies of Europe. It was called "unfair trade" for the United States to be so—by comparison—"tax friendly" to individuals and businesses.

Europeans continued to complain about the new farm subsidy legislation and the imposition of tariffs on steel imports to protect the domestic industry against dumping and were distraught that the Senate version of Fast Track would allow Congress to block any trade deals that negate laws protecting domestic industries.

There was continued sniping at the United States because Bush "unsigned" the Kyoto global warming treaty that, economists warned, would generate sky-high inflation while requiring nothing of most nations. Spitefully, the 15-nation European Union ratified the treaty on June 1 as Bilderberg was meeting.

This prompted a graying Bilderberg luminary to moan that George Bush is "the worst president since [Richard] Nixon." Never has Bush received a higher tribute.

NATO has been functioning as the standing army of the United Nations since celebrating its 50th anniversary in Washington during the invasion of Yugoslavia. NATO's first shot fired in anger was not in defense, as its charter required, but in an offensive war. At that time, leaders announced that NATO was no longer confined to

Europe but would undertake military ventures anywhere in the world—at the direction of the UN Security Council.

Bilderberg is reinforcing this world army doctrine while doing early work on the third great region of the world: the emerging "Asian-Pacific Union."

It is already being bound together as APEC—the Asian-Pacific Economic Union. Even as Bilderberg met, one of its own, Sen. Chuck Hagel (R-Neb.) was attending a meeting of Asian-Pacific defense ministers. Ultimately, there are to be three great regions for the administrative convenience of the world government: the European Union, American Union and Asian-Pacific Union.

Bilderberg ended a day earlier than normal, abandoning Westfields early on Sunday afternoon, June 2. Normally, they would have said their farewells on Monday. This must have been a sudden decision, because staffers of Bilderberg participants in nearby Washington had been told they would be out of their offices until Tuesday.

Europeans Penetrate U.S. Media Blackout

Bilderberg has succeeded in scaring off the American mainstream press—with the exception of *American Free Press* and *Insight* magazine—but the European media's interest persists.

All newspapers in Maryland and Virginia received a press release well in advance advising them of the meeting and the history of Bilderberg with the assurance they would have much help in covering the global event. *The Washington Post, New York Times* and *Washington Times* were hand-delivered the release.

Only *The Washington Times* responded, sending a reporter, Dan Doyle, from its weekly news magazine, *Insight*. Neither *The New York Times* nor *The Washington Post* are ignorant of Bilderberg. Both have long been represented at Bilderberg, keeping their promise to publish nothing.

British Broadcasting Corporation interviewed me twice while I was still billeted with Bilderberg at Westfields and subsequently. Star television of Turkey interviewed me several times. They, in turn, were helping colleagues in Europe.

A reporter for an Estonian newspaper, *Gesti Paevalehi*, Arui Tapuer, who is based in New York, rode a Greyhound bus to Washington, took a metro train to Vienna, Va., and then a cab to Westfields where, as he expected, he was blocked by the palace guard. He said the cab driver was shocked to see the shutdown.

Estonia is only becoming accustomed to a free press after shedding the shackles of the former Soviet Union.

BBC's first concern was that Bilderberg had warded off their hounds by shifting the meeting to another site. Westfields had told BBC that nothing was happening but "a couple of weddings." I was asked about this in an on-air interview.

"Bilderberg is lying," I said, after advising the British public that Bilderberg is probably listening in because of its long-standing practice of bugging my phone during my days at Bilderberg sites.

The term "lying" or "lie" is used here in the full sense. To "lie" is to willfully tell an untruth with the intent of enriching yourself, injuring another or both. In this case, Westfields was trying to injure the people's right to know.

"Bilderberg is here; the palace guard is deployed," I said before giving listeners details about the agenda and luminaries known, at that time, to be present.

European cities have a lot of highly competitive newspapers and they have collaborated with the court-killed *Spotlight*—and now *American Free Press*—to swamp Bilderberg in a blizzard of publicity in recent years. But their budgets are limited, so much of this year's coverage must be long-range in Europe.

Policy of Secrecy Forced on Record

There were two formal attempts, for the record, to get Bilderberg to provide, voluntarily, its secret list of participants and its agenda.

One-half hour before the 2 p.m. departure deadline for the unwashed multitudes on Thursday, May 30, Dr. M. Raphael Johnson, then editor of *The Barnes Review*, the bimonthly Washington-based revisionist historical journal, approached the long table where staff awaited to hand Bilderberg participants' portfolios containing these documents.

Johnson explained that he was a graduate student working on a doctoral thesis on international affairs and his paper would not be published for months, if at all. A large Swedish woman kept repeating, "No."

Five minutes before deadline, I approached the table, addressing a man in a dark suit.

"I am an American journalist," I said. "May I have a copy of the Bilderberg agenda and a list of participants?"

The big blonde Swedish woman elbowed the middle-aged man aside and kept repeating "No."

"You are conducting public business behind closed doors," I said.

"No, this is a private meeting," Blondie replied.

"This meeting is attended by public officials from the United States and it is subsidized by the taxpayers—"

"Time to leave," said a burly security man and I was escorted out with one on each arm.

Press Pretends Ignorance of Bilderberg

The Washington Post and *The New York Times*, which have had representatives at Bilderberg meetings on many occasions, explained their lack of coverage by pleading ignorance.

The Washington Times explained that it was unable to cover Bilderberg because access to the Westfields Marriott was denied. However, its weekly news magazine, *Insight*, sent a reporter to the scene and planned an extensive story. Unfortunately, *Insight* is now defunct.

The Westfields Marriott refused to discuss its lies in denying that Bilderberg was meeting at its heavily secured luxury hotel in Chantilly, Va. When pressed, the phone was hung up.

"I'm not sure . . . I really don't know. What's it about?" said a man on the national desk at the *Post*.

He was given a brief summary of the meeting and luminaries who attended and referred the call to "Mr. Kayman." Al Kayman's voice mail was given the same civics lesson.

"I don't know if we'll be covering it but I will look into it," said a man on *The New York Times* national desk. He had also expressed bewilderment and was given a quick history of Bilderberg.

"It was closed," said *The Washington Times* man. "We can't write about something we can't get into."

A call was placed to Kieran Atlow, senior sales manager at Westfields. He was unavailable, said a woman who identified herself only as "Barbara."

"My name is Jim Tucker and I am covering Bilderberg for *American Free Press*," she was told. "I was told several times by Westfields staff that there was no such group as 'Bilderberg' meeting there. On Thursday, May 30, as Bilderberg was gathering at Westfields, you told the British Broadcasting Corporation that there was no such meeting, 'only a couple of weddings' going on. Why did Westfields people lie?"

"I, I, I really couldn't answer that—I'm sorry," said "Barbara" as she hung up the phone.

Bilderberg Documents Confirm AFP Reports

Under threat of extensive media attention in Europe to its refusal to provide the agenda and list of participants at its secret meeting in Chantilly, Va., Bilderberg surrendered.

Tony Gosling, a European Bilderberg hound, promptly faxed the documents to *American Free Press*. Gosling is one of many in Europe who have collaborated with the court-killed *Spotlight*—and now *American Free Press*—in exposing Bilderberg. His web site, www.bilderberg.org, provides extensive coverage.

Bilderberg had hoped to keep all its secrets because the major media in the United States collaborated in the blackout. When meeting in Europe, Bilderberg now confronts a lot of coverage in the major media initially prompted by *The Spotlight.*

When compelled to make its list public, Bilderberg always adds a "press release." The press release is the same each year, rationalizing its conducting public business in private, with the exception of a first-paragraph update. It reads:

"The 50th Bilderberg meeting will be held in Chantilly, Va. Among other subjects the conference will discuss terrorism, trade, post-crisis reconstruction, Middle East, civil liberties, U.S. foreign policy, extreme right, world economy, corporate governance."

These topics were reported regularly to AFP by a Bilderberg source inside Westfields.

The list forced out of Bilderberg is incomplete, as always. Every time the list has been obtained by whatever means, there are people who attended but are not mentioned. For example, this year, AFP was able to get a call through to Andrew Parisiliti at Westfields during the meeting but he is not on Bilderberg's list.

Parisiliti is foreign affairs advisor to Sen. Chuck Hagel (R-Neb.), a Bilderberg regular who was attending an Asian peace summit at the time. Parisiliti was representing Hagel at Bilderberg.

Bilderberg has, at one time or another, had representatives of all major U.S. newspapers and network news outlets attend. They do so on their promise to report nothing. This is how Bilderberg keeps its news blackout virtually complete in the United States.

This year's crop included *The Washington Post*'s Hoagland (a regular) and Charles Krauthammer, both columnists for *The Washington Post*, Jean de Belot of France, editor of *le Figaro*; John Bernder of Norway, director-general of Norwegian Broadcasting Corp.; Paul Gigot, editorial page editor of the "conservative" *Wall*

Street Journal; Charlie Rose, producer of Rose Communications who appears on public radio; Toger Seidenfaden of Denmark, editor-in-chief of *Politiken* and Kenneth Whyte of Canada, editor of *The National Post.*

Conrad Black, owner of a string of newspapers around the world, attended as a regular.

Every year, there are a few newcomers who are part of the Bilderberg fringe. Roughly 100 are regulars who have attended for many years. Fringe people are invited because Bilderberg thinks they may be useful tools. If not, they are cast aside.

When Douglas Wilder was serving his term as governor of Virginia, he was summoned by Bilderberg because he was the first black ever elected a governor in the United States. However, Wilder's presumed presidential ambitions never were fulfilled, despite his initial entree into Bilderberg circles.

Wilder ran in the Democratic presidential primary in 1984 but got less than one percent of the vote in lily-white New Hampshire and was cast aside by Bilderberg. Similarly, Christine Todd Whitman, as governor of New Hampshire was invited and later cast aside.

The absence of Hagel does not mean he was cast aside because his representative attended and the senator had hoped to. But he was carrying on Bilderberg business at the Asian defense meeting and remains in good standing.

So these newcomers may be emerging Bilderberg stars or future castoffs, depending on events: Sen. Kay Bailey Hutchison (R-Tex.) and Rep. John LaFalce (D-N.Y.).

But for the first time, the chairmen of the two major parties were summoned to Bilderberg. Terry McAuliffe, chairman of the Democratic National Committee and Mark Racicot, chairman of the Republican National Committee, both attended Bilderberg.

Leaders of the Democratic and Republican parties now know what Bilderberg wants them to do. They also know the vast sums of money and global influence that are at stake.

A Venue for Royalty ...

2003—Versailles, France: The lobby of the Trianon Palace Hotel was the welcoming site of the annual Bilderberg meetings that year. Topics of discussion included the war in Iraq, U.S. support of Israel, peace in the Middle East and global taxes. Bilderbergers were photographed casually walking the grounds of the Trianon, providing reporters with unprecedented access to Bilderbergers.

CHAPTER TWENTY-TWO

2003

Versailles, France

The annual meeting of the global elites kicked off mid May in secrecy. However, we were there to greet them, unveiling to the world what goes on behind closed doors when the world's most powerful meet to discuss pressing issues of the day.

he rift between American and European Bilderberg participants grew greater over both the U.S. invasion of Iraq and blind, blank check support of Israeli aggression against Palestinians. These were hotly debated topics as Bilderberg luminaries began filling the posh Trianon Palace Hotel in Versailles, France, on May 14 for its May 15-18 meeting.

Another issue high on the Bilderberg agenda was the proposed European Union army independent of NATO. Unlike the other two major issues, this is not a confrontation between Americans and Europeans. All Americans oppose the EU army, but so do many Europeans. Leading the anti-army European faction is "Lord" George Robertson, secretary-general of NATO.

French President Chirac, as head of the host state, delivered a welcoming speech during Bilderberg's first full working day on Thursday, May 15. Chirac tried to calm tensions by recalling that, despite dissension over the invasion of Iraq, Americans and Europeans are traditional allies. France was among the harshest critics of the war and the U.S. administration is bent on "punishing" the French.

Germany and Russia were harsh critics too, like most European states, but Secretary of State Colin Powell, even as Bilderberg was meeting, traveled to both those countries for make-up sessions.

Bilderberg's annual secret meeting that year was delayed for hours by people they scorn as the unwashed multitudes—workers in France. Their strike on May 13 allowed only one in five planes to land at Charles de Gaulle International Airport and at the older Orly Field in Paris.

Versailles is a short distance from Paris. The "one day strike" was so successful—with millions of supporters filling the streets of Paris and other cities—that it was extended through Thursday, May 15.

Bilderberg staff had started slipping inconspicuously into the Trianon on May 13, preparing for the planned shutdown about noon the following day. On Thursday morning, May 15, the last of the Bilderberg luminaries arrived in long, black limos, behind police escorts and shrieking sirens.

Bilderberg had planned to shut down the Trianon Palace at noon on May 13, as usual, so their functionaries could arrive absent the masses. Instead, the Trianon was open to the public until late Wednesday evening and the shutdown occurred early Thursday morning. Then Bilderberg commenced its work.

Three sources within the Trianon Palace provided detailed information about what transpired behind the guarded, sealed-off resort.

Bilderberg remained united on the common goal of establishing a world government under the United Nations while retaining control over the wealth of the Earth and all inhabitants.

But anger over the U.S. war ran high. Europe opposed U.S. war plans a year ago, extracting a promise from Secretary of Defense Rumsfeld not to invade Iraq in 2002. But the Europeans like the war no more this year than last. There was taunting, such as "where are all these awful weapons of mass destruction?"

Europeans were also skeptical of U.S. plans to "control" Iraq's oil

2003—Versailles, France: AFP correspondent Christopher Bollyn snapped this photo "up close and personal," capturing one of the world's most powerful Bilderbergers on film for the ages. Few U.S. media outlets besides *American Free Press* newspaper in Washington seemed interested. Bilderberg masters insist their puppets in the media obey a "Bilderberg blackout" order.

for the "benefit" of the Iraqi people. "Who are the 'other' beneficiaries?" one asked sarcastically. So Iraqi oil money will be used to rebuild what Americans destroyed? "How many fat contracts will go to Europeans?" came the question.

But emotions ran even higher on the issue of U.S. Middle East policy. At the moment Bilderberg was gathering in Versailles, Israeli

Prime Minister Ariel Sharon was contemptuously rejecting the "road map" to peace introduced by Bush and endorsed by the other members of the "quartet"—the UN, EU and Russia.

Powell had just visited Sharon to beg him to accept the peace plan. But Sharon dismissed as "not on the horizon" any discussion of dismantling Israeli settlements in Palestinian territory.

In *The Jerusalem Post*, Sharon ridiculed any idea that U.S. aid may be reduced. He said no U.S. administration had ever supported settlements in the West Bank and Gaza Strip, which Israel occupied after launching the Six-Day War in 1967.

Referring to Sharon's arrogance toward the country that has given Israel countless billions of dollars over the past half century while asking nothing in return, a European Bilderberg luminary told a grim-faced American: "you are too stupid to know when you've been insulted by a moral midget."

Adding to the embarrassment of Americans at Bilderberg was the fact that the peace plan thrown back into Powell's face asked only modest moves by Israel. It only asks that Israel abandon settlements built on Palestinian lands since March 2001. Israel, in this initial "peace move," is not required to give up the land it seized in doubling its size in the1967 war.

The idea of an independent EU army arose from Europe's resentment over U.S. domination of NATO. Some suggest it be a separate force but party of, and controlled by, NATO. But opponents in Europe as well as the United States argued that a separate EU force would make NATO's role as the UN's world army incoherent.

NATO said repeatedly that it is no longer confined to defending Europe but will deploy troops anywhere in the world at the direction of the UN Security Council. At the time, UN "peacekeepers" were on patrol at 16 far-flung missions throughout the world.

Bilderberg Security Traps Itself

Bilderberg security was so intense it drove sources to come forward earlier than usual—on *American Free Press*'s first day in France on Monday, May 12. This reporter checked into the Novotel, a short distance from the Trianon Palace, where Bilderberg was scheduled to begin filtering in on Wednesday afternoon. I went straight to the Trianon, did some scouting and settled in for coffee at the bar.

As I have for more than 20 years of Bilderberg bird-dogging, I began low-key conversations about how "something important" must be happening because I was unable to make reservations for the full week.

The first day had always been a "softening up" operation, when employees are encouraged to discuss the awesome events unfolding. The Trianon had been filled for big events in the past. But never was it sealed off with armed guards, or employees told to see and hear nothing on pain of being fired and blacklisted and never to look the luminary in the eye nor speak unless spoken to.

By the following day, workers knew something sinister was about to take place. Newer people had been furloughed. Longer-term employees were warned again about secrecy.

By the second and third day, some brave folks stepped forward and became my eyes and ears. Their quick hands also obtained documents. They met with me at pre-arranged locations.

But for the first time, they came forward on the first day—because of Bilderberg's overbearing security.

I had mentioned that "something big" was happening because I had tried to make reservations for the entire week but was told I would have to leave on Wednesday, May 14, because the Trianon was booked up for a "private event."

The staffer looked puzzled and shook his head. This was no surprise; employees are told as late as possible, on a "need to know" basis, to reduce the risk of leaks.

The employee picked up a phone to inquire. He hung up, looking stunned. Within moments—not minutes—a security guard was on either side of me, talking intensely. One gave me a sidelong glance. Bilderberg security has had numerous photos of me on

2004: Stresa, Italy: Many people would say that this photograph, more than any others, clearly demonstrates the coming together of the powerful elites at Bilderberg. Far right is Richard Perle the architect of the Iraq war. Second from right is Jessica Mathews from the Carnegie Endowment for Peace. Seated with backs to camera are David Rockefeller and Clinton advisor Vernon Jordan.

file for years.

Dutifully, the employee ignored me. But another two stepped forward to say they, too, would collaborate in informing me.

"They can fire one of us, but to fire three of us would give them problems," Pipeline explained.

Security failed to take into account that hotel employees here have strong unions, with typical benefits such as paid vacations. In most places, including the United States, they do not—no vacation, health insurance or other benefits. As a result, Trianon employees are unaccustomed to being spoken to as animals.

It was arranged that I would meet daily with Pipeline. I would meet separately with another at still another location. They provided detailed information and dialogue and identified many of the people involved.

Reporters from numerous media outlets in Europe met with me daily at 5 p.m. at the Novotel bar. All information was pooled, compared and confirmed.

They Can't Hide Their Faces

Reporters and photographers, sometimes working in shifts, patrolled outside the Trianon Palace all day, every day, as Bilderberg met in 2003.

Every day, they gathered at the Novotel bar to compare notes and pool information. Copies of *American Free Press*'s first story, filed from Versailles for the May 26, 2003 edition, were provided to the European journalists.

The only other American "journalists" at the meeting were Bilderberg participants.

Hundred of photos were circulated on a table for all to examine. Most would not be published—just a face behind a darkened window in a limo.

But Gunnar Blondal, a journalist from Norway, had a laptop computer that could enhance photos, leading to many positive identifications—usually by two or more reporters.

Others were identified by sight as they ventured outside into the brisk, spring air.

Others were identified by subterfuge—such as contacting the Trianon with an "emergency call from home" and getting the participant on the phone.

By these means, the following have been positively identified as participating:

Queen Beatrix of The Netherlands; Ali Babacan, minister of the economy in Turkey; King Juan Carlos and Queen Sophia of Spain; Jacques Chirac, president of France; Kenneth Clark, former British chancellor of the exchequer and member of Parliament; Etienne D'avignon, Societe General of Belgium; Jean Louis Debre, president of the French National Assembly; Kermal Dervis, Turkey; Sevein Gjerem, CEO of the National Bank of Norway; Pascual Lamy, European Union; Egil Myklebust, chairman of the aircraft firm Norsk Hydro SAS; Richard Perle, Defense Policy Board; Andres Fogh-Rasmussen, prime minister of Denmark; Dominique de Villepin, French foreign minister; Wolfgang Schaulde, opposition leader in Germany; Otto Schilly, minister of the home office in Germany; Paavo Lipponen, former prime minister of Finland; Jarmd Ollila, CEO of Nobid in Finland; Anna Lindh, foreign minister of Sweden; Peter Sutherland, chairman of Goldman Sachs International and chairman of BP Amoco and Marty Taylor, secretary of Bilderberg.

Bilderberg Presses Sharon Into Oral Flip-Flop

In a rare moment in its half-century of secret meetings to plan the world, Bilderberg has accomplished some good: by pressuring the Israeli government to at least publicly back off its policy of expanding Israel and oppressing Palestinians.

Even as Bilderberg was meeting inside the Trianon Palace, the Israeli prime minister was rejecting the "road map" to peace with contempt. Sharon told *The Jerusalem Post* and other Israeli media that Israel would never return any of the Palestinian lands seized in the past half-century. Sharon laughed at suggestions that U.S. aid may be reduced or eliminated unless his policy of expanding the occupation ended. He boasted that all U.S. administrations have opposed Israeli settlements while blank-check aid never stopped.

European Bilderberg participants were outraged at Sharon's attitude and complained vociferously to American participants. Europeans placed angry calls to their own government officials and to Israel.

A week later, on May 26, Sharon reversed himself—at least publicly. He told his stunned countrymen that he was determined to reach a peace agreement and end the "occupation" of the West Bank and Gaza Strip.

It was the first time Sharon had publicly uttered the word "occupation"—which is anathema to many Israelis who claim the land as their own for religious reasons.

"To keep 3.5 million people under occupation is bad for us and them," Sharon told outraged members of his Likud Party in comments broadcast on Israeli radio. "This can't continue endlessly. Do you want to remain forever in Ramallah, Jenin, Nablus?" he asked, naming towns in the West Bank.

Sharon's startling reversal of rhetoric was in direct response to European Bilderberg luminaries because he feared the U.S. government could be pressured into punishing Israel's occupation by reducing or ending the annual foreign aid.

While Sharon's comments were widely viewed with cynicism by those who expect him to find some way to escape the "road map" he has officially embraced, some held out hope that the Israeli leader might be sincere.

"Sharon is a pragmatist," said Efraim Inbar, director of the Begin-Sadat Center for Strategic Studies at Bar Ilan University in Tel Aviv. "He is capable of change when circumstances require."

But Yossi Sarid, a member of the Israeli Knesset (parliament), was more cynical, saying Sharon wanted the U.S. government to assume that he was committed to the peace plan while his hawkish allies could assume he was just making a tactical move to appease the Europeans and Americans.

"Ariel Sharon likes to walk in the fog, because then no one knows where he is headed," Sarid wrote in the *Yediot Ahronot* newspaper.

Bilderberg Blackout ...

2004—Stresa, Italy: *Washington Post* publisher Donald Graham (center above) was photographed by AFP cameramen at the 2004 meeting in Stresa. Yet Donald's *Washington Post* didn't think the meeting newsworthy enough for detailed coverage.

CHAPTER TWENTY-THREE

2004

Stresa, Italy

In 2004, Bilderberg again demanded that Americans raise their taxes and increase foreign aid although the United States is, by far, the world's greatest donor and debtor nation.

t the 2004 secret Bilderberg meeting at the Grand Hotel des Iles Borromees near Stresa, Italy, some of the world's most powerful elite focused on U.S. taxes and foreign giveaways, as well as the increasingly violent Iraq occupation and the role the United Nations should play in all future outbreaks of violence. The gathering took place at the posh resort overlooking Lake Maggiore June 3-6.

Prior to the meeting, a Bilderberg memo promised that its members would deal mainly with European-American relations and in that context, with U.S politics, Iraq, the Middle East, European geopolitics, NATO, China, energy and economic problems.

During the conference, Britain came in for harsh criticism for supporting the invasion of Iraq. It was also lambasted for failing to embrace the euro, despite Prime Minister Tony Blair's promise to do so at a Bilderberg meeting some years ago in the Scottish resort of Turnberry.

Bilderberg members also expressed frustration with the rising clamor in Britain to quit the European Union.

As expected, the United States was heavily criticized for the fact that its foreign aid was a smaller percentage of gross domestic product than that of other nations. That marked the third straight meeting at which Bilderbergers' decades of almost total congeniality was marred by hostility among the Americans, Britons and continental Europeans.

The first evidence of division in the ranks was apparent in 2002 when Bilderbergers met at Chantilly, Va., near Washington. Then, Europeans were angry that the United States was preparing for an invasion of Iraq. Secretary of Defense Donald Rumsfeld tried to placate them with a promise not to invade "this year." Instead, the war began in March 2003.

Bilderbergers, however, remained united in their long-term goal to strengthen the role the UN plays in regulating global relations. Aside from that objective, other matters on this year's conference agenda included the following:

• British elites are to press on with membership in the European Union despite growing domestic opposition.

• The Free Trade Area of the Americas (FTAA) should be enacted and include the entire Western Hemisphere except for Cuba until Fidel Castro is gone. It should then evolve into the "American Union" as a carbon copy of the European Union.

• An "Asian-Pacific Union" is to emerge as the third great super state, neatly dividing the world into three great regions for the administrative convenience of banking and corporate elites. The United States and other international financial institutions should facilitate and administrate these global trade pacts.

Another much-discussed subject at this year's conference was the concept of imposing a direct UN tax on people worldwide. In order to achieve it, some Bilderbergers presented two proposals: a tax on oil at the wellhead and a tax on international financial transactions.

Bilderberg leaders tilted strongly toward the oil tax because everyone who drives a car, rides public transportation or flies in a plane will end up paying the tax. That will represent more people than those engaged in international financial transactions across the globe.

On the issue of Iraq, European Bilderbergers were more upset that the United States invaded without the UN's blessing than the fact that many thousands of American soldiers and Iraqis have been killed.

Word reached the conference from Rumsfeld, who was unable to attend this year's meeting, that the U.S. military would assume a more defensive stance in Iraq, rather than the more provocative operations of door-to-door searches and widespread detention.

Rumsfeld was, however, represented in Stresa by Douglas Feith, his undersecretary for policy, and William Luti, deputy undersecretary for Near Eastern and South Asian affairs. Former Pentagon advisor Richard Perle, one of the major architects of the war in Iraq, was also present. It had been Perle, Feith and Paul Wolfowitz who, from the mid 1990s, had fashioned the Middle East policy later adopted by Bush, Cheney and Rumsfeld.

European Bilderbergers also protested the fact that the Pentagon was considering reducing troop levels in Germany and tried hard to convince their American counterparts to resist the move.

They argued it would "undermine unity" and, irrespective of the military implications, the German economy benefited annually from the millions of dollars spent by U.S. servicemen there.

Resistance in Britain to the euro, and to membership in the European Union, caused much concern and was deemed an obstacle to the solidification of the super state.

Bilderberg participants ended their secret sessions on an upbeat note with a ferry ride to a luxury island on Lake Maggiore, where John Elkman, the latest vice president of the Fiat motor company, married his new bride in September.

Italian Cops Cage Bilderberg Hound

On Monday, May 31, 2004, I was arrested by Italian plainclothes policemen on my first day in Stresa, covering Bilderberg. I had gone to the five-star Grand Hotel des Iles Borromees, where the conference was to be held, hoping to pry information from hotel staff. On my way out, of the hotel, three plainclothes cops blocked my path, seized my passport and led me to an unmarked car.

The officer in charge, Antonio Bacinelli, told me they were taking me for a five-minute ride because their commander wanted to talk to me. But it was more like 40 minutes as the car whizzed through small towns to police headquarters.

At police HQ, I was led from the car and placed in an interrogation room.

I told the cops that I was sure the State Department wasn't happy about me covering Bilderberg, but they were unlikely to approve of Italian police putting me in jail for doing my job. My interrogator was a craggy-faced officer in his 60s, dressed in a business suit.

He interviewed me through translators, including Bacinelli and a young woman, and asked me if I had any particular reason for being in Stresa. I replied: "You know exactly who I am, but I will tell you anyway. I'm here to cover Bilderberg for the American newspaper, *American Free Press.*"

I then handed over my American press credentials, which they examined.

The female officer read aloud, in English, what was printed on the back of my plastic-sealed press card. The wording contained the following: "The holder hereof agrees to assume all risks incident to use of this pass" but "members of the police force shall be courteous and cooperative on all occasions to the bearer of this pass."

There was then a burst of Italian chatter in which the word "journalist" was heard several times, before the female officer smiled, returned my passport and press card and told me I would face no further harassment from the police.

To my surprise, Bacinelli and the commander drove me back to the hotel, after three hours in custody. They even followed me into the hotel and sat in the lobby while I went into a lounge area where

I could keep my eyes on them. I had said to them: "If you chaps are so interested in Bilderberg, you are invited to join me again in the days ahead. I will be happy to tell you what the Bilderberg boys are doing."

They had replied: "Oh no. We're regulars at this hotel."

Later, a hotel employee, who agreed to talk anonymously, told me the police were not regulars.

Mainstream Still Covering

After more than a half-century of silence, *The New York Times* carried a story on the secret Bilderberg Group July 11—but it was inaccurate and failed to disclose its own long-term collaboration. *The Times* has had officials at many Bilderberg meetings over the years and, until now, has kept its vow of silence.

While the *Times* had accidentally mentioned Bilderberg in a news story about a participant who died at a meeting years ago, it was the first time the newspaper had actually written about the secretive group of international financiers and political leaders.

The *Times* quoted the woman who helps coordinate Bilderberg meetings in Europe, Maja Banck-Polderman of Leiden, Netherlands. Over the years, Banck-Polderman has routinely resisted efforts to provide details about Bilderberg meetings.

"They do not have to sign anything, but they understand that they do not talk," she was quoted regarding Bilderberg's secrecy, or "Chatham House," rule.

The story predictably bleats about "conspiracy theories" as if secret Bilderberg meetings were not an established fact for 50 years.

It celebrated Sen. John Edwards's (D-N.C.) attendance, suggesting it propelled him into the role of vice presidential candidate.

Others papers picked up the story from the New York Times Wire Service.

For example, the Itar-Tass News Agency reported that Russian oil was a major topic. Tass's recent report detailed the 2004 Bilderberg meeting in Stresa, Italy.

Washington Post Challenged

On May 11, 2004 I sent a letter to *The Washington Post*, inviting the newspaper to report on the 2004 Bilderberg meetings. The following is a copy of the letter I sent to Michael Getler, the *Post*'s ombudsman. The ombudsman's role is to examine readers' complaints and determine, in his independent judgment, which are valid. He is then to address valid complaints in his op-ed column every Sunday and recommend corrective actions.

To this day, there has been no response.

> Dear Mr. Getler:
> May I suggest that *The Washington Post* publish a comprehensive story about an important international meeting that will take place June 3-6 at the Grand Hotel des Iles Borromees in Stresa, Italy?
> High officials from the departments of Defense, Treasury and State and from the White House typically attend these meetings. Heads of state, political leaders and international financiers from Europe will also attend.
> Covering this event would cost nothing. Your associate editor, Jimmy Lee Hoagland, and your publisher, Donald Graham, routinely attend these meetings. *Post* publishers Philip Graham and Katharine Graham attended these annual meetings during their lifetimes.
> Is it not newsworthy when 120 of the world's most powerful men meet in a sealed-off resort behind armed guards for three days each year? They are obviously planning policy that affects all Americans and most Europeans.
> Yet, the media giants who attend—which, at different times, included *The New York Times, Los Angeles Times* and all four major networks—pledge secrecy. Not a word describing Bilderberg meetings has appeared.
> I have covered Bilderberg for more than 20 years, first for the defunct *Spotlight* and Liberty Lobby, and now for

ISLAND LAKE MAGGIORE: This posh venue was the site of the Bilderberg conference for 2004, held near Stresa, Italy.

American Free Press. However, Bilderberg has been inhospitable to me. I spent 20 happy years with daily newspapers—the late *Washington Daily News, Richmond Times-Dispatch* and *The Akron Beacon Journal,* among others—without ever reading or hearing the world "Bilderberg."

Jimmy Lee and Donald will tell you that nothing important transpires at Bilderberg; perhaps that it is a marathon poker game. But, by covering Bilderberg, I was able to write advance stories on the end of the Cold War, the first gulf war, on President Bush the Elder breaking his "read my lips: no new taxes" promise, on the downfall of Margaret Thatcher as British prime minister and other exclusives. Were these events not important?

Thank you for hearing me out, and I eagerly await your response.

Cordially,
Jim Tucker
AFP Senior Editor

Bilderbergers Make Me Angry ...

2005—Rottach-Egern, Germany: I got my "game face on" as I arrived at the 2005 Bilderberg confabulation, standing in front of the Seehotel Uberfahrt in Rottach-Egern, Germany. The 2005 meeting should be very important to all Americans, as U.S. neo-cons tried to defend the Iraq war debacle and convince their European brothers that needless war and bloody imperialism benefit the global elites and world government.

CHAPTER TWENTY-FOUR

2005

Rottach-Egern, Germany

At the 2005 Bilderberg meeting at the the Dorint Sofitel resort in Rottach-Egern, Germany, Kissinger was overheard informing longtime U.S. diplomat Richard Holbrooke that the price of oil may reach $150 a barrel in two years, according to two friendly sources inside the secret Bilderberg meeting.

This year, Bilderbergers met at the Dorint Sofitel Seehotel Uberfahrt, a five-star conference and business hotel with 188 luxury rooms. It is on a lake and near a golf course—typical Bilderberg requirements.

"It should not be long," Kissinger reportedly told Holbrooke, vice chairman of Perseus LLC and longtime Bilderberg luminary. Kissinger said the demand for oil has far exceeded the supply. Oil, and who gets it, is part of the bitter Bilderberg dispute over Middle East policy.

One source said James Baker had made the same prediction while representing the Carlyle Group at an earlier business conference, saying "look for $150 a barrel."

Baker represented the White House at Bilderberg meetings under former Presidents Reagan and Bush the Elder, where he served as chief of staff and treasury secretary, respectively.

The economic impact of tripling already-high oil prices would be staggering. Inflation would soar, because transportation—from raw material to finished product to marketplace—has a significant impact on virtually everything you buy—from neckties to houses.

Bilderberg hunkered down May 5-8 to decide how the world should deal with European-American relations, the Middle East powder keg, the Iraq war, the global economy and potential war in Iran.

The first appearance of Virginia Gov. Mark Warner (D) indicated Bilderberg considered him a presidential contender.

The absence of former Sen. John Edwards (N.C.), John Kerry's presidential running mate in 2004, indicated the Sun has set on his political career. Last year was Edwards's first appearance and, like most of the "fringe" invitees, he had been cast aside like an old shoe.

European hostility toward Americans for the invasion of Iraq was rekindled by reports in the European press that British Prime Minister Blair had secretly agreed with President Bush to go to war months in advance of the U.S. invasion.

The Guardian of London, among other newspapers, carried detailed accounts of a transcript of conversations between Blair and President Bush three months before the March 2002 invasion. The transcript clearly showed. Blair promising, in advance, to join the United States in the war on Iraq.

This prompted hostile comments while Kissinger was presiding over a panel discussion on the meaning of "peace." Europeans demanded to know if "Iran is next," and "when does it end?" America was repeatedly warned not to "rush to war with Iran."

But history demonstrates that Americans are no more the "war party" than the European Bilderbergers. Europeans joined in supporting the 1991 invasion of Iraq by Bush the Elder, celebrating the end of "America's Vietnam syndrome." Europeans also supported former President Clinton's invasion of Yugoslavia, bringing NATO into the operation. The first shot ever fired in anger by NATO troops were in Yugoslavia. Bilderberg had made NATO, effectively, the UN's standing army.

BILDERBERG NEWSWORTHY: Above Etienne Davignon, honorary chairman of Bilderberg (left) and the powerful banker behind the push for Europe to adopt the euro, talked with Paul Wolfowitz, the former assistant secretary of defense and current head of the World Bank. Were they discussing global government and finance, or just exchanging soufflé recipes?

The British election results in 2005 pleased Europeans, who grudgingly supported Blair because of his commitment to the European Constitution (EC). Britons were to vote in 2006 on ratifying the EC. But they were happy that Blair's Labor Party's majority in Parliament shrank from 160 to 60 and there was speculation that he would be replaced as prime minister within two years.

To address the Mideast issue in 2005, Bilderberg brought together Eival Gilady and Natan Sharansky of Israel and Palestinian Ziad Abu-Amr.

Gilady was strategic adviser to Prime Minister Ariel Sharon. Sharansky was a former minister for Jerusalem and diaspora affairs. Sharansky is the Israeli extremist who 21st Century Republicans now model themselves after ideologically. Sharansky is also known to have helped craft President Bush's second inaugural address and has shaped the Republicans' push to "democratize" the world.

Abu-Amr is a member of the Palestinian Legislative Council, president of the Palestinian Council on Foreign Relation and professor of political science at Birzeit University.

This year, Bilderberg ordered Israel to keep its promise to withdraw from some settlements in the West Bank and Gaza. Also, they noted that Palestinians must be grateful for the portion of their territory they get back and not insist on pre-1967 borders.

"We must get along, despite our harsh differences, because we now live in an interdependent, global economy," said a lanky, gray-haired European in a discussion of "trans-Atlantic Relations." Poverty in Africa or South America "or wherever" is a "threat to all of us, anywhere in the world," he said.

Again, the United States was denounced for "not providing a fair share" of economic aid to poor countries. Again, Kissinger and Rockefeller, among other Americans, beamed and nodded approval. Bilderberg argued that, as a percentage of gross national product, Americans were "stingy."

Again, there was discussion of timing for a vote in the United Nations on establishing a direct global tax by imposing a 10-cents-a-barrel levy on oil at the well-head. This was important to the Bilderberg goal of establishing the UN as a formal world government. Such a direct tax on individuals is symbolically important.

Bilderberg's global tax proposal had been pending before the UN for three years but the issue had been blacked out by the Bilderberg-controlled U.S. media.

Said one Bilderberger of the pending UN tax: "Let the tax pass the UN with absolutely no publicity. Talk with the [news] boys in

2005—Rottach-Egern, Germany: A line of "polizei" vans arrived on the grounds of the Bilderberg conference. German security was in full force that year, as concerns over terrorism figured prominently. Among other subjects, Bilderbergers were after a global tax on oil. This has been an important goal of the world shadow government as a step toward world government.

---

advance and warn them about triggering right-wing hysteria. People won't even notice that fraction of a penny per gallon. When people do become aware, perhaps in three years, they'll simply say 'ain't that sumphin.' "

Other topics of discussion this year included "China and energy," "Russia's role in the world," "economic liberation" and U.S. Social Security "reform." Bilderberg's interest in how the United States deals with Social Security remains unclear. China's demand for oil had increased dramatically in recent years, contributing to the current $50 price per barrel. Bilderbergers debated whether a proposed pipeline should move oil to Japan or China from Russia.

Bilderbergers were downcast when word came that some Senate Democrats, in May 2005, who had voted for "free" trade bills in the past, were threatening to kill the Central America Free Trade Agreement (CAFTA) because of insufficient worker protections. CAFTA is a crucial step in expanding NAFTA into the Free Trade Area of the Americas.

Bilderberg Found

In 2005 European Bilderberg hunters found the hiding place of this secretive cabal at a posh resort in this charming little city 40 miles from Munich.

Three times the Dorint told AFP they were fully booked—but that Bilderberg was not there. All but Bilderberg participants and their staffs, wives or, in some cases, someone else's wife, will be required to leave. The hotel staff will be warned to reveal nothing of what they see and hear.

Cat & Mouse

It's an annual ritual: For the record, I ask the same female Bilderberg staffer for a list of participants and the agenda but is refused. At the same moment, this time, she screamed at freelance photographer Danny Estulin to stop taking pictures. He obligingly took her arm-waving photo. But the fun continued.

As a huge luxury bus unloaded platoons of Bilderberg security—dark suits and ties—a young man dressed like a college boy on vacation approached me and identified himself as "U.S. security." He said he was not allowed to give his name or agency.

Doing my duty as a citizen, I explained that public officials from the United States who participate in secret meetings with private citizens to make public policy are committing criminal acts.

He pointed out that then-first lady Hillary Clinton gathered a group of federal bureaucrats and "experts" from the private sector behind closed doors to develop a plan to reform the nation's health system. U.S. District Judge Royce Lamberth denounced Mrs.

2005—Rottach-Egern, Germany: The luxurious Dorint Sofitel hotel on the Tegernsee lake, approximately 30 miles outside of Munich. It is a popular Bavarian resort town, famous for its golf courses and food.

Clinton, saying she had violated the law, and levied a criminal fine.

The security man said he remembered the case but lacks jurisdiction to arrest U.S. officials in Germany.

"I understand," I said. "But you could have arrested Secretary of Defense Donald Rumsfeld and others three years ago when Bilderberg met in Chantilly, Va. I will tell you the next time Bilderberg meets in the United States and I'll carry your handcuffs."

The officer smiled. He was unable to identify himself but AFP can: He is Special Agent Robert Harvey of the Protective Services unit of the Army's Criminal Investigation Command at Ft. Belvoir, Va.

Security was massive. After the platoons of Bilderberg necktied security men unloaded, and with numerous uniformed local police already on patrol, five buses filled with German police in riot gear arrived. Most disappeared inside the Dorint, never to be seen again. In addition to U.S. Secret Service, the Mossad was also on hand, according to a report by a German official.

AFTERWORD
BY WILLIS A. CARTO

Introduction to Afterword by Jim Tucker

Had it not been for Willis A. Carto, who hired me as editor of *The Spotlight* and then put me on the track of Bilderberg, I would probably—almost assuredly—never have heard the word "Bilderberg."

Having had the opportunity, through Carto's good offices as founder of Liberty Lobby, publisher of *The Spotlight*, to begin what ultimately proved to be a generation of world-wide Bilderberg-hunting, I was able to bring news about Bilderberg to literally millions of folks who would like myself have otherwise remained in the dark about these globalist schemers.

In consideration of Willis Carto's central part in unmasking Bilderberg, it seems appropriate to close this volume with a commentary from Willis himself: his reflections upon what Bilderberg means to all who care about our world's future.

With all humility, conscious of the warm praise Willis imparts for my efforts, I thus turn these pages over to Mr. Carto for a final word.

hat you have suspected for years—that a conspiracy of international plutocrats is out to get you—is proven by this book.

Jim Tucker deserves the highest praise for his amazing persistence, year after year, in tracking down this coven of carnivores, reporting on their secret activities in the only newspapers in America with the guts to use his dispatches, first *The Spotlight* and then in *American Free Press*.

And in part due to *The Spotlight*'s effort to expose Bilderberg that our newspaper was illegally shut down by a corrupt federal judge acting on behalf of conspirators with ties to the internationalist elite. But *American Free Press* has picked up and kept Jim Tucker's Bilderberg reportage alive.

From the unique and hitherto-hidden facts presented in Jim's book we learn:

• There is in fact a highly organized conspiracy between influential politicians and bankers to give each more of what they crave, power and money;

• That both of these have to be contributed by you and millions of other deluded taxpayers and voters;

• That the conspiracy includes bringing down all national governments, and, by fraud and bribery, substituting a world government;

• That the consumers, taxpayers and voters are victimized by their so-called "free press," which is literally part of the conspiracy;

• That wars are started to advance the interests of these acolytes of evil who routinely send thousands of deceived young men to die while they pocket the wages of sin;

• That they write the history books to justify their crimes and to pave the way for future profitable wars and an ultimate world government.

This last point is also the reason for the birth of Revisionist (authentic) history after World War I.

Dedicated historians all—these men and others dared to look into the real facts about the events that led to that war:

• Dr. Harry Elmer Barnes	• Prof. Charles A. Beard,
• Prof. Sidney B. Fay	• C. Hartley Grattan,
• Henry Wickham Steed	• Sisley Huddleston,
• Edwin D. Schoonmaker	• H.C. Peterson,
• William Seaver Woods	• Francis Nielson

And this list is hardly complete. However, after World War II, many of these distinguished names continued in their work which was supplemented by the efforts of many other Revisionists, including:

• Dr. James J. Martin	• John Toland,
• Benjamin Colby	• Prof. Charles Callan Tansill,
• Dr. David Hoggan	• Dr. Arthur Butz,
• George N. Crocker	• Capt. Russell Grenfell,
• Gen. Albert C. Wedemeyer	• Dr. Austin J. App,
• Ralph Franklin Keeling	• Dr. Wilhelm Staeglich,
• John Sack	• Alfred M. deZayas,

- Carlos Porter
- John T. Flynn
- Lawrence R. Brown
- Francis P. Yockey
- William Henry Chamberlin
- David Irving
- Michel Sturdza
- Sen. William Langer
- Col. Charles A. Lindbergh
- Prof. Wayne S. Cole
- Justus Doenecke

- Louis FitzGibbon,
- Lawrence Dennis,
- William Gayley Simpson,
- Edward Delaney,
- Arthur Ponsonby,
- A.J.P. Taylor,
- Conrad K. Grieb,
- Sen. Burton K. Wheeler,
- F.J.P. Veale,
- Chesley Manly,
- Boake Carter

This is to name but a few.

Now, you ask—and rightly so—why I've burdened you with this list of distinguished historians, many of whose names you may not know. It is for this reason: When the complete and authentic history of the 20th century is finally written, no serious scholar can recount that panorama without referring to the remarkable work of one man, the courageous journalist, Jim Tucker, who was on the scene to record, first-hand, the secret dealings of those behind-the-scenes intriguers—who call themselves "Bilderberg"—who were ultimately responsible for making history—hidden history—happen as it did during the 20th century, and beyond.

No sane person with the national interests of the United States and the personal welfare of every man woman and child in mind can fail to see at this time—the year 2005—that American intervention into the two European wars of 1914 and 1939 have been unmitigated disasters, setting this country on a downward spiral in every aspect: economic, monetary, cultural, moral, racial and political. The ongoing debacle in Iraq is just part and parcel of the tragedy.

Thus, readers will judge Jim Tucker's work against this sordid backdrop, as the outline of the criminal conspiracy which has guided America's foreign and domestic policies becomes tragically clear.

—WILLIS A. CARTO
Washington, D.C., July 2005

APPENDIX 1

Sample Lists of Attendees

Bilderberg Participants 1996

The following is the official list of participants who attended the 1996 Bilderberg Conference, held May 20 to June 2 at the CIBC Leadership Centre in Toronto, Canada.

Chairman: Carrington, Peter, Former Chairman of the Board, Christie's International plc; Former Secretary General, NATO, Great Britain
Honorary Secretary General for Europe and Canada: Halberstadt, Victor, Professor of Public Economics, Leiden University, Netherlands
Honorary Secretary General for U.S.A.: Yost, Casimir A., Director, Institute for the Study of Diplomacy, School of Foreign Service, Georgetown University, Washington D.C., USA

Agnelli, Giovanni, Honorary Chairman, Fiat S.p.A., Italy
Ahtisaari, Martti, President of the Republic of Finland, Finland
Allaire, Paul A., Chairman, Xerox Corporation, USA
Andreas, Dwayne, Chairman, Archer-Daniels-Midland Company, USA
Aslund, Anders, Senior Associate, Carnegie Endowment for International Peace, Sweden
Axworthy, Lloyd, Minister for Foreign Affairs, Canada
Balsemao, Francisco, Pinto Professor of Communication Science, New University, Lisbon, Portugal
Barnevik, Percy, President and Chief Executive Officer, ABB Asca Brown Boveri Ltd., Sweden
Bentsen, Lloyd M., Former Secretary of the Treasury; Partner, Verner Liipferi Bernhard McPherson and Hand, Chartered, USA
Bernabe, Franco, Managing Director and CEO, Ente Nazionale Idrocarburi, Italy
Bertram, Christoph, Diplomatic Correspondent, *Die Zeit*; Former Director International Institute for Strategic Studies, Germany
Beyazit, Selahaltin, Director of Companies, Turkey
Bildt, Carl, The High Representative, International
Black, Conrad M., Chairman, *The Telegraph* plc, Canada
Bolkestein, Frits, Parliamentary Leader VVD (Liberal Party), Netherlands
Bottelier, Pieter P., Chief of Mission, The World Bank, Resident Mission in China, International
Bryan, John H., Chairman and CEO, Sara Lee Corporation, USA
USA Buckley, Jr., William F., Editor-at-Large, *National Review,* USA
Carras, Costa, Director of Companies, Greece
Cartellieri, Ulrich, Member of the Board, Deutsche Bank, A.G., Germany
Carvajal Urquijo, Jaime, Chairman and General Manager, Iberfomento, Spain
Chretien, Jean, Prime Minister, Canada
Collomb, Bertrand, Chairman and CEO, Lafarge, France
Corzine, Jon S., Senior Partner and Chairman, Goldman Sachs & Co., USA
Cotti, Flavio, Minister for Foreign Affairs, Switzerland
Dam, Kenneth W. Max, Pam Professor of American and Foreign Law, The University of Chicago Law School, USA
David, George, Chairman, Hellenic Bottling Company S.A., Greece
Davignon, Etienne, Executive Chairman, Societe Generale de Belgique; Former Vice Chairman of the Commission of the European Communities, Belgium
Drouin, Marie-Josee, Executive Director, Hudson Institute of Canada, Canada
Eaton, Fredrik S., Chairman, Executive Committee, Eaton's of Canada, Canada
Ellemann-Jensen, Uffe, Member of Parliament, Denmark
Ercel, Gazi, Governor, Central Bank of Turkey, Turkey
Feldstein, Martin S., President, National Bureau of Economic Research, USA
Fischer, Stanley, First Deputy Managing Director, International Monetary Fund, International
Flood, A.L., Chairman, Canadian Imperial Bank of Commerce, Canada
Freeman, Jr., Chas W., Former Assistant Secretary of Defense for International Security; Chairman of the Board, Projects International Associates, Inc., USA
Garton Ash, Timothy, Fellow of St. Antony's College, Oxford, Great Britain
Gigot, Paul, Washington Columnist, *The Wall Street Journal,* USA

Gonensay, Emre, Minister for Foreign Affairs, Turkey
Gotlieb, Allan E., Former Ambassador to the United States of America, Canada
Griffin, Anthony G.S., Honorary Chairman and Director, Guardian Group, Canada
Harris, Michael, Premier of Ontario, Canada
Haussmann, Helmut, Member of Parliament, Free Democratic Party, Germany
Hoegh, Westye, Chairman of the Board, Leif Hoegh & Co. A.S.A.; Former President, Norwegian Shipowners' Association, Norway
Holbrooke, Richard, Former Assistant Secretary for European Affairs, USA
Huyghebaert, Jan, Chairman, Almanij-Krediet-bank Group, Belgium
Iloniemi, Jaakko, Managing Director, Centre for Finnish Business and Policy Studies; Former Ambassador to the United States of America, Finland
Job, Peter, Chief Executive, Reuters Holding PLC, Great Britain
Jordan, Jr., Vernon E., Senior Partner, Akin, Gump, Strauss, Hauer & Feld, LLP (Attorneys-at-Law), USA
Jospin, Lionel, First Secretary of the Socialist Party; Former Ministre d'Etat, France
Karner, Dietrich, Chairman of the Managing Board, Erste Allgemeine-Generali Aktiengesellschaft, Austria
Kissinger, Henry R., Former Secretary of State; Chairman, Kissinger Associates, Inc., USA
Knight, Andrew, Non Executive Director, News Corporation, Great Britain
Kohnstamm, Max, Senior Fellow, European Policy Centre, Brussels; Former Secretary General, Action Committee for Europe; Former President, European University Institute, International
Kothbauer, Max, Deputy Chairman, Creditanstalt-Bankverein, Ausria
Kravis, Henry R., Founding Partner, Kohlberg Kravis Roberts & Co., USA
Lauk, Kurt, Member of the Board, Veba A.G., Germany
Lellouche, Pierre, Foreign Affairs spokesman, Rassemblement pour la Republique, France
Levy Lang, Andre, Chairman of the Board of Management, Banque Paribas, France
Lord, Winston, Assistant Secretary for East Asian and Pacific Affairs, USA
Marante, Margarida, TV Journalist, Portugal
Martin, Paul, Minister of Finance, Canada
Matlock, Jack F., Former U.S. Ambassador to the U.S.S.R., USA
Maystadt, Philippe, Vice-Prime Minister, Minister of Finance and Foreign Trade, Belgium
McHenry, Donald F., Research Professor of Diplomacy and Int'l Affairs, Georgetown University, USA
Melkert, Ad P.W., Minister for Social Affairs and Employment, Netherlands
Monks, John, General Secretary, Trades Union Congress (TUC), Great Britain
Montbrial, Thierry de, Director, French Institute of Int'l Relations; Professor of Economics, Ecole Polytechnique, France
Monti, Mario, Commissioner, European Communities, International
Her Majesty the Queen of the Netherlands
Nunn, Sam, Senator (D-Ga.), USA
Olechowski, Andrzej, Chairman of the Supervisory Board, Bank Handlowy W. Warszawie S.A.; Former Minister for Foreign Affairs, Poland
Ostry, Sylvia, Chairman, Centre for International Studies, University of Toronto, Canada
Pangalos, Theodoros G., Minister for Foreign Affairs, Greece
Perry, William J., Secretary of Defense, USA
Petersen, Jan, Parliamentary Leader, Conservative Party, Norway
Podhoretz, Norman, Editor, *Commentary,* USA
Pury, David de, Director of Companies; Former Co-Chairman of the ABB Group and former Ambassador for Trade Agreements, Switzerland
Rifkind, Malcolm, Foreign Secretary, Great Britain
Robertson, Simon, Chairman, Kleinwort Benson Group plc, Great Britain
Rockefeller, David, Chairman, Chase Manhattan Bank International Advisory Committee, USA
Rogers, Edward S., President and CEO, Rogers Communications, Inc, Canada.
Roll, Eric, Senior Advisor, SBC Warburg, Great Britain
Ruggiero, Renato, Director General, World Trade Organization; Former Minister of Trade, International
Sahlin, Mona, Member of Parliament, Sweden
Schrempp, Jurgen F., Chairman of the Board of Management, Daimler-Benz AG, Germany
Schwab, Klaus, President, World Economic Forum, International
Seidenfaden, Toger, Editor-in-Chief, Politiken A/S, Denmark
Sheinkman, Jack, Chairman of the Board, Amalgamated Bank, USA
Sommaruga, Cornelio, President, International Committee of the Red Cross, Switzerland
Soros, George, President, Soros Fund Management, USA
Her Majesty the Queen of Spain
Stephanopoulos, George, Senior Advisor to the President, USA
Strubo, Jurgen, CEO, BASF Aktiengesellschaft, Germany
Suranyi, Gyorgy, President, National Bank of Hungary, Hungary

Sutherland, Peter D., Chairman and Managing Director, Goldman Sachs International; Former Director General, GATT and WTO, Ireland
Tabaksblat, Morris, Chairman of the Board, Unilever N.V., Netherlands
Taylor, J. Martin, Chief Executive, Barclays Bank plc, Great Britain
Trotman, Alexander J., Chairman, Ford Motor Company, USA
Veltroni, Valter, Editor, L'Unita, Italy
Vitorino, Antonio, Deputy Prime Minister and Minister of Defense, Portugal
Voscherau, Henning, Mayor of Hamburg, Germany
Vranitzky, Franz, Federal Chancellor, Austria
Vuursteen, Karel, Chairman of the Board, Heineken N.V., Netherlands
Wallenberg, Marcus, Executive Vice President, Investor AB, Sweden
Weiss, Stanley A., Chairman, Business Executives for National Security, Inc., USA
Whitehead, John C., Former Deputy Secretary of State, USA
Wilson, L.R., Chairman, President and CEO, BCE Inc., Canada
Wolfensohn, James D., President, The World Bank; Former President and CEO, James D. Wolfensohn, Inc., International
Wolff von Amerongen, Otto, Chairman and CEO of Otto Wolff GmbH, Germany
Wolfowitz, Paul Dean, Nitze School of Advanced International Studies; Former Under Secretary of Defense for Policy, USA
Yanez-Barnuovo, Juan A., Permanent Representative of Spain to the UN, Spain
Observers
Orange, H.R.H. the Prince of, Netherlands
Philippe, H.R.H., Prince, Belgium

Rapporteurs
Micklethwait, John, Business Editor, *The Economist,* Great Britain
Victor, Alice, Executive Assistant, Rockefeller Financial Services, Inc., USA

Bilderberg Participants 1998

The following is the official list of participants who attended the May 14-17, 1998, Bilderberg meeting at the Turnberry Hotel in Ayrshire, Scotland. The list, marked "confidential; not for circulation," is the official guest list. Some of the attendees indicated cannot be confirmed.

Chairman: Peter Carrington, former chairman of the board, Christie's International plc; former secretary-general, NATO, Great Britain
Honorary Secretary General: Victor Halberstadt, professor of public economies, Leiden University., Netherlands
Alphabetical list of attendees:
Agnelli, Giovanni, honorary chairman, Fiat S.P.A., Italy
Allaire, Paul A., chairman, Xerox Corporation., USA
Almunia Amann, Joaquin, secretary-general, Socialist Party., Spain
Balsemao, Francisco Pinto, professor of communication science, New University, Lisbon; chairman, IMPRESA, S.G.P.S., former prime minister., Portugal
Barnevik, Percy, chairman, (AB)B Asea Brown Boveri Ltd., Sweden
Bayar, Ugur, chairman, Privatization Administration, Turkey.
Bernabe, Franco, managing director, ENI S.p.A., Italy
Bertram, Christoph director, Foundation Science and Policy; former diplomatic correspondent *Die Zeit.,* Germany
Beugel, Ernst H. van der, emeritus professor of international relations, Leiden University; former honorary secretary-general of Bilderberg meetings for Europe and Canada., Netherlands
Black, Conrad M. chairman, *The Telegraph* plc, Canada.
Bonino, Emma, member of the European Commission, International
Brittan, Leon, vice president of the European Commission, International
Browne, E. John P., group chief executive, British Petroleum Company plc, Great Britain
Bruton, John, leader of Fine Gael, Ireland
Buchanan, Robin W.T., senior partner, Bain & Company Inc. UK, Great Britain
Burda, Hubert, chairman, Burda Media, Germany
Carvajal Urquijo, Jaime, chairman, Dresdner Kleinwort Benson S.A. Spain.
Cavalchini, Luigi G., permanent representative to the European Union, Italy
Cem, Ismail (TR), minister for foreign affairs, Turkey
Chretien, Raymond A.J., ambassador to the U.S., Canada

224 Bilderberg Diary

Chubais, Anatoli B., former first vice prime minister, chairman, RAO EES., Russia
Clarke, Kenneth, member of Parliament, Great Britain
Collomb, Bertrand, chairman and CEO, Lafarge, France
Courtis, Kenneth S., first vice president, research department, Deutsche Bank Asia Pacific., International
Coutinho, Vasco Pereira, chairman, IPC Holding, France
Crockett, Andrew, general manager, Bank for International Settlements, International
David, George A., chairman of the board, Hellenic Bottling Company S.A., Greece
Davignon, Etienne, executive chairman, Societe Generale de Belgique; former vice chairman of the Commission of the European Communities, Belgium
Deutch, John M., institute professor, Massachusetts Institute of Technology, Department of Chemistry; former director general, Central Intelligence Agency; former deputy secretary of defense, USA
Dion, Stephane, Queen's Privy Council for Canada and minister of intergovernmental affairs, Canada
Donilon, Thomas E., partner, O'Melveny & Myers; former assistant secretary of state and chief of staff, U.S. Department of State, USA
Ellemann-Jensen, Uffe, chairman, Liberal Party, Denmark
Engelen-Kefar, Ursula, deputy chairman of the Board of Management, Deutscher Gewerkschaftsbund, DGB, Germany
Feldstein, Martin S., president and CEO, National Bureau of Economic Research, Inc., USA
Fischer, Stanley, first deputy managing director, International Monetary Fund, International
Forester, Lynn, president and CEO, FirstMark Holdings, Inc., USA
Godiesh, Orit, chairman of the board, Bain & Company, Inc., USA
Gergorin, Jean-Louis, member of the board of directory, Matra Hachette, France
Gezgin Eris, Meral, president IKV (Economic Development Foundation), Turkey
Goossens, John J, president and CEO, Belgacom., Belgium
Grierson, Ronald, former vice chairman, GEC, Great Britain
Grossman, Marc, assistant secretary, U.S. Department of State, USA
Guetta, Bernard, editor-in-chief, Le Nouvel Observateur., France
Hague, William, leader of the opposition (Conservative Party), Great Britain
Hannay, David, Prime Minister's personal envoy for Turkey; former permanent representative to the United Nations., Great Britain
Hoagland, Jim, associate editor, The Washington Post, USA
Hoegh, Westye, chairman of the board, Leif Hoegh & Co. ASA; former president, Norwegian Shipowners' Association., Norway
Hoeven, Cess H. van der, president, Royal Ahold, Netherlands.
Hoge, Jr., James F., editor, Foreign Affairs., USA
Hogg, Christopher chairman, Reuters Group plc., Great Britain
Holbrooks, Richard C., former assistant secretary for European affairs; vice chairman, CS First Boston., USA
Horta e Costa, Miguel, vice president, Portugal Telecom, Portugal
Ischinger, Wolfgang, political director, Foreign Office, Germany
Issing, Otmar, member of the board, Deutsche Bundesbank, Germany
Jenkins, Michael, vice chairman, Dresdner Kleinwort Benson, Great Britain
Johnson, James A. chairman and CEO, Fannie Mae, USA
Jordan, Vernon E. Jr., senior partner, Akin, Gump, Strouse, Hauer & Feld, LLP, USA
Kaletsky, Anatole, associate editor, The Times, Great Britain
Karamanlis, Koetas A., leader of the opposition, Great Britain
Kirac, Suna, vice chairman of the board, Koc Holding A.S, Turkey
Kissinger, Henry A., former secretary of state; chairman, Kissinger Associates, Inc., USA
Kohnstamm, Max, senior consultant, the European Policy Center, International
Kopper, Hilmar, chairman of the supervisory board, Deutsche Bank A.G., Germany
Korteweg, Pieter, president and CEO, Robeco Group, Netherlands
Kovanda, Karel, head of mission of the Czech Republic to NATO and the WEU, Czechoslovakia
Kravis, Henry R., founding partner, Kohlberg Kravis Roberts & Co., USA
Kravis, Marie-Josee, senior fellow, Hudson Institute, Inc., USA
Leschly, Jan CEO, SmithKline Beecham plc., USA
Levy-Lang, Andre, chairman of the board of management, Paribas, France
Lipponen, Paavo, prime minister, Finland
Lykketoft, Mogens, minister of finance, Denmark
MacMillan, Margaret O., editor, International Journal, Canadian Institute of International Affairs, University of Toronto, Canada
Manning, Preston, leader of the Reform Party, Canada
Masera, Rainer S., director general, I.M.I. S.p.A., Italy
Mathews, Jessica Tuchman, president, Carneigie Endowment for International Peace, USA

McDonough, William J., president, Federal Reserve bank of New York, USA
Nass, Matthias (D), deputy editor, *Die Zeit*, Germany
Netherlands' Queen Beatrice, Netherlands
Olechowski, Andrzej, chairman, Central Europe Trust, Poland.
Ollila, Jorma, president and CEO, Nokia Corporation, Finland
Padoa-Schioppa, Tommaso, chairman, CONSOB, Italy
Papandreou, George A., Alternate Minister for Foreign Affairs, Greece
Prendergast, Kieran, under secretary-general for political affairs, United Nations, International
Prestowitz, Clyde V., president, Economic Strategy Institute, USA
Puhringer, Othmar, chairman of the managing board, VA-Technologie AG, Austria
Purves, William, group chairman, HSBC Holdings plc., Great Britain
Pury, David de, chairman, de Pury Pictet Turrettini & Co. Ltd., Switzerland
Randa, Gerhard, chairman and the managing board, Bank of Austria, Austria
Rhodes, William R., vice chairman, Citibank, N.A., USA
Robertson, George, secretary of state for defense, Great Britain
Rockefeller, David, chairman, Chase Manhattan Bank International Advisory Committee, USA
Rodriguez Inciarte, Matias, vice chairman, Banco de Santander, Spain
Roll, Eric, senior adviser, SBC Warburg Dillon Read, Great Britain
Rothschild, Evelyn de, chairman, N.M. Rothschild & Sons, Great Britain
Schrempp, Jurgen E., chairman of the board of management, Daimler-Benz A.G., Germany
Seidenfaden, Toger, editor in chief, Politiken A/S, Denmark
Siniscalco, Domenico, professor of economics; director of Fendazione ENI Enrico Mattei., Italy
Solana Madarings, Javier, secretary general, NATO, International
Sousa, Marcelo Robelo de, leader of the PSD Party, Portugal
Storvik, Kjell, governor, Bank of Norway, Norway
Suchocka, Hanna, minister of justice, Poland
Summers, Lawrence H., deputy secretary for international affairs, U.S. Department of the Treasury, USA
Sutherland, Peter D., chairman, Goldman Sachs International; chairman, British Petroleum Company plc., Ireland
Taylor, J. Martin, group chief executive, Barclays plc., Great Britain
Thoman, G. Richard, president and CEO, Xerox Corporation, USA
Udgaard, Nils M., foreign editor, *Aftemposten.*, Norway
Vasella, Daniel, CEO, Novartis, Switzerland
Vink, Lodewijk J.R. de, president and CEO, Warner-Lambert Company, USA.
Virkkunen, Janne, senior editor-in-chief, *Helsingin Sanomat.*, Finland
Vits, Mia de, general secretary, ABVV-FGTB, Belgium
Vranitzky, Franz, former federal chancellor, Austria
Vries, Gijs M. de, leader of the Liberal Group, European Parliament, International
Wallenberg, Jacob, chairman of the board, Skandinaviska Enskilda Banken, Sweden
Whitman, Christine Todd, governor of New Jersey, USA
Wissmann, Matthias, federal minister for transport, Germany
Wolfansohn, James D., president, the World Bank, International
Wolff von Amarongen, Otto, chairman and CEO of Otto Wolff GmbH, Germany
Wolfowitz, Paul, dean, Nitze School of Advanced International Studies; former under secretary of defense for policy, USA
Yost, Casimir A., directory, Institute for the Study of Diplomacy, School of Foreign Service, Georgetown University, Washington, USA
Rapporteurs:
Micklethwait, John, business editor, *The Economist*, Great Britain
Wooldridge, Adrian, foreign correspondent, *The Economist*, Great Britain

Bilderberg Participants 2002

The following is the official list of participants who attended the 2002 Bilderberg Conference, held May 20 to June 2 at the Westfields Marriot in Chantilly, Va.

Honorary Chairman: Davignon, Etienne, Vice Chairman, Société Générale de Belgique
Allaire, Paul A, Former Chairman and CEO, Xerox Corporation, USA
Armgard, Beatrix Wilhelmina, Queen of the Netherlands, Netherlands
Baillie, A. Charles, Chairman and CEO, TD Bank Financial Group, Canada
Balls, Edward, Chief Economic Advisor to the Treasury, United Kingdom
Balsemão, Francisco Pinto, Professor of Communication Science, New University, Lisbon; Chairman of

IMPRESA, S.G.P.S., Portugal
Belot, Jean de, Editor-in-Chief, Le Figaro, France
Bergsten, C. Fred, Director, Institute for International Economics, USA
Bernander, John G., Director General, Norwegian Broadcasting Corporation, Norway
Black, Conrad M, Chairman, Telegraph Group Ltd., Canada
Bolkestein, Frits, Commissioner, European Commission, International
Borges, Antonio, Vice Chairman and Managing Director, Goldman Sachs, Portugal
Boyd, Charles G., President and CEO, Business Executives for National Security, USA
Castries, Henri de, Chairman of the Board, AXA, France
Cebrián, Juan Luis, CEO, Prisa (El Pais), Spain
Collomb, Bertrand, Chairman and CEO, Lafarge, France
Couchepin, Pascal, Federal Councillor; Head of the Federal Department of Economic Affairs, Switzerland
Courtis, Kenneth S., serves on the International Research Council of the Center for International and
Strategic Studies, Canada
Dahrendorf, Ralf, Member, House of Lords; Former Warden, St. Antony's College, Oxford, Great Britain
Dam, Kenneth W., Deputy Secretary, US Department of Treasury, USA
David, George A., Chairman of the Board, Coca-Cola H.B.C. S.A. ., Greece
David-Weill, Michel A., Chairman, Lazard Frères & Co., USA
Dervis, Kemal, Minister of Economic Affairs, Turkey
Deutch, John M., Institute Professor, MIT, USA
Dinh, Viet D., Assistant Attorney General for Office of Policy Development, USA
Dodd, Christopher J., Senator, D. Connecticut, USA
Donilon, Thomas E., Executive Vice President, Fannie Mae, USA
Draghi, Mario, Vice Chairman and Managing Director, Goldman Sachs International [Chairman of the
Deputies of the Group of Ten, Bank of International Settlements], Italy
Eizenstat, Stuart, Covington & Burling, USA
Eldrup, Anders, Chairman of the Board of Directors, Danish Oil & Gas Consortium, Denmark
Feldstein, Martin S., President and CEO, National Bureau of Economic Research, USA
Ferreira, Elisa Guimarães, Member of Parliament, Former Minister of Planning, Portugal
Fischer, Franz, commissioner for agriculture and rural development, European Union
Foley, Thomas S., Partner, Akin, Gump, Strauss, Hauer & Feld, USA
Fortescue, Adrian, Director General, Justice and Internal Affairs, European Commission, International
Frum, David, American Enterprise Institute; Former Special Assistant to President Bush, Canada
Gergorin, Jean-Louis, Executive Vice President, Strategic Coordination, EADS, France
Gigot, Paul A., Editorial Page Editor, The Wall Street Journal, USA
Glickman, Dan, former sec. Of agriculture; former Rep. (D.-Kan.), USA
Graham, Donald E., Washington Post, USA
Greenspan, Alan, Chairman, Federal Reserve System, USA
Groenink, Rijkman W.J, Chairman of the Board, ABN AMRO Bank N.V., Netherlands
Gusenbauer, Alfred, Member of Parliament; Chairman, Social Democratic Party, Austria
Halberstadt, Victor, Professor of Economics, Leiden University; Former Honorary Secretary General of
Bilderberg Meetings, Netherlands
Hills, Carla A., Chairman and CEO, Hills & Company, International Consultants, USA
Hoagland, Jim, Associate Editor, The Washington Post, USA
Hubbard, Allan B., President, E&A Industries, USA
Hutchison, Kay Bailey, Senator (Republican, Texas), USA
Huyghebaert, Jan, Chairman, Almanij N.V., Belgium
Ischinger, Wolfgang, Ambassador to the US, Germany
James, Charles A., Assistant Attorney General for Antitrust, USA
Johansson, Leif, Volvo, Sweden
Johnson, James A., Vice Chairman, Perseus, L.L.C., USA
Jordan, Jr., Vernon E., Managing Director, Lazard Frères & Co. LLC, USA
Kissinger, Henry A., Chairman, Kissinger Associates, Inc., USA
Kist, Ewald, Chairman of the Board ING N.V., Netherlands
Kleisterlee, Gerard J., President and CEO, Royal Philips Electronics, Netherlands
Kopper, Hilmar, Chairman of the Supervisory Board, Deutsche Bank AG, Germany
Krauthammer, Charles, Columnist, The Washington Post, USA
Kravis, Henry R, Founding Partner, Kohlberg Kravis Roberts & Co., USA
Kravis, Marie-Josée, Senior Fellow, Hudson Institute Inc. ., USA
Kudelski, André, Chairman of the Board & CEO, Kudelski Group, China
LaFalce, John J., Congressman (Democrat, New York), USA
Lamy, Pascal, European commissioner, European Union
Leschly, Jan, Chairman & CEO, Care Capital LLC, USA

Lévy-Lang, André, Former Chairman, Paribas, France
Lewis, Bernard, professor of Mideast studies at Princeton University, USA
Lippens, Maurice, Chairman, Fortis, Belgium
Lipponen, Paavo, Prime Minister, Finland
MacMillan, Margareth, Dean of University of New Castle, United Kingdom
Mathews, Jessica T., President, Carnegie Endowment for International Peace., USA
McAuliffe, Terry, Chairman, Democratic National Committee, USA
McDonough, William J., President and CEO, Federal Reserve Bank of New York, USA
Miguel, Ram, Secretary of State for Foreign Affairs, Spain
Mitchell, Andrea, Chief Foreign Affairs Correspondent, NBC News, USA
Mo'si, Dominique, Deputy Director, French Institute of International Relations, France
Montbrial, Thierry de, Director, French Institute of International Relations, France
Moskow, Michael H., President, Federal Reserve Bank of Chicago., USA
Myklebust, Egil, Chairman, Norsk Hydro ASA, Norway
Ollia, Jorma, Chairman of the Board and CEO, Nokia Corporation, Finland
Özaydinl', Bulend, CEO, Koç Holding A.S., Turkey
Padgrotsky, Leif, trade minister, Sweden
Padoa-Schioppa, Tommaso, Member of the Executive Board, European Central Bank, International
Papahelas, Alexis, Foreign policy columnist. TO VIMA, Greece
Parisiliti, Andrew, Foreign Affairs advisor to Sen. Chuck Hagel (R-Neb.), USA
Pearl, Frank H., Chairman and CEO, Perseus, L.L.C., USA
Pehe, Jiri, former advisor to president, Czech Republic
Perle, Richard N., Resident Fellow, American Enterprise Institute for Public Policy Research, USA
Polenz, Ruprecht, Member of Parliament, CDU/CSU, Germany
Prestowitz, Jr., Clyde V., President, Economic Strategy Institute, USA
Prodi, Romano, President of the European Commission, Italy
Racicot, Mark, Chairman, Republican National Committee, USA
Raines, Franklin D., Chairman and CEO, Fannie Mae, USA
Randa, Gerhard, Chairman and CEO, Bank Austria AG, Austria
Rattner, Steven, Managing Principal, Quadrangle Group LLC, USA
Reisman, Heather, President and CEO, Indigo Books and Music Inc., Canada
Robertson, Lord George, Secretary-General of NATO, Scotland
Rockefeller, David, Member, JP Morgan International Council, USA
Rodriguez Inciarte, Mat'as, Executive Vice Chairman, Banco Santander Central Hispano, Spain
Roll, Eric, Senior Adviser, UBS Warburg Ltd., United Kingdom
Rose, Charlie, Producer, Rose Communications, USA
Roy, Olivier, University Professor and Researcher, CNRS, France
Rumsfeld, Donald H. Secretary of Defense, USA
Sanberk, Özdem, Director, Turkish Economic and Social Studies Foundation, Turkey
Schrempp, Jurgen E, Chairman of the Board of Management, DaimlerChrysler AG., Germany
Schulz, Ekkehard, Chairman, ThyssenKrupp AG, Germany
Schweitzer, Louis, Chairman and CEO, Renault S.A., France
Seidenfaden, Tøger, Editor-in-Chief, Politiken, Denmark
Seillière, Ernest-Antoine, Chairman and CEO, CGIP, France
Sheinkman, Jack, Chairman of the Board, Amalgamated Bank, USA
Shevtsova, Lilia, Senior Associate, Carnegie Moscow Center, Russia
Sieghart, Mary A, editorial writer for *Times of London*, United Kingdom
Siegman, Henry, Council on Foreign Relations, USA
Sofia, Queen of Spain
Soros, George, Chairman, Soros Fund Management, USA
Steinberg, James B, Vice President and Director, Foreign Policy Studies Program, USA
Stoltenberg, Jens, Leader of the Opposition (Social Democratic Party), Netherlands
Summers, Lawrence H., President, Harvard University, USA
Sutherland, Peter D, Chairman and Managing Director, Goldman Sachs International; Chairman BP
Amoco, Ireland
Taxell, Christoffer, President and CEO, Partek Oyj, Finland
Taylor, J. Martin, chairman WH Smith Group; Adviser, Goldman Sachs, United Kingdom
Thoman, G. Richard, Senior Advisor, Evercore Partners Inc., USA
Thornton, John L., President and co-CEO, The Goldman Sachs Group Inc., USA
Tiilikainen, Teija H, Director of Research, Centre for European Studies., Finland
Treschow, Michael, Chairman, Ericsson, Sweden
Trichet, Jean-Claude, Governor, Banque de France, France
Vasella, Daniel L, Chairman and CEO, Novartis AG, China

Vink, Lodewijk J. R. de, Chairman, Global Health Care Partners; Credit Suisse First, USA
Vranitzky, Franz. Former Federal Chancellor, Austria
Wallenberg, Jacob, Chairman of the Board, Skandinaviska Enskilda Banken, Sweden
Wallenberg, Marcus, CEO of Investor, Sweden
Whyte, Kenneth, Editor, *The National Post*, Canada
Williams, Gareth, Leader, House of Lords; Member of the Cabinet, United Kingdom
Wolfensohn, James D., President, The World Bank, Australia
Zumwinkel, Klaus, Chairman of the Board of Management, Deutsche Post AG, Denmark

2004 Partial List of Major Attendees

In 2004, no complete list of attendees could be obtained. However, a partial list was compiled thanks to sources inside Bilderberg. The following is the partial list of participants who attended the 2004 conference, held June 3 to June 6 at the Grand Hotel des Iles Borromees in Stresa, Italy.

Ackermann, Josef, Chairman, Deutsche Bank AG, Germany
Ambrosetti, Alfredo, Chairman, Abbrosetti Group, Italy
Babacan, Ali, Minister of Economic Affairs, Turkey
Balsemao, Francisco Pinto, Former PM, Portugal
Barnavie, Elie, Department of General History, Tel-Aviv University, Israel
Bernabe, Franco, Vice Chairman, Rothschild Europe, Italy
Beytout, Nicolas, Editor In Chief, Les Echos, France
Boot, Max, CFR, Features Editor, *Wall Street Journal*, USA
Borel, Daniel, Chairman, Logitech International S.A., Switzerland
Browne, John, Group Chief Executive, BP, Great Britain
Camus, Phillipe, CEO, European Aeronautic Defense & Space, France
Caracciolo, Lucio, Director, Limes Geopolitical Review, Italy
Castries, Henri de, Chairman, AXA Insurance, France
Cebrian, Juan Luis, CEO, PRISA, former Chairman, International Press Institute, Spain
Cemal, Hasan, Senior Columnist, *Milliyet* newspaper, Turkey
Clarke, Kenneth, Member of Parliament (Con.), Deputy Chairman, British American Tobacco, Great
Britain
Corzine, Jon S., Sen. (D-N.J.), USA
David, George A., Chairman, Coca-Cola Hellenic Bottling Co, Greece
Davignon, Etienne, Hon. Chairman, Belgium
Dehaene, Jean-Luc, Former Prime Minister, Mayor of Vilvoorde, Belgium
Dervis, Kemal, Parliament, former senior World Bank official, Turkey
Donilon, Thomas L., Vice-President, Fannie Mae, CFR, USA
Draghi, Mario, Goldman Sachs, Italy
Edwards, John, Senator (D. NC), USA
Feith, Douglas J., Undersecretary for Policy, Department of State, USA
Galateri, Gabriele, Chairman, Mediobanca, Italy
Gates, Bill, Microsoft Corp., USA
Gates, Melinda F., Co-Founder, Gates Foundation, wife of Bill Gates, USA
Geithner, Timothy F., President, Federal Reserve Bank of NY, USA
Giavazzi, Francesco, Prof. of Economics, Bocconi Univ.; adviser, World Bank and European Central
bank, Italy
Gleeson, Dermot, Chairman Allied Irish Bank Group, Ireland
Graham, Donald E., Chairman and CEO, Washington Post Company, USA
Haas, Richard N., President, CFR, former Director of Policy & Planning, State Department, USA
Halberstadt, Victor, Prof. of Economics, Leiden University, Netherlands
Hansen, Jean-Pierre, Chairman, Suez Tractabel SA, Belgium
Heikensten, Lars, Governor, Swedish Central Bank, Sweden
Holbrooke, Richard C., former Director, CFR, former Ass't Sec. of State, USA
Hubbard, Allen B., President E&A Industries, USA
Issacson, Walter, President and CEO, Aspen Institute, USA
Janow, Merit L., Professor, International Economic Law and Int'l Affairs, Columbia University, member
of appellate body, WTO, USA
Jordan, Vernon E., Senior Managing Dir., Lazard Freres & Co LLC, USA
Kagan, Robert, Senior Associate, Carnegie Endowment for Int'l Peace, USA
Kerr, John, Director, Shell, Rio Tinto and Scottish American Investment Trust, Great Britain
Kissinger Henry A., Chairman, Kissinger Associates Inc., USA
Koc, Mustafa V., Chairman, Koc Holdings AS, Turkey

Koenders, Bert (AG), Parliament, president, Parliamentary Network of the World Bank, Netherlands
Kovner, Bruce, Chairman, American Enterprise Institute, USA
Kravis, Henry R., Founding Partner, Kohlberg Kravis Roberts & Co., acquisitions financier, USA
Kravis, Marie Josee, Senior Fellow, Hudson Institute Inc., USA
Lehtomaki, Paula, Minister of Foreign Trade and Development, Finland
Lipponen, Paavo, Speaker of Parliament, Finland
Long, Yongtu, Secretary General, Boao forum for Asia, China
Luti, William J., Deputy Under Secretary of Defense for Near Eastern and South Asian Affairs, USA
Lynch, Kevin G., Deputy Minister, Department of Finance, Canada
Mathews, Jessica T., President, Carnegie Endowment, USA
McDonough, William J., former president, Federal Reserve N.Y., USA
McKenna, Frank, former premier of New Brunswick, Canada
Monti, Mario, Competition/Antitrust Commissioner, Euro. Comm., International
Mundie, Craig J., Microsoft Corp., USA
Naas, Matthias, Deputy Editor, *Die Zeit*, Germany
Beatrix HM Queen of the, Netherlands
Neville-Jones, Pauline, Chairman, Quineti Q, gov. of the BBC, former Chairman Joint Intel. Comm., UK
Nooyi, Indra K., President and CEO, PepsiCo Inc., USA
Ollila, Jorma, Chairman, Nokia Corporation, Finland
Padoa-Schioppa, Tommaso, Director, European Central Bank, International
Pantelides, Leonidas, Ambassador to Greece, Cyprus
Passera, Corrado, CEO, Banca Intesa SpA, Italy
Perle, Richard N., Resident Fellow, American Enterprise Institute, former Likud policy adviser, USA
Phillipe, HRH Prince, Belgium
Rachman, Gideon, Brussels Correspondent, *The Economist,* Great Britain
Reed, Ralph E., President, Century Strategies, former head of Christian Coalition, USA
Reisman, Heather, Pres. and CEO, Indigo Books and Music Inc., Canada
Riotta, Gianni, Editorialist, *Corriere della Serra*, Italy
Rockefeller, David, Member JP Morgan International Council, Chairman, Council of the Americas, USA
Ross, Dennis B., Director, The Washington Institute for Near East Policy, USA
Sandschneider, Eberhard, Director, Research Institute, German Society for Foreign Policy, Germany
Schilly, Otto, Minister of the Interior, Germany
Schnabel, Rockwell A., Ambassador to the EU, USA
Schrempp, Jurgen E., Chairman, DaimlerChrysler AG, Germany
Shevtsova, Lilia, Senior Associate. Carnegie Endowment for International Peace, Russia
Sikora, Slawomir, President and CEO, Citibank Handlowy, Poland
Siniscalo, Domenico, Director General Ministry of the Economy, Italy
Socrates, Jose, Member of Parliament, Portugal
Strmecki, Marin J., Smith Richardson Foundation, USA
Struye de Swielant, Dominique, Permanent representative of Belgium, NATO, Belgium
Sutherland, Peter D., Chairman, Goldman Sachs International, Ireland
Taylor, Martin, Honorary Secretary General, International Adviser, Goldman Sachs, International
Thornton, John L., Chairman, Brookings Institution, Professor, Tsinghua University, USA
Tremonti, Giulio, Minister of Economy and Finance, Italy
Trichet, Jean-Claude, President, European Central Bank, International
Veer, Jeroen van der, Chairman, Committee of Managing Directors, Royal Dutch/Shel, Netherlands
Wallenberg, Jacob, Chairman, SEB investments; Chairman, W Capital Management AB, Sweden
Weinberg, Peter, CEO, Goldman Sachs International Great Britain, USA
Wolf, Martin H., Associate Editor/Economic Commentator, *The Financial Times,* Great Britain
Wolfensohn, James D., President, The World Bank-International, USA
Wooldridge, Adrian D., Foreign Correspondent, *The Economis,* Great Britain
Yavlinsky, Grigory A., Member of Parliament, Russia
Yergin, Daniel, Chairman, Cambridge Energy Research Associates, USA
Zumwinkel, Klaus, Chairman, Deutche Post Worldnet AG; Chairman, Deutche Telecom, Germany

The Bilderberg Blackout

The following pages contain important documents gathered over the years by reporters and concerned citizens, who have worked tirelessly to expose the secretive nature of the meetings and an agenda dedicated to influencing public policies in favor of world government. Included in this section are articles by the first columnist to mention Bilderberg, a lengthy report buried in a congressional publication, documented claims of ignorance of Bilderberg by editors and government officials, and letters attacking this reporter. All serve to show the concerted effort to hide Bilderberg from the public eye, enforce a media blackout and mislead the public as to the true nature of Bilderberg.

Westbrook Pegler Exposes Bilderberg

PEGLER

Spooky Parley On Georgia Island

By WESTBROOK PEGLER
Copyright. 1957. King Features Syndicate, Inc.

SOMETHING very mysterious is going on when a strange assortment of 67 self-qualified, polyglot designers and arbiters of the economic and political fate of our western world go into a secret huddle on an island off Brunswick, Ga., and not a word gets into the popular press beyond a little routine AP story.

These gumshoe superstate architects and monetary schemers were drawn from all the NATO countries.

The fact of this weird conclave, as spooky as any midnight meeting of the Klux in a piney wood, was bound to get known to the' world eventually.

I got my first -word of it from a reader who happened onto St. Simon Island, Brunswick, on her way to West Palm Beach.

She wrote that the hotel on St. Simon was almost deserted, but that when she commented on this, the clerk said the place had been alive with mysterious characters a few days earlier and with Secret Service and FBI, too.

He Was There

I have not verified whether Secret Service and FBI were there, but I did brace Ralph McGill, the editor of the Atlanta Constitution, by long distance, and he put on a bland face and said why yes, he had been there but ves, he had been there but had not thought the occasion required him, as a journalist, to write anything.

Ralph said he divested himself of his journalistic nature for the conference and wanted me to treat his discussion confidentially.

But, after all, I was phoning him as reporter to get information, whereas he had made some mental and ethical arrangement with him-

self which allowed him to dejournalize himself for this extremely newsy meeting.

However, I did agree not to quote him and will leave the facts to your judgment.

Two Invited

McGill and Arthur Hays Sulzberger, the publisher of the New York Times, were the only journalists invited to this thing and I observed to Ralph that it was pretty dam funny that with so many thousands of reporters and professional opionarians in this country, this conference tagged only those two and no others and they suppressed the story.

Elsewhere I was told that Sulzberger flew down from New York in his own ship.

Senator Harry Byrd of Virginia, a statesman who certainly rates consultation in such a seminar, had not heard a word about it.

He and the Judiciary Committee's subcommittee on subversion were highly interested.

I keep emphasizing the secrecy because it was obviously planned that way.

Counsel Startled

Judge Robert Morris, the counsel for the subcommittee, had received side-long tips and he was startled when I was able to put in his hands further information which was verified by my talk with McGill.

I told Byrd and Morris and I am telling you now about a queer parallel between this thing and a conference on Jekyll Island, Ga., a similar retreat, way back in 1908 in which the currency of the United States and of the world was manipulated, to

what effect, whether for good or evil, opinions vary.

Senator Aldrich, of Rhode Island, called this one into being. He was the father of Winthrop Aldrich.

There have been many excited versions of that ancient hoe-down on Jekyll Island in 1908, but relatively few have ever heard of it at all. Byrd frankly admitted that he had not. Neither had Morris

But long ago, B. C. Forbes, the biographer of American big business, told the wild, weird truth in a book and his version stands undisputed to this day.

Secret Session

He wrote that Aldrich and a small, select group of American and European financiers, with a strong Kuhn-Loeb, Hamburg, representa-

tion, sneaked onto Jekyll Island and stayed a week in such secrecy that not even the servants knew who they were. They called one another by only their first names.

There were 68 on the roster for the recent meeting at St. Simon Island, but one who was there has told me that Ike's protege, Paul Hoffman, now of the UN, did not accept. Tom Dewey did.

And those present included the mysterious Gabriel Haugé, a "Lutheran lay minister, professor and economist," in the Wall Street Journal's description of the guy. He was there in the role of Eisenhower's "economic adviser." The Wall Street Journal said Haugé "helped teach Ike what to think."

---

12   S. F. CALL-BULLETIN   ☆☆   Fri., April 12, 1957

PEGLER

How Federal Reserve System Began

By WESTBROOK PEGLER
Copyright. 1957. King Features Syndicate, Inc.

THE MYSTERIOUS congress of American and European wiseguys at St. Simon Island, Brunswick, Ga., on February 15, 16 and 17 recalls irresistibly the secret, fateful deliberations of a similar and smaller but equally presumptuous group of self-acknowledged superintellects on nearby Jekyll Island off the Georgia coast in the spring of 1908.

This meeting was called by Senator Nelson W. Aldrich, of Rhode Island, whose family is now entwined with the Rockefeller clan.

It resulted in the adoption of the Federal Reserve System, whether for better or worse no man can say with finality.

The similarity of the secret meeting of 49 years ago and the recent whispering session is irresistible.

The late B. C. Forbes, editor of Forbes' magazine and for many years the biographer of giants of American finance and industry, wrote a disturbing account of the Jekyll Island conference which was published in a collection entitled "Men Who Are Making America" in 1917.

Few Americans of this time have heard of that weird meeting.

Through the courtesy of Mr. Forbes' son, Bruce, who still operates the Forbes financial publishing interests, I am able to present the gist and some of the graphic text of the elder Forbes' account, which still was news to the

---

Reproduced above is a portion of journalist Westbrook Pegler's 1957 article on Bilderberg. This is the very article Willis A. Carto read which motivated him to begin tracking the Bilderbergers. Pegler said: "Something very mysterious is going on when a strange assortment of 67 self-qualified, polyglot designers and arbiters of the economic and political fate of our western world go into a secret huddle on an island off Brunswick, Ga., and not a word gets into the popular press beyond a little routine AP story. These gumshoe superstate architects and monetary schemers were drawn from all the NATO countries. The fact of this weird conclave, as spooky as any midnight meeting of the Klux in a piny wood, was bound to get known to the world eventually."

No Such Thing as Bilderberg Exists

VOICE OF THE MOUNTAINS

P.O. BOX 2090   ASHEVILLE   ASHEVILLE NORTH CAROLINA 28802

CITIZEN-TIMES
PUBLISHING COMPANY

July 10, 1992

Dear Mrs.

Thank you for your letter. Apparently, the only publication
that has access to information on the so-called "Bilderbergs"
is The Spotlight.

To my knowledge, such an organization does not exist and a
media conspiracy to keep its existence a secret would be
ludicrous.

Sincerely,

Larry Pope
Executive Editor

Some supposedly "well-informed" newspaper editors don't even know what
Bilderberg is, or they feign ignorance at the behest of their Bilderberg masters.
The letter reproduced here is not an attempt at humor. The author of the letter,
Larry Pope, then the executive editor of the *Asheville Citizen-Times*, was respond-
ing to a letter writer's inquiry as to why the newspaper never reported on the activ-
ities of the Bilderberg Group.

Bilderberg in the Congressional Record

Congressional Record

United States
of America

PROCEEDINGS AND DEBATES OF THE 92^d CONGRESS, FIRST SESSION

| Vol. 117 | WASHINGTON, WEDNESDAY, SEPTEMBER 15, 1971 | No. 133 |

House of Representatives

CONGRESSIONAL RECORD — *Extensions of Remarks*   E 9615

BILDERBERG: THE COLD WAR INTERNATIONALE

HON. JOHN R. RARICK

OF LOUISIANA

IN THE HOUSE OF REPRESENTATIVES

Wednesday, September 15, 1971

Mr. RARICK. Mr. Speaker, on several occasions during recent months, I called the attention of our colleagues to activities of the Bilderbergers—an elite international group comprised of high Government officials, international financiers, businessmen and opinionmakers—see CONGRESSIONAL RECORD, E4016–8 of May 5, 1971, entitled "Bilderbergers' Woodstock Meeting;" H3701 to H3707 of May 10, 1971, entitled "U.S. Dollar Crisis—A Dividend of Internationalism;" E4979 to E4985 of May 24, 1971, entitled "Secret Bilderberg Meeting and the Logan Act;" and E7786 to E7787 of July 16, 1971, entitled "Bilderberg Case: Reply From U.S. Attorney General's Office."

This exclusive international aristocracy holds highly secretive meetings annually or more often in various countries. The limited information available about what transpires at these meetings reveals that they discuss matters of vital importance which affect the lives of all citizens. Presidential Adviser Henry Kissinger, who made a secret visit to Peking from July 9 to 11, 1971, and arranged for a Presidential visit to Red China, was reported to be in attendance at the most recent Bilderberg meeting held in Wood-

stock, Vt., April 23–25, 1971. The two points reportedly discussed at the Woodstock meeting were "the contribution of business in dealing with current problems of social instability" and "the possibility of a change of the American role in the world and its consequences."

Following these secret discussions, which are certainly not in keeping with the Western political tradition of "open covenants openly arrived at," the participants return to their respective countries with the general public left uninformed, notwithstanding the attendance of some news media representatives, of any of the recommendations and plans agreed upon as a result of the discussions—or for that matter even the occurence of the meeting itself.

Because the American people have a right to know of any projections for a change in America's role in the world and because Henry Kissinger and other Government officials and influential Americans met with high Government officials and other powerful foreign leaders, I sought to have more information about the recent Bilderberg meeting made public by raising the question to the U.S. Attorney General of a possible violation of the Logan Act by American participants and asked if the Justice Department anticipated taking any action in the matter.

The reply from the Justice Department, in effect, was that all of the elements constituting a violation of the Logan Act were present and that the Department contemplated no action but

Congressional Record

The public proceedings of each House of Congress, as reported by the Official Reporters thereof, are printed pursuant to directions of the Joint Committee on Printing as authorized by appropriate provisions of Title 44, United States Code, and published for each day that one or both Houses are in session, excepting very infrequent instances when two or more unusually small consecutive issues are printed at one time. ¶ The Congressional Record will be furnished by mail to subscribers, free of postage, for $3.75 per month, $45 per year, or 25 cents per copy, payable in advance. Remit check or money order, made payable to the Superintendent of Documents, directly to the Government Printing Office, Washington, D.C. 20402. ¶ Following each session of Congress, the daily Congressional Record is revised, printed, permanently bound and is sold by the Superintendent of Documents in individual parts or by sets. ¶ With the exception of copyrighted articles, there are no restrictions on the republication of material from the Congressional Record.

This entry in the *Congressional Record* of Sept. 15, 1971, from an outraged John R. Rarick (D-La.) puts Bilderberg in the official U.S. record. Rarick wanted to know why Bilderbergers were discussing matters of vital importance to American taxpayers but insisted on doing it in secret, and also why taxpayers were footing the bill for the travel expenses of U.S. public officials. The document was 10 pages long. The first page has been reproduced here.

Sen. Buckley Denies Bilderberg Exists

United States Senate

COMMITTEE ON
INTERIOR AND INSULAR AFFAIRS
WASHINGTON, D.C. 20510

July 12, 1974

R.O. Gorman
242-15 44 Avenue
Douglas Town, New York 11363

Dear Mr. Gorman:

Thank you and your family for your letter. Frankly, I don' subscribe to the theory that there exists an organization of international bankers called the Bilderbergers or that certain members of our government are involved in a conspiracy of its making.

I appreciate knowing your views.

Sincerely,

James L. Buckley

Although then-Sen. James L. Buckley (R-N.Y.) was quick to assure one of his constituents that the existence of Bilderberg was some sort of myth—a conspiracy theory—Buckley's own brother, ex-CIA man and much-promoted media personality William F. Buckley Jr., attended the 1975 Bilderberg meeting in Cesme, Turkey.

Ike Urges Staffer to Attend Bilderberg

THE WHITE HOUSE
WASHINGTON

March 11, 1955.

MEMORANDUM FOR

GABRIEL HAUGE

I understand that next week Prince Bernhard
is having a meeting at Barbizon, continuing
his exploration looking toward improving
European and American relations.

If personally you can fit such a trip into
your schedule, I suggest you find the money (govt)
and go to France.

D.D.E.

D.D.E.

On official White House stationery, President Dwight D. Eisenhower wrote a memorandum to his then-administrative assistant Gabriel Hauge, making reference to the upcoming Bilderberg meeting in Barbizon, France, in 1955. He does not refer to it as "Bilderberg" as the name had not yet been adopted by the group to describe their yearly gathering. Note Eisenhower urges Hauge to travel to the meeting and to "find the money." Next to that Ike adds in handwriting the abbreviation "govt," meaning Hauge should travel on the taxpayers' expense. Following the meeting Hauge gave Eisenhower a lengthy report on the proceedings but, as per Bilderberg requests, did not identify the participants, just their comments, supplied to Eisenhower "anonymously."

Maryland Taxpayers Quiz Their State Senator

Hon. Charles McC. Mathias
U.S. Senate

Dear Senator Mathias:

As your constituents, we have a question for you: What are you hiding? With all due respect we find it strange that you refuse to disclose any information concerning your trip to the Bilderberg meeting in Megeve, France, April 19-21, 1974.

We did notice the letter you sent to the Washington *Post* in which you claim to have promised you would keep the meeting contents confidential. But any questions sent you by Maryland constituents are totally ignored if they involve the Bilderberg meeting and we find that strange and disturbing.

Don't you feel that as a United States Senator you have an *obligation* to disclose fully your activities to Maryland voters?

Do you really believe that you can attend a meeting also attended by principals of foreign governments and consider yourself a "private citizen" and speak "off the record"?

You have indicated the State Department paid your fare to France. Who paid for your return trip?

Is it possible for us, your constituents, to know what subjects were discussed at the Hotel Mont d'Arbois, where the secret conferences were held?

Were any conclusions reached at the meeting? Isn't it logical for us to assume conclusions *were* reached and if we knew what those conclusions were we would not approve? Why else the secrecy?

We know that more than 100 of the world's richest and most powerful men attended this meeting. You are not an oil man, nor a banker, nor are you a billionaire. Most of those attending were. Obviously you were invited because you are a United States Senator. As a Senator your loyalty lies with your constituents, not to international bankers.

Or, do you feel your Senatorial oath of office is superseded by your oath to the Bilderbergers?

As your constituents, we want the answers to these questions.

Concerned
Maryland Voters

In this letter, concerned citizens in Maryland demanded to know why taxpayers had paid for Sen. Charles Mathias to attend a private, secret meeting of global elites. It is a violation of U.S. law for American officials to partake in gatherings at taxpayer expense without disclosing what was discussed. However, Mathias was never prosecuted for his attendance at the annual confab of the world shadow government.

Bilderberg Worries About Adverse Publicity

CARNEGIE ENDOWMENT FOR INTERNATIONAL PEACE
UNITED NATIONS PLAZA AT 46TH STREET   NEW YORK 17, NEW YORK   CABLE ADDRESS INTERPAX   OXFORD 7-3131

OFFICE OF THE PRESIDENT

June 19, 1962

Dear Gabe:

Thank you for sending me the copy of the Eastern Banker with the little note about the Bilderberg Meetings.

There have been a number of unfavorable stories, originally stemming I think from a Swedish newspaper account of the meeting of "multi-millionaires." The AP, in an instance of almost unparalleled irresponsibility, picked this up and the Times and Washington Post printed it. I have just now been shown a copy of an article in the London Observer for 3 June, which is not nearly so critical, although it does start out by speaking of "a curious conclave (that) just ended." It talks about Retinger and the Prince and mentions the Reston piece, so someone must have talked more than he should have.

Frankly, I am a bit concerned about this adverse publicity. It should be wonderful grist for Westbrook Pegler's and/or Fulton Lewis, Jr.'s mills.

The piece you sent is the first one that dignifies me by mentioning my name. But so it goes. I guess we will just have to ride this one out.

Sincerely yours,

Joseph E. Johnson

Gabriel Hauge, Esq.
Manufacturers Hanover Trust Co.
350 Park Avenue
New York, New York

In the rather intriguing letter reproduced above, longtime Bilderberg functionary Joseph E. Johnson, president of the Carnegie Endowment for International Peace, complains about "unfavorable" stories on Bilderberg that have appeared in the media. Johnson also comments that "someone must have talked more than he should have" and that he is a "bit concerned about this adverse publicity." In other words, a Bilderberg Group member had a big mouth and revealed too much.

Official Cover-Up or Unbelievable Ignorance?

DEPUTY ASSISTANT ATTORNEY GENERAL
OFFICE OF LEGAL COUNSEL

Department of Justice
Washington, D.C. 20530

APR 8 1975

Dear Ms. McArthur:

Your letter to the President of March 10, 1975, has been referred to this Office for reply, because no one in the White House has any information regarding "The Bilderburgers." Unfortunately, after some investigation, we have not been able to discover any information regarding "The Bilderburgers" either.

I am sorry I cannot be of more help.

Sincerely,

Mary C. Lawton
Deputy Assistant Attorney General
Office of Legal Counsel

Above, this letter from Mary C. Lawton, then deputy assistant attorney general in the Office of the Legal Counsel, was written to a supporter of *The Spotlight* newspaper who wrote for information on Bilderberg. In the letter Lawton denies any knowledge of Bilderberg or that anyone in the president's office had ever heard of Bilderberg.

First Bilderberger to Gain White House

GERALD R. FORD, JR.
FIFTH DISTRICT, MICHIGAN

WASHINGTON, D.C. ADDRESS:
HOUSE OF REPRESENTATIVES
WASHINGTON, D.C.

GRAND RAPIDS, MICHIGAN, ADDRESS:
425 CHERRY STREET SE.
GRAND RAPIDS 2, MICHIGAN

COMMITTEE ON APPROPRIATIONS

Congress of the United States
House of Representatives
Washington, D. C.

February 21, 1961

Mr. Gabriel Hauge
Chairman, Finance Committee
Manufacturers Trust Company
44 Wall Street
New York 15, New York

Dear Gabe:

Many thanks for your kind and thoughtful letter inquiring
whether or not it would be possible for me to accept an
invitation from H.R.H. Prince Bernhard of The Netherlands
to join the next meeting of the Bilderberg Group near Quebec
from April 21st to 23rd.

I am sure this would be a very wonderful and interesting experience and I certainly appreciate your kindness in thinking
of me. However, during the past few weeks our children have
been quite ill with scarlet fever. After they had almost
recovered, our youngest boy, Steve, had a recurrence which our
physician tells us could be very serious. As a result the
doctor has advised us to keep him very quiet for the next
several weeks.

Because of this and since my committee work and the legislative
program is particularly heavy during the latter part of April,
I feel that it would be unwise for me to make such a commitment.

I am most grateful for your invitation and certainly hope you
will keep me in mind for a meeting with the Bilderberg Group at
some future date.

Thank you again and warmest personal regards

Sincerely,

Gerald R. Ford, Jr., M. C.

ml

*P. S. When you are in Washington call + I can show it
pick me & . . . fully. J-*

In this letter, then-Congressman Jerry Ford of Michigan sends Gabriel Hauge his regrets about not being able to attend the 1961 Bilderberg meeting. No problem, however. Ford did attend the 1964 and 1966 Bilderberg meetings and by 1974 became the first Bilderberg Group member to achieve the U.S. presidency. In 1995, another Bilderberger, Bill Clinton, also gained the White House after attending the 1991 Bilderberg meeting in Baden-Baden, Germany.

Liberty Lobby Gave You the Lowdown

LIBERTY LOWDOWN

A Confidential Washington Report Supplied Only to LIBERTY LOBBY Pledgers

SECRET WORLD SUMMIT CONFERENCE: 1975

June 1975
Number 141

The 1975 conference of the mysterious Bilderberg Organization took place in Turkey, Apr. 25-27. A LIBERTY LOBBY reporter was on hand throughout this year's meeting, which in many ways was different from previous Bilderberg meetings* and marked a turning point in them.

The 1975 meeting took place against the background of the most massive exposure the Bilderbergers have ever suffered. In 1974 the meeting was at Megeve, France. A LIBERTY LOBBY reporter was there and although no news whatever of this important gathering was carried by either the Associated Press, United Press International or any newspaper in the U.S., LIBERTY LOBBY alerted millions of Americans to the facts through the media of its publications and radio program. Because of these efforts, numerous editors of daily newspapers asked AP and UPI about previous Bilderberg meetings and demanded coverage of later ones.

Finding themselves in the embarrassing position of having been caught in what had every appearance of a conspiracy to suppress important news, officials of both wire services made certain that a competent correspondent was on the scene at the 1975 meeting. Mr. John Lawton therefore represented UPI and Mrs. Emel Amil the AP.

LOCATION OF THE 1975 CONFERENCE

The 1975 meeting took place at Cesme (pronounced CHESS-ma), Turkey, a small village on a dead-end road 50 miles east of Izmir. The sole attraction of Cesme is its huge, new luxury hotel . . . amidst the area's contrasting poverty. This is the Golden Dolphin, located in Cesme because the Aegean Sea is pure and clear there, and the sun usually shines. Presumably the Bilderbergers found other attractions beckoning from Cesme, however--its location marks it as one of the more inaccessible places in the world. Unless one takes a private plane directly to Izmir, or comes by private yacht to the dock of the Golden Dolphin, the only way to reach this out-of-the-way spot is by commercial airline to Istanbul, transfer in the dingy airport there to another plane for Izmir, then by rented car, taxi or donkey cart to Cesme via a two-lane road intermittently blockaded by Turkish Army troops and police, carrying sub-machine guns.

Following previous custom, a press conference was held the day prior to the meeting. The location was the Efes Hotel, in Izmir, which housed the Bilderberg wives, who also were not allowed to attend the tightly guarded Golden Dolphin conference.

Press conference at Efes Hotel, 50 miles from Golden Dolphin, site of Bilderberg Conference. H.R.H. Bernhard in center, flanked by Ernst H. van der Beugel and Selahattin Beyazit.

Entrance to luxurious Golden Dolphin, Cesme, Turkey. This picture taken only minutes before guests were evicted, hotel was closed and sealed off to receive Bilderbergers.

Turkish guards at hotel entrance. Note two Army men with submachine guns. Local police, national security plainclothes men and hotel security representatives also pose.

*See Liberty Lowdown Nos. 100, 129-133, 137.

Above, a reproduction of the front page of the June 1975 *Liberty Lowdown*, a publication of *Liberty Lobby*, founded by veteran agitator Willis A. Carto—who wrote the issue of *Liberty Lowdown* above after visiting Cesme with Mrs. Carto during the 1975 meeting. Had Carto not insisted his reporters cover Bilderberg, it is most likely Bilderberg meetings would have gone forever unreported in the United States.

Did Bilderberg Anoint Bill Clinton in 1991?

Governor's visits abroad paid with private money

BY RACHEL O'NEAL
AND LARRY RHODES
Democrat Staff Writers

Private sponsors picked up the tab for Gov. Bill Clinton's recent trips to Germany and the Soviet Union – a journey he made without staff aides, spokesmen said Tuesday.

Mike Gauldin, the governor's spokesman, said the Bilderberg Conference paid for Clinton's trip to Germany and a Washington, D.C., philanthropist paid for the Soviet Union visit.

Susie Whitacre, another Clinton spokesman, said Clinton usually travels with staff members, but he chose to go to Europe alone.

"The reason he didn't have staff with him was due to limited space and limited provisions," Whitacre said. "The sponsors asked that they not bring staff members with them."

Clinton left the United States June 5 to attend the Bilderberg Conference, a three-day meeting in Baden-Baden, Germany.

Clinton's trip to Germany was a result of an invitation for the governor to visit the Soviet Union.

Clinton was in Moscow on Monday where he met with John Matlock Jr., the U.S. ambassador to the Soviet Union.

The governor was invited to attend the meeting in the Soviet Union by Ester Coopersmith, a Washington philanthropist and former U.S. representative to the United Nations.

Coopersmith and other American philanthropists arranged the trip to Moscow to present antibiotics to the Soviet government for the children of Chernobyl, the site of a massive radioactive disaster in

1986.

"He had planned for the trip to Moscow, but it was not confirmed until after he had left," Gauldin said.

Clinton returned to Little Rock on Tuesday night.

The June 6-9 conference focused on issues involving the Middle East, the Soviet Union and Eastern Europe.

Clinton's interests in the conference were trade and economic development for Arkansas which will be made possible by the unification of European economics under the European Economic Community in 1992, the emergence of Eastern European nations from communism and recent economic changes in the Soviet Union, a news release said.

"It was a natural extension of the trip to Baden-Baden," Gauldin said.

Clinton attended the conference at the invitation of Vernon Jordan, the former president of the National Urban League.

In 1991, an Arkansas newspaper reported that then-Governor Bill Clinton was traveling to Baden-Baden, Germany, for a trade conference. That year he was the lone American governor to attend Bilderberg—and he from a small, poor, rural state. Clinton was invited by Bilderberg regular Vernon Jordan, a Clinton friend and the former president of the National Urban League. And although when Clinton began his run for the presidency few Americans knew who he was, Bilderbergers certainly did. Was Clinton "anointed" president at the Baden-Baden meeting, Bilderberg watchers ask? At least Clinton paid for the trip with private money.

Bilderberg Strikes Back

I received this letter in 1998 following the meeting in Scotland from someone who claimed to be a Bilderberg. The source has yet to be determined.

I t matters not who I am or where I might "fit" into your limited and distorted view of the world scheme of things. but it can be said that I was among the few to have again received THE INVITATION to attend a certain conference on world affairs, which we (as a <u>private</u> group) chose to hold this year in Scotland, and which was necessarily restricted to those who had earned THE RIGHT or THE PRIVILEGE to be there—your imbecilic "reporter" notwithstanding. The odious little man you repeatedly send every year to try and crash our very <u>private</u> proceedings has none of the above! You should remember that.

James P. Tucker is typical of all too many who are part of the present-day "Fourth Estate"—lower class "wannabees" with little or no real education, whose literacy level borders on the ludicrous—who use the dubious profession of journalism to stalk the corridors of power (where they do not belong), and rub shoulders with the elite. He is way out of his class. And when we block Tucker in his puerile efforts to poke his nose into where it isn't wanted, and where <u>he hasn't been invited</u>, he vents his frustration in your newspaper. Is this the best you can do?

For one thing, don't expect us to admit someone that anyone can see is obviously not from a private school, <u>and</u> from the upper classes, or a member of the power elite. Such men and women have strived hard to achieve their status in life, and there is that intangible air of authority about them, if not a certain charisma, that commands entrance to a Group such as ours. But to send us your smelly little nail biting leper of a chain-smoking "journalist," attired in his usual ill-fitting baggy suit, his body covered with eczema and dermatitis, is asking too much of anybody (no matter what class!) to "warm" up to him, let alone shake his scabby, nicotine-stained hands!

As it is with all journalists who, it seems, have never learned a basic respect for their elders and betters, Mr. Tucker shamelessly ignores the basic rights of every decent man or woman, prying into things he has no

Page 1 of 2

Turnberry

HOTEL, GOLF COURSES AND SPA

Mr. Willis Carto, Publisher
THE SPOTLIGHT,
300 Independence Ave. SE,
Washington, D.C. 20003

June 12, 1998

Dear Sir,

It matters not who I am or where I might 'fit' into your limited and distorted view of the world *scheme* of things, but it can be said that I was among the few to have again received **THE INVITATION** to attend a certain conference on world affairs, which we (as a private Group) chose to hold this year in Scotland, and which was necessarily restricted to those who had earned **THE RIGHT** or **THE PRIVILEGE** to be there—your imbecilic 'reporter' notwithstanding. The odious little man you repeatedly send every year to try and crash our *very* private proceedings has none of the above! You should remember that.

James P. Tucker is typical of all too many who are part of the present-day 'Fourth Estate'—lower class 'wannabees' with little or no real education, whose literacy level borders on the ludicrous—who use the dubious profession of journalism to stalk the corridors of power (where they do not belong), and rub shoulders with the elite. He is way out of his class. And when we block Tucker in his puerile efforts to poke his nose into where it isn't wanted, and where he hasn't been invited, he vents his frustration in your newspaper. Is this the best you can do?

For one thing, don't expect us to admit someone that anyone can see is obviously not from a private school, and from the upper classes, or a member of the power elite. Such men and women have strived hard to achieve their status in life, and there is that intangible air of authority about them, if not a certain charisma, that commands entrance to a Group such as ours. But to send us your smelly little nail biting leper of a chain-smoking 'journalist,' attired in his usual ill-fitting baggy suit, his body covered with eczema and dermatitis, is asking too much of anybody (no matter what class!) to 'warm' up to him, let alone shake his scabby, nicotine-stained hands!

As it is with all journalists who, it seems, have never learned a basic respect for their elders and betters, Mr. Tucker shamelessly ignores the basic rights of every decent man or woman, prying into things he has no business to, all the while demanding for himself the very same rights he denies others, as he bleats out the tired old fallacy that his mythical 'public' has a "*right* to know." Most of the time this imaginary public, or 'populists' as your filthy rag of a newspaper calls them—usually the 'have-nots' and white trash of the illiterate lower classes—do not "*need* to know," nor do they really "*want* to know."

Such is the case with the private considerations of our Group who, since being founded by Prince Bernhardt of the Netherlands, have now *deliberately* met privately (away from the prying eyes of the working class worms of the press), every year for the past 43 years. And, what is more, we will continue to do so no matter what means you employ to try and force us to reveal ourselves to the world at large. Even though some of us might be very public people, we not only have a right to *personal* privacy but we have the basic right to meet in private whenever we want to.

Over the past three weeks, following the end of our Conference on May 18, 1998, I took full advantage of four weeks long overdue leave to spend this precious time with many of my friends in Scotland and the north of England, before returning here to Westminster to resume my official governmental duties. But all

THE TURNBERRY LETTER: This is a copy of the infamous "Turnberry letter." It was dated June 12, 1998, and sent on letterhead from the Turnberry Hotel, the site of the Bilderberg meetings that year. In the letter the anonymous writer, believed to be a top Bilderberger, attacked me, and my editor for doing what real journalists do: Report the truth. The source of the letter remains a mystery to this day, though I have my suspicions.

---

business to, all the while demanding for himself the very same rights he denies others, as he bleats out the tired old fallacy that his mythical "public" has a "right to know." Most of the time this imaginary public, or "populists" as your filthy rag of a newspaper calls them—usually the "have-nots" and white trash of the illiterate lower classes—do not *"need* to know," nor do they really *"want* to know."

Such is the case with the private considerations of our Group who, since being founded by Prince Bernhard of the Netherlands, have now *deliberately* met privately (away from the prying eyes of the working class worms of the press), every year for the past 43 years. And, what is more, we will continue to do so no matter what means you employ to try and force us to reveal ourselves to the world at large. Even though some of us might be very public people, we not only have a right to *personal* privacy but we have the basic right to meet <u>in private</u> whenever we want to.

Over the past three weeks, following the end of our Conference on May 18, 1998, I took full advantage of four weeks long overdue leave to spend this precious time with many of my friends in Scotland and the north of England, before returning here to Westminster to resume my official governmental duties. But all the while it has been on my mind to write to you and express my extreme disgust at your efforts to make public what our Group wants to remain secret, simply because there are few in the world who have the knowledge required to understand why we exist, and what our true aims are. Who and what our small Group represents is far from being what your correspondent makes us out to be.

This letter is not a "red herring" designed to throw you off the track, nor is it a disguised vehicle for deliberate mis-information. I am just venting my personal frustration (on behalf of the Group) at the Press in general, your newspaper in passing, and your employee in particular. But there is a limit to our gentlemanly tolerance of an immature journalist who has deluded himself and others into thinking he's a latter day James Bond, as he plays his little secret agent games, peering through the keyholes of life, listening outside our conference room doors, and doing whatever he can to corrupt the integrity and honor of those who have been sworn to absolute secrecy—never to divulge any aspect of our annual Group Conference, who came, who went, who spoke, what they said, or what we discussed <u>in private</u>.

Now tell me, can we not as a Group keep our deliberations secret if we <u>want</u> to, even though we might not *need* to? If you really needed to know, we might even consider telling you, but I can assure you that your readers would not find what we talk about more interesting than your invented suppositions. What we do and what our Group represents is interesting to us and <u>us alone</u>.

It was at our Athens Conference in 1995 that I first saw this infamous "Mr. Tucker of *The Spotlight*" [now *American Free Press*], whom our security staff had been talking about. I am told that we succeeded admirably in stopping him cold for the next two years, but after his abominable behaviour at our 1996 Group Conference in Canada, we decided to teach the little man a lesson and show him that the big boys knew how to play games too. And so on Lake Lanier Island last year we let him think he could stay at the Pine Isle, by having the hotel staff move him to a new room, but not before we had placed what looked like a "bug" where we knew he would find it! And find it he did, trumpeting his self-righteous frustration like a wounded elephant, up and down the halls of the hotel—or should I say, characteristically braying like the ass that he is—until he was thrown out! He would have been anyway, but he never thought for one moment why we, of all people, would even want to listen in on his private conversations, so filled was he with his own puffed up self-importance.

Because of Mr. James Tucker and a couple of others on your staff, your newspaper has unfortunately succeeding in convincing many of your readers that our Group is connected with David Rockefeller's Trilateral Commission. It isn't! That's all about money; our Group is concerned about other things. Neither are we connected in any way with the Council on Foreign Relations or the Brookings Institution, although a very small number of our Group belong to both and sometimes attend their meetings. Neither are we the proponents of a new World Order, or secretly involved in an evil conspiracy to form a one world government. The Zionists are doing a very good job in that department, thank you, while you and your correspondents play into the hands of Israel by conveniently diverting the public's attention to us and other insignificant global brouhahas.

We are an organization that is devoted to the good of the world, in the same way as is the even more shadowy world organization of The Round Table, a small but powerful group that is on a level with—if not higher than—the exclusive *"Order of The Garter."* If you want exclusivity, you will find that they far outclass our Group. They are more devoted to secrecy than even your NSA at Fort Meade, Maryland! I would not be surprised if you have yet to hear of this immensely powerful group, but I can tell you that, like us, *The Round Table* have no "Head Office" as such, but they have chapters in selected countries of the world. Their membership is smaller than ours by far, and not one will admit to even knowing about such an organization even existing. The Duke of Edinburgh, Prince Charles, Ian Douglas-Hamilton (the Premier Duke of Scotland), Baroness Thatcher, Lord Vincent, and the former Bishop of Winchester are said to be members and, to the best of my knowledge, so was Sir Winston before his death in 1965. Your former U.S. President, Ronald Reagan was also an active member, until Alzheimer's Disease prevented him from traveling overseas, and so was John Menzies of Australia before he retired.

In closing, I will also tell you this. *The Round Table* met very <u>secretly</u> for the first time this year not too far from you, in a large private home close to Washington DC, in the green fields of northern Virginia, from March 25-27, 1998! I am in no way whatsoever advocating that you do so, but if you want to find out who (or what) is the primary and most promising force to counteract the world evil of a godless conglomerate *endeavouring* to gain control of everything you and I hold dear—then you can assuredly let your readers know that there is a Greater Force PRESENT in the world than the petty politics and world threat you have shamelessly branded our honourable Group to be. Therefore, may I suggest again that you renew your hope in the future, your faith in what you know to be true, and your trust in what I have just told you. More than that I am not prepared to tell you at this time.

But . . .

As a recognised [sic], obedient—and sometimes most often—a very <u>public</u> servant of The Realm, am bound by honour and obedience to remain faithfully yours,

(Signature indecipherable)

Jim Tucker Responds (Open Letter)

Dear Bilderberg Pretender:

I believe you are a phony, but respond in case you are a Rockefeller chambermaid acting on his orders.

As evil as Bilderberg participants are; they are not illiterate, hysterical fools, which are characteristics you so thoroughly demonstrate in your literary attempt.

You suggest Bilderberg has a right to a private meeting. I have heard Bilderberg boys and their apologists in the kept press make this stupid argument for 20 years. There is no right to a private meeting when public officials, whose expenses and salaries are paid by taxpayers, participate, as many do. Their salaries are immodest and they don't fly coach or stay at Holiday Inn.

Even if all privately funded, I would challenge the right of public officials to conduct public business behind closed doors. Destroying a head of state and killing our young men in manufactured wars is definitely public business.

Your disdain for those born poor who worked for their education is

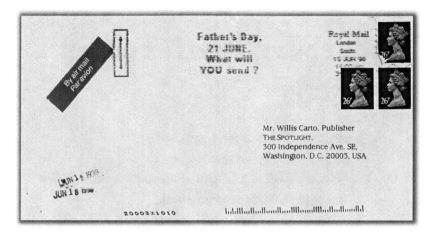

Father's Day,
21 JUNE.
What will
YOU send ?

Royal Mail
London

Mr. Willis Carto, Publisher
THE SPOTLIGHT,
300 Independence Ave. SE,
Washington, D.C. 20003, USA

Above, the envelope in which the "Turnberry Letter" was mailed, bearing the postmark of the Royal Mail, London.

---

interesting and probably typical of the Bilderberg mentality. How many nights did you sit up deciding not to be born Chinese? Or in Abraham Lincoln's log cabin? Or a manger?

Thanks for your solicitude over my health. After baffling dermatologists for years, my skin has been greatly improved by a wholistic medication. On your advice, I have fired my tailor and will henceforth have my suits designed by Omar the Tentmaker.

I want to look my best when I attend the Bilderberg meeting next year. While the Bilderberg brass gives me less than a warm welcome, I have attended more of their meetings than some of the Bilderbergs.

You seem badly confused over the common goals of Bilderberg, the Trilateral Commission and their propaganda ministry, the Council on Foreign Relations, and other offshoots. It can be difficult to follow the game when one is handicapped by a low IQ.

So you can understand Bilderberg better, may I recommend subscribing to *The Spotlight*? Have a friend read it to you—very slowly—and light will dawn even in the darkest, emptiest cellars of Earth.

Thank you for your gracious letter.

Cordially,

James P. Tucker Jr. LLB

Bilderberg Conferences 1954-2005

May 29-31, 1954: Oosterbeek, Netherlands

March 18-20, 1955: Barbizon, France

September 23-25, 1955: Garmisch-Partenkirchen, West Germany

May 11-13, 1956: Fredensborg, Denmark.

February 15-17, 1957: St. Simons Island, Georgia, U.S.A.

October 4-6, 1957: Fiuggi, Italy

September 13-15, 1958: Buxton, England

September 18-20, 1959: Yesilkey, Turkey

May 28-29, 1960: Burgenstock, Switzerland

April 21-23, 1961: St Castin, Canada

May 18-20, 1962: Saltsjobaden, Sweden

May 29-31, 1963: Cannes, France.

March 20-22, 1964: Williamsburg, Virginia, U.S.A.

April 24, 1965: Villa d'Este, Italy

March 25-27, 1966: Wiesbaden, West Germany

March 31 - April 2, 1967: Cambridge, England

April 26-28, 1968: Mont Tremblant, Canada

May 9-11, 1969: Marienlyst, Denmark

April 17-19, 1970: Bad Ragaz, Switzerland

April 23-25, 1971: Woodstock, Vermont, U.S.A.

April 21-23, 1972: Knokke, Belgium

May 11-13, 1973: Saltsjobaden, Sweden.

April 19-21, 1974: Megive, France

April 25-27, 1975: Cesme, Turkey

1976: No conference was held.

April 22-24, 1977: Torquay, England

April 21-23, 1978: Princeton, New Jersey, U.S.A.

April 27-29, 1979: Baden, Austria

April 18-20, 1980: Aachen, West Germany

May 15-17, 1981: Burgenstock, Switzerland

May 14-16, 1982: Sandefjord, Norway

May 13-15, 1983: Montebello, Canada

May 11-13, 1984: Saltsjobaden, Sweden

May 10-12, 1985: Rye Brook, New York U.S.A.

April 25-27, 1986: Gleneagles, Scotland

April 24-26, 1987: Villa d'Este, Italy

June 3-5, 1988: Telfs-Buchen, Austria

May 12-14, 1989: La Toja, Spain

May 11-13, 1990: Glen Cove, New York, USA.

June 6-9, 1991: Baden-Baden, Germany

May 21-24, 1992: Evian-les-Bains, France

April 22-25, 1993, Vouliagmeni, Greece

June 2-5 1994: Helsinki, Finland

June 8-11, 1995: Zurich, Switzerland

May 30 - June 2, 1996: Toronto, Canada

June 12-15, 1997: Lake Lanier, Ga., U.S.A.

May 14-17, 1998: Turnberry, Ayrshire, Scotland

June 3-6, 1999: Sintra, Portugal

June 1-3, 2000: Brussels, Belgium

May 24-27, 2001: Gothenburg, Sweden

May 30-June 2, 2002: Chantilly, Virginia, U.S.A.

May 15-18, 2003: Versailles, France

June 3-6, 2004: Stresa, Italy

May 5-8, 2005: Rottach-Egern, Germany

JIM TUCKER'S
BILDERBERG DIARY

Proper Name Index

Jim Tucker's Bilderberg Diary

I f you've never heard the word "Bilderberg," don't feel as though you are uninformed. Some of the best-read, most-widely-traveled folks on the face of the planet have no knowledge whatsoever regarding the existence of the group—formally known by its leadership and members as "The Bilderberg Meetings."

In existence for more than 50 years, acting as a virtual global ruling elite, Bilderberg's very name and activities remain largely hidden in the shadows, despite its immense clout in directing the course of world affairs.

Now with the release of *Bilderberg Diary* by veteran journalist James P. Tucker, Jr., those who've never known of Bilderberg will get a first-hand account of its history from the one journalist who has doggedly tailed the Bilderbergers all over the United States and Europe for the last quarter of a century.

Although the mass media in the United States—both print and broadcast—has determinedly suppressed news and information about— even the very existence of—Bilderberg, Tucker has established himself as the world's foremost authority on Bilderberg, reporting on their intrigues in the pages of the Washington-based *American Free Press.*

In *Bilderberg Diary* Jim Tucker lays out—for the first time—his entire remarkable history of covering Bilderberg, literally infiltrating Bilderberg meetings, procuring their private documents, and working relentlessly to shine the spotlight of public scrutiny on Bilderberg's shadowy affairs.

Tucker's colorful prose will introduce you to the little-known arena of the Bilderberg elite, a memorable and panoramic journey that lays bare the realities behind modern-day international power politics in a way never seen before.

ORDERING FORM

❑ **PLEASE SEND ME** _____ **COPIES of** *Jim Tucker's Bilderberg Diary: One Reporter's 25-Year Battle to Shine the Light on the World Shadow Government.* **(Softcover, 272 pages.) No charge for shipping & handling.**

BOOK PRICING:

ONE COPY is $25

TWO COPIES are $40

THREE COPIES are $50

FOUR COPIES are $60

FIVE OR MORE COPIES are $12.50 each.

❑ **SIGN ME UP FOR A TWO-YEAR SUBSCRIPTION (104 issues)** to *American Free Press* **newspaper for $89 (INTRO PRICE)**

❑ **SIGN ME UP FOR A ONE-YEAR SUBSCRIPTION (52 issues) to** *American Free Press* **newspaper for $49 (INTRO PRICE).**

❑ **PLEASE SIGN ME UP FOR A 16-WEEK TRIAL SUBSCRIPTION** to *American Free Press* **newspaper for $17.76 (INTRO PRICE)**

PAYMENT OPTIONS: **I ENCLOSE: $** _____

❑ Check ❑ Money Order ❑ Visa ❑ MasterCard

Card # _____

Expires _____ Sig. _____

NAME _____

ADDRESS _____

CITY _____

STATE, ZIP _____

RETURN THIS FORM TO: AFP, 645 Pennsylvania Ave. SE,
Suite 100, Washington, D.C. 20003.
Call **1-888-699-NEWS** toll free charge to
Visa or MasterCard.

BB69

LaVergne, TN USA
03 April 2010
178000LV00002B/2/P

9 780981 808680